UNDERSTANDING CRITICAL RACE RESEARCH METHODS AND METHODOLOGIES

Despite the growing urgency for Critical Race Theory (CRT) in the field of education, the "how" of this theoretical framework can often be overlooked. This exciting edited collection presents different methods and methodologies, which are used by education researchers to investigate critical issues of racial justice in education from a CRT perspective. Featuring scholars from a range of disciplines, the chapters showcase how various researchers synthesize different methods—including qualitative, quantitative and mixed methods, and historical and archival research—with CRT to explore issues of equity and access in the field of education. Scholars discuss their current research approaches using CRT and present new models of conducting research within a CRT framework, offering a valuable contribution to ongoing methodological debates. Researchers across different levels of expertise will find the articulations of CRT and methods insightful and compelling.

Jessica T. DeCuir-Gunby is Professor of Educational Psychology and University Faculty Scholar in the Teacher Education and Learning Sciences Department at NC State University.

Thandeka K. Chapman is Associate Professor in the Department of Education Studies at University of California, San Diego.

Paul A. Schutz is Professor in the Department of Educational Psychology at the University of Texas, San Antonio.

UNDERSTANDING CRITICAL RACE RESEARCH METHODS AND METHODOLOGIES

Lessons from the Field

Edited by Jessica T. DeCuir-Gunby,
Thandeka K. Chapman, and Paul A. Schutz

Routledge
Taylor & Francis Group

NEW YORK AND LONDON

First published 2019
by Routledge
52 Vanderbilt Avenue, New York, NY 10017

and by Routledge
2 Park Square, Milton Park, Abingdon, Oxon, OX14 4RN

Routledge is an imprint of the Taylor & Francis Group, an informa business

© 2019 Taylor & Francis

The right of Jessica T. DeCuir-Gunby, Thandeka K. Chapman, and Paul Schutz to be identified as the authors of the editorial material, and of the authors for their individual chapters, has been asserted in accordance with sections 77 and 78 of the Copyright, Designs and Patents Act 1988.

Library of Congress Cataloging-in-Publication Data
A catalog record for this title has been requested

ISBN: 978-1-138-29469-1 (hbk)
ISBN: 978-1-138-29470-7 (pbk)
ISBN: 978-1-315-10094-4 (ebk)

Typeset in Bembo
by Apex CoVantage, LLC

CONTENTS

Foreword: Moving Critical Race Theory in Education from
A Problem-Posing Mindset to a Problem-Solving Orientation   *viii*
       Marvin Lynn
Contributors   *xiii*

PART I
Introduction   **1**

  1 Critical Race Theory, Racial Justice, and Education:
     Understanding Critical Race Research Methods
     and Methodologies   3
     Jessica T. DeCuir-Gunby, Thandeka K. Chapman,
     and Paul A. Schutz

PART II
Critical Race Archival and Historical Analysis   **11**

  2 Understanding the Why of Whiteness: Negrophobia,
     Segregation, and the Legacy of White Resistance
     to Black Education in Mississippi   13
     Jamel K. Donnor

  3 CRT in Education: Historical/Archival Analyses   24
     Jerome E. Morris and Benjamin D. Parker

4 Can You Hear (and See) Me Now? Race-ing American
Language Variationist/Change and Sociolinguistic
Research Methodologies 34
Sonja L. Lanehart

PART III
Critical Race Qualitative Methods 49

5 A Match Made in Heaven: Tribal Critical Race Theory
and Critical Indigenous Research Methodologies 51
Bryan McKinley Jones Brayboy and Jeremiah Chin

6 Taking it to the Streets: Critical Race Theory,
Participatory Research and Social Justice 64
Adrienne D. Dixson, ArCasia James, and Brittany L. Frieson

7 The Commitment to Break Rules: Critical Race Theory,
Jazz Methodology and the Struggle for Justice in Education 76
David Stovall

8 Critical Race Perspectives on Narrative Research
in Education: Centering Intersectionality 86
Theodorea Regina Berry and Elizabeth J. Bowers Cook

9 Not One, but Many: A CRT Research Team Approach to
Investigate Student Experiences in Racially Diverse Settings 97
*Thandeka K. Chapman, Nicholas D. Hartlep, May Vang, Talonda
Lipsey-Brown, and Tatiana Joseph*

10 Bridging Theories to Name and Claim a Critical
Race Feminista Methodology 109
*Dolores Delgado Bernal, Lindsay Pérez Huber,
and María C. Malagón*

PART IV
Critical Race Quantitative and Mixed Methodologies 123

11 Quants and Crits: Using Numbers for Social Justice
(Or, How *Not* to be Lied to with Statistics) 125
*Claire E. Crawford, Sean Demack, David Gillborn,
and Paul Warmington*

12 Expanding Educational Pipelines: Critical Race Quantitative
    Intersectionality as a Transactional Methodology   138
    Alejandro Covarrubias, Pedro E. Nava, Argelia Lara, Rebeca
    Burciaga, and Daniel G. Solórzano

13 Critical Race Cartographies: Exploring Map-Making
    as Anti-Racist Praxis   150
    Verónica N. Vélez and Daniel G. Solórzano

14 Critical Race Mixed Methodology: Designing a Research
    Study Combining Critical Race Theory and Mixed
    Methods Research   166
    Jessica T. DeCuir-Gunby and Paul A. Schutz

PART V
Future Directions in Critical Race Methods
and Methodologies   **181**

15 "Where Do We Go From Here?" A Future Agenda for
    Understanding Critical Race Research Methods
    and Methodologies   183
    Thandeka K. Chapman and Jessica T. DeCuir-Gunby

Index   *193*

FOREWORD

Moving Critical Race Theory in Education from A Problem-Posing Mindset to a Problem-Solving Orientation

Marvin Lynn

In the last two decades, Critical Race Theory (CRT) research has risen to prominence in the field of education. CRT is a substantive critique of race and racism in the law and in the broader society that extends mainly from the work of Derrick Bell, Richard Delgado, and Kimberlé Crenshaw. The late Derrick Bell, aptly referred to as the "Father of CRT" by Gloria Ladson-Billings (2010), was perhaps the most prolific CRT scholar – long recognized for his subversive scholarship, teaching, and activism in the legal field. Concepts developed by Bell such as "the permanence of racism" and "interest convergence theory" serve as conceptual and theoretical cornerstones of CRT (Lynn, Jennings & Hughes, 2013). Additionally, Bell's popular counternarratives were not only utilized in his scholarly work but were also used in his popular books published in the late 80s and 90s. Bell's work was counterbalanced by Richard Delgado who popularized "chronicles" as a form of legal storytelling which, like Bell's counternarratives, centered the experiences and perspectives of folks of color on "race matters" in the United States. Kimberlé Crenshaw's concept of "intersectionality" also became a key building block for CRT. Her contention that race and gender must be understood as mutually reinforcing and indelibly connected markers of experience for people color in a racist and patriarchal society helped to broaden CRT's scope and reach – both within the law and in education.

First-generation CRT in Education scholars Gloria Ladson-Billings and William Tate were faculty members at the University of Wisconsin-Madison in the early 90s. Danny Solórzano, another first-generation scholar, was a faculty member at UCLA. According to Brown and Jackson (Lynn & Dixson, 2013), Wisconsin was the site of the conference where the concept of Critical Race Theory was birthed and UCLA was the professional home to Kimberlé Crenshaw and Cheryl Harris. UCLA is also home to a Critical Race Legal Studies program. As a result,

Ladson-Billings, Tate, and Solórzano likely had relationships with legal scholars who were at the forefront of the movement. They quickly advanced a "Critical Race Theory of Education" (Ladson-Billings & Tate, 1995) and forever changed the field.

Since 1995, there have been dozens of books, dissertations, research articles, and book chapters that have drawn on CRT as a concept to address a range of educational issues. Since 2008, there also has been an annual conference entitled the Critical Race Studies in Education Association Conference. It is designed to give developing education scholars a space to advance their emergent scholarship in this area. It has served thousands and continues to provide a safe space for emerging scholars of color in education to develop strong critiques of racism in schools without the fear that their work will be summarily dismissed or that they might suffer some professional challenges as a result.

Drawing on empirical and theoretical traditions within education research, CRT in Education scholars have offered strong criticisms of educational policy and practice across the P-20 educational pipeline. A bevy of research studies have proliferated the use, often times inappropriately, of CRT as tool of analysis to further contextualize and illuminate the ways in which race and racism are historically rooted and presently operating in society's institutions. As such, CRT is primarily used as a "problem-posing" heuristic – to borrow Freire's language (2004) – that helps shape research questions that are focused on further exposing problems that arise from and are further complicated by White supremacy. This is useful because it has helped the field of education develop some important understandings about the nature of race and education. It is no longer acceptable, for example, for educational researchers to dismiss race and racism as factors that shape the outcomes of their research. Concepts like *Community Cultural Wealth* (Yosso, 2005), *The Education Debt* (Ladson-Billings, 2006), and *Critical Race Pedagogy* (Lynn, 1999) have been born out of these important discussions and have brought greater conceptual and theoretical clarity to discussions about inequality and education. With the development of Critical Race Pedagogy, my intention was to move beyond a critique of racism to an analysis of teacher beliefs and practices that would illuminate how we could connect CRT to principles of liberatory and effective educational praxis to advance a new conversation in our field about what it means to teach in diverse contexts. There was also an effort to give voice to teachers of color who have strong critiques of racism embedded within their practice.

While our research has become more mainstream, it has not, in my view, helped to resolve major educational crises that persist, such as the increasing disparities between Black and White children throughout the educational pipeline. Our research has made it clear that race and racism are important factors that shape these outcomes. However, we don't yet know how to resolve these seemingly intractable problems facing many Black, Brown, and Native youth in our schools. I argue that CRT has not been sufficiently advanced as a tool to help us resolve this ongoing and increasingly complex crisis.

Another key example of this challenge involves the way in which our research frames the problems associated with the diversification of the teacher pipeline. While the numbers of teachers of color have grown in the last 20 years, the pace of that growth has been significantly outmatched by the growth in numbers of students of color (Ingersoll, May & Collins, 2017). There continue be great disparities between the numbers of teachers of color and White teachers both in P-12 and higher education settings. The disparities are exacerbated by the fact that teachers of color leave the profession at significantly higher rates than White teachers. Critical race researchers (Kohli, 2018) and others (White, 2018) have pointed to racism in schools as a key factor impacting these teachers' decisions to leave the profession.

In my view, critical race research in education hasn't changed a great deal in the last two decades. We appear to be perpetually stuck in a "problem-posing" pattern and, by and large, fail to see the importance of using CRT as a tool to frame *solutions* to these longstanding problems. In other words, critical race researchers must turn from a problem-*posing* orientation to problem-*solving* orientation. To be clear, I don't mean to bifurcate "problems" and "solutions" in a rationalist, technocratic, and overly simplistic manner. Both "problems" and "solutions" exist within the constellation of ideas about our condition and may be mutually developed, constituted, reinforcing and overlapping. I also recognize the challenge any scholar faces when they situate their work within a radical and insurgent discourse that, by its very nature, focuses on *critique* as the chief mechanism through which it addresses any set of problems, issues or concerns at multiple levels and in connection to a set of other discourses, critiques and movements for political, social and economic change. I'm calling on education scholars to envision the ways in which CRT might be used as a problem-solving tool and to be dissatisfied with offering critique for the sake of critique. The body of scholarship we've developed has provided ample evidence of the role of race and racism in education. Does it continue to be necessary for us to focus exclusively on developing and writing up studies that illuminate the existence of racism in schools? Although this continues to be important, I would however urge scholars to draw on existing analyses of racism in schools within the existing CRT in Education literature to construct new methods, pedagogies, policies, and ways of knowing that have the possibility for helping schools to transform themselves in ways that improve educational outcomes for Black, Brown and Native children and their families.

I'm somewhat encouraged by the work happening at Portland Community College in Oregon. The college has made an effort to use CRT as a foundation of their strategic planning efforts. In addition, campus officials are attempting to use CRT as a basis for planning for facilities at various campuses. They are considering a number of key questions such as "How does the built environment foster key forms of racial marginalization for students of color on campus and how can we develop a facilities plan that alleviates this in some way?" With questions like this in mind, they have made an effort to construct learning spaces that are open and easily accessible. They have also done so in consultation with students of color. The process is ongoing so it is difficult to determine whether the effort has been successful. But I find it a promising example of how some have begun to make the effort to use CRT to solve problems rather than stand on the rooftops yelling about them.

In order to be successful, when using CRT to inform the problem-solving process, it will be important to be aware of and use the variety of research methods we have at our disposal. With that in mind, this edited book, *Understanding Critical Race Research Methods and Methodologies: Lessons From the Field*, provides an excellent review of the potential variety of research methods currently being used by CRT scholars. It includes contributions from a number of prominent CRT scholars, and will provide both the seasoned and beginning researcher with a window into a number of useful research methods to help in the development of CRT problem-solving informed research.

I have the fervent hope that further attention to how we use CRT to inform the research process may help us re-conceptualize our approaches to framing educational problems and, in turn, lead to the development of educational policy and practice that vastly improves educational outcomes for Black, Brown, and Native children in the United States. Solórzano and Yosso's (2002) call for advancing "critical race method" was meant to incite these conversations sixteen years ago. Despite their call to advance an empirical movement, there has been little attention paid to a liberatory project focused on the development of research methods in education. This edited volume brings renewed energy to this movement. It also gives me hope that focusing a critical race lens on how we conduct research will lead to better outcomes for racially marginalized children in schools that are increasingly polarized.

References

Freire, P. (2004). The banking concept of education. In A. Canestrari & B. Marlow (Eds.), *Educational foundations: An anthology of critical readings* (pp. 99–111). London: Sage.

Ingersoll, R., May, H., & Collins, G. (2017). *Minority teacher recruitment, employment, and retention: 1987 to 2013*. Palo Alto, CA: Learning Policy Institute.

Kohli, R. (2018). Behind School Doors: The impact of hostile racial climates on urban teachers of color. *Urban Education*, 53(3), 307–333.

Ladson-Billings, G. (2006). From the achievement gap to the education debt: Understanding achievement in US schools. *Educational Researcher*, 35(7), 3–12.

Ladson-Billings, G. (2010). Race to the top, again: Comments on the genealogy of critical race theory. *Connecticut Law Review*, 43, 1439.

Ladson-Billings, G. & Tate, W. F. (1995). Toward a critical race theory of education. *Teachers College Record*, 97(1), 47–68.

Lynn, M. (1999). Toward a critical race pedagogy: A research note. *Urban Education*, 33(5), 606–626.

Lynn, M., & Dixson, A. D. (Eds.). (2013). *Handbook of critical race theory in education*. New York: Routledge.

Lynn, M., Jennings, M. E., & Hughes, S. (2013). Critical race pedagogy 2.0: Lessons from Derrick Bell. *Race Ethnicity and Education*, 16(4), 603–628.

Solórzano, D. G., & Yosso, T. J. (2002). Critical race methodology: Counter-storytelling as an analytical framework for education research. *Qualitative Inquiry*, 8(1), 23–44.

White, T. (2018). Teachers of color and urban charter schools: Race, school culture, and teacher turnover in the charter sector. *Journal of Transformative Leadership and Policy Studies*, 7(1), 27.

Yosso, T. J. (2005). Whose culture has capital? A critical race theory discussion of community cultural wealth. *Race Ethnicity and Education*, 8(1), 69–91.

CONTRIBUTORS

Theodorea Regina Berry is Professor and Chair, Department of African American Studies at San Jose State University. Dr. Berry is a pioneer scholar on critical race feminism in the context of curriculum studies whose scholarship appears in such journals as the *Review of Educational Research, International Journal of Qualitative Studies in Education,* and *Race Ethnicity and Education.* She is the author of *States of Grace: Counterstories of a Black Woman in the Academy* (Peter Lang, 2018), lead editor and contributing author of *From Oppression to Grace: Women of Color and their Dilemmas Within the Academy* (Stylus Publishing, 2006) and co-editor of *The Evolving Significance of Race in Education: Living, Learning, and Teaching* (with Sherick Hughes, Peter Lang, 2012).

Bryan McKinley Jones Brayboy is President's Professor of Indigenous Education and Justice in the School of Social Transformation at Arizona State University. At ASU, he is senior advisor to the president, director of the Center for Indian Education, associate director of the School of Social Transformation, and co-editor of the *Journal of American Indian Education.* From 2007 to 2012, he was visiting President's Professor of Indigenous education at the University of Alaska Fairbanks. He was elected as a fellow of the American Educational Research Association and as a member of the National Academy of Education in 2018.

Rebeca Burciaga is an associate professor of Educational Leadership and Mexican American Studies at San Jose State University. Her research and practice centers on three strands of interrelated inquiry related to Chicana/o and Latina/o students, families, communities—and the educators who serve them: Chicana feminist epistemologies and pedagogies in the field of education; sociohistorical analyses of deficit interpretations of academic achievement for youth of color; and critical professional development for teachers, educational leaders, and community members to innovate youth engagement in and outside of the classroom.

Thandeka K. Chapman conducts research with teachers and students in urban and racially diverse settings to examine and resolve the ways that institutional racism is manifested in school climate, curriculum, adult and student relationships, and school policies. Using a Critical Race Theoretical Framework, Dr. Chapman has examined various education reforms which were designed to produce educational equity for students of color after the United States Supreme Court Brown v. Board Verdicts of 1954/1955. Her scholarship includes research on African American college access, charter school reform, student outcomes in racially desegregated schools, and multicultural education for social justice curricular initiatives in urban school settings. Her current research focuses on the academic, social, behavioral, and psychological outcomes of K-12 Ethnic Studies programs in California. In keeping with her social justice agenda for school reform at all levels of education, Dr. Chapman uses her research findings to assist districts, traditional schools, and charter schools in alleviating barriers to student learning and developing policies, teaching practices, and curricula that better serve the social and academic needs of all students.

Jeremiah Chin is a Postdoctoral Research Fellow at the Center for Indian Education at Arizona State University. He received a joint J.D./Ph.D. from Arizona State University's Sandra Day O'Connor College of Law and Justice and Social Inquiry in 2017. His dissertation focused on the intersection of social science, race, and law at the Supreme Court, using Critical Race Theory and Institutional Ethnography to analyze scientific evidence in opinions of the Supreme Court on housing discrimination and higher education.

Elizabeth J. Bowers Cook completed her doctoral studies under the support of the Gaye Theresa Johnson African American Studies Doctoral Fellowship at the University of Texas at San Antonio (UTSA). Her research interests are led by a social justice praxis and pedagogy, which is centered on Intersectionality, Critical Race Theory, Critical Race Feminism, Black Feminist Thought, and Black Feminist epistemologies. Earning degrees from both Duke University (B.A.) and the University of Oklahoma (M. Ed.), Dr. Cook is intentional about connecting theory to praxis and doing good work through both writing and leadership.

Alejandro Covarrubias engages in praxis that confronts persistent and pervasive White supremacy in American institutions, policies, and practices. Dr. Covarrubias studies intersectional institutionalization of educational (in)opportunities with a focus on the experiences of refusal and resistance by students who have been pushed out of high school, the policies that lead to removal, displacement, criminalization, and commodification/elimination of indigenous brown bodies, and the community-based places that (re)engage high school pushouts in alternative educational projects.

Claire E. Crawford is a BRIDGE Research Fellow (Birmingham-Illinois Partnership for Discovery, Engagement and Education) and member of the Centre for Research in Race & Education (CRRE) at the University of Birmingham, UK. She is also an affiliate member of the Center for Office of Community College Research and Leadership at the University of Illinois Urbana-Champaign, USA. Claire's research interests focus on the critical examination of education policies, standardized testing, inequity of opportunity, and educational outcomes by race and ethnicity in the UK and USA.

Jessica T. DeCuir-Gunby is a professor of Educational Psychology and University Faculty Scholar in the Department of Teacher Education & Learning Sciences at NC State University. She also serves as a faculty mentor with the multidisciplinary and inter-institutional Center for Developmental Science at the University of North Carolina, Chapel Hill and is an associate editor for the *American Educational Research Journal*. Her research interests include race and racial identity development, Critical Race Theory, mixed methods research, and emotions in education.

Dolores Delgado Bernal is Professor of Education and Chicana/o Latina/o Studies at California State University, Los Angeles. She has worked for 30 years with schools and communities to disrupt the miseducation of Chicanx/Latinx students. She has published over 30 articles and chapters, and her books include *Transforming Educational Pathways for Chicana/o Students: A Critical Race Feminista Praxis* (2017); *Chicana/Latina Testimonios as Pedagogical, Methodological, and Activist Approaches to Social* Justice (2015); and *Chicana/Latina Education in Everyday Life: Feminista Perspectives on Pedagogy and Epistemology* (2006). Her scholarship has been recognized with a Derrick Bell Legacy Award and an AERA Distinguished Scholar Award.

Sean Demack is a senior lecturer in sociological research methods and member of the Centre for Education and Inclusion Research (CEIR) at Sheffield Hallam University, UK. Sean is a statistician who has been involved in teaching and leadership of research methods in higher education for over 10 years. His research interests are in educational inequality, secondary data analysis, randomized controlled trials, design and analysis of surveys, and critical quantitative enquiry. He is a peer reviewer for the *Educational Endowment Foundation* (EEF) and *European Sociology Association*, and is on the editorial board of *Race Ethnicity and Education*.

Adrienne D. Dixson is Professor of Education Policy, Organization and Leadership at the University of Illinois College of Education. Her primary research interest focuses on how issues of race, class, and gender intersect and impact educational equity in urban schooling contexts, as located within the theoretical frameworks of Critical Race Theory and Black feminist theories. Her robust research record includes numerous edited volumes, including one of the first book-length texts on CRT in education, *CRT in Education: All God's Children Got a Song* (2006, 2016 Routledge), and numerous peer-reviewed journal articles. Recently, she has started examining how educational equity is mediated by school reform policies in the urban South, specifically regarding school reform in post-Katrina New Orleans, how local actors make sense of and experience those reform policies and how those policies become or are "racialized."

Jamel K. Donnor A leading scholar on critical race theory and education, Dr. Donnor's research investigates the inextricable ties between the law, race, and inequality in America. Specifically examining the evolutionary links between ideology, interests, and politics in shaping opportunity, Dr. Donnor's scholarship expands our understanding on the intersections between race, education, and opportunity in a democratic society.

Brittany L. Frieson is a doctoral student in the Curriculum & Instruction department at the University of Urbana-Champaign. She completed her undergraduate degree at Meredith College and her master's degree in Curriculum and Instruction at North Carolina State University in Raleigh, North Carolina. Her current research interests focus on the lived experiences and rich linguistic repertoires of minoritized populations in elementary dual-language bilingual programs. As a former elementary teacher of emergent bilinguals, the inspiration for her scholarly work continuously draws upon her past experiences as an educator and a student to highlight the complexities in which women of color face in the classroom.

David Gillborn is Professor of Critical Race Studies and the Director of the Centre for Research in Race & Education (CRRE) at the University of Birmingham, UK. David is founding editor of the international peer-reviewed journal *Race Ethnicity and Education* and twice winner of the Society for Educational Studies' Book of the Year award. David received the Derrick Bell Legacy Award from the Critical Race Studies in Education Association (CRSEA), and was recently named to the Laureate Chapter of the Kappa Delta Pi International Honor Society.

Nicholas D. Hartlep is currently an Associate Professor of Urban Education and the Chair of the Early Childhood and Elementary Education Department at Metropolitan State University in Saint Paul, Minnesota. Routledge published his co-edited book *The Neoliberal Agenda and the Student Debt Crisis in US Higher Education*, which received an Outstanding Book Award from the Society of Professors of Education. The American Association of State Colleges and Universities presented him with the John Saltmarsh Award for Emerging Leaders in Civic

Engagement for his work on student loan debt and anti-racist teacher preparation. Hartlep researches the model-minority stereotype of Asian Americans.

ArCasia James is a doctoral student at the University of Illinois at Urbana-Champaign, where she studies the Black history of education. She completed her undergraduate degree at the University of Texas at Austin and her master's degree at the University of Pennsylvania in Philadelphia. As a former secondary humanities teacher, she has taught both domestically and abroad. Her dissertation project will examine Black student perspectives of desegregation in Waco, Texas, through oral history interviews and archival research. Her other scholarly interests include the history of social studies curriculum and Black Feminism and Critical Race Theory in education.

Tatiana Joseph is an assistant professor in Curriculum and Instruction at the School of Education, University of Milwaukee-Wisconsin. Her research interests center on the idea of quality educational opportunities for urban students, especially English Language Learners. Specifically, her research focuses on First Language Maintenance, Culturally Responsive Teaching, Critical Race Theory, curriculum development, and teacher preparation. Dr. Joseph received a B.A in Secondary Education and Spanish from Marquette University, a M.S. in Curriculum and Instruction with an emphasis in ESL/Bilingual Education from the University of Wisconsin-Milwaukee and Ph.D. in Urban Education from the University of Milwaukee-Wisconsin. She also has extensive experience teaching languages in the K-12 setting. In addition, Dr. Joseph also served as a School Board Director for Milwaukee Public Schools, representing the community she where she grew up.

Sonja L. Lanehart is Professor and Brackenridge Endowed Chair in Literature and the Humanities at the University of Texas at San Antonio. She is author of *Sista, Speak! Black Women Kinfolk Talk about Language and Literacy* (2002); editor of *Sociocultural and Historical Contexts of African American English* (2001), *African American Women's Language: Discourse, Education, and Identity* (2009), and the *Oxford Handbook of African American Language* (2015); and former co-editor of *Educational Researcher: Research News and Comment*. Her research interests include sociolinguistics, African American language and identity, and applications of Critical Race Theory and Intersectionality in sociolinguistics and educational research.

Argelia Lara is an Assistant Professor in the School of Education at Mills College. She received her Ph.D. from UCLA's Graduate School of Education and Information Systems in the division of Social Science and Comparative Education with a specialization in race and ethnic studies. Argelia's research interests examine immigrant education, undocumented students along the K-PHD pipeline, college choice, access and equity for students of color, and first-generation college students. Argelia's work has been published in *Urban Education, Association of Mexican American Educators Journal, Race Ethnicity and Education,* and the *Journal of Hispanics in Higher Education.*

Talonda Lipsey-Brown is currently an Assistant Professor at Edgewood College in Madison, Wisconsin and is the liaison for a new partnership between Edgewood College and Milwaukee Public Schools University. In addition, she also teaches courses in Urban Education at the Milwaukee Area Technical College. In addition to using Critical Race Theory and narrative inquiry to explore the experiences of students of color in majority-White suburban schools, her research also examines teachers' identities and ideologies, and the impact of school climate on their relationships with students of color in both urban and suburban schools.

Marvin Lynn is the Dean of the Graduate School of Education. He is an internationally recognized expert on race and education, and the lead editor of the *Handbook of Critical Race Theory in Education*—published simultaneously in the USA and the UK with Routledge Press. He serves as an editorial board member of several journals, and has published more than two-dozen research articles and book chapters.

María C. Malagón is an Assistant Professor of Sociology at California State University, Fullerton. She received her Ph.D. in Social Sciences and Comparative Education at UCLA. Her research interests examine various segments along the Latina/o educational pipeline, using feminist analysis to interrogate how discourses of racialized femininities and masculinities manifest in educational policy and practice. She has a professional background in gender education programs, high school outreach, and juvenile "delinquency" prevention and intervention programs. She is currently working on a book manuscript that explores the experiences of Mexican American girls in a California reformatory school during the 1940s.

Jerome E. Morris is the *E. Desmond Lee Endowed Professor of Urban Education* (in conjunction with St. Louis Public Schools) and a Fellow with the Public Policy Research Center at the University of Missouri-St. Louis. His research provides empirically grounded models for understanding race and education in post-*Brown* America. In addition to authoring *Troubling the Waters: Fulfilling the Promise of Quality Public Schooling for Black Children* (2009, Teachers College Press), Morris has published in research journals such as the *American Educational Research Journal, Educational Researcher, Teachers College Record, Review of Research in Education, Anthropology & Education Quarterly, Urban Education,* and *Kappan.*

Pedro E. Nava, is an Assistant Professor of Education in the Educational Leadership Program at Mills College in Oakland, California. Pedro completed his Ph.D.

from UCLA's Graduate School of Education in the Urban Schooling division. The focus of his research and teaching are in urban and rural schooling inequality, critical pedagogy and critical race theory, immigration and education, family-school engagement, and participatory action research.

Benjamin D. Parker is a Gifted Education Teacher in Pennsylvania and serves as an Adjunct Instructor of Educational Foundations at Millersville University. He is an affiliate with the Urban Education and Community Studies Research Group at the University of Missouri-St. Louis. Dr. Parker's research and teaching focus on educational access and equity with regard to critical schooling environments. His previously published works can be found in *Radical Pedagogy*, *Perspectives on Urban Education*, and the *Journal of Language and Literacy Education*.

Lindsay Pérez Huber is Associate Professor in Social and Cultural Analysis of Education (SCAE) in the College of Education at California State University, Long Beach and a Visiting Researcher at the UCLA Chicano Studies Research Center. Broadly, her research analyzes racial inequities in education, the impact on marginalized students of color, and how students and their communities respond to those inequities through strategies of resistance for social change. Dr. Pérez Huber received her Ph.D. in Social Science and Comparative Education (SSCE), with a specialization in Race and Ethnic Studies from the UCLA Graduate School of Education and Information Studies.

Paul A. Schutz is currently a Professor in the Department of Educational Psychology at the University of Texas at San Antonio. His research interests include the nature of emotion, emotional regulation, and teachers' understandings of emotion in the classroom. He is a past president for Division 15: Educational Psychology of the American Psychological Association, a former co-editor of the *Educational Researcher: Research News and Comments*, and a co-editor of the upcoming *Handbook of Educational Psychology, Volume 4.*

Daniel G. Solórzano is Professor of Social Science and Comparative Education at the Graduate School of Education and Information Studies and Director of the Center for Critical Race Studies at UCLA. His teaching and research interests include Critical Race Theory in education, racial microaggressions, critical race pedagogy, and critical race spatial analysis. He has authored over 100 research articles and book chapters on issues related to educational access and equity for underrepresented student populations in the United States.

David Stovall is Professor of Educational Policy Studies and African-American Studies at the University of Illinois at Chicago (UIC). His scholarship investigates three areas: (1) Critical Race Theory; (2) the relationship between housing and education; and (3) the intersection of race, place and school. In the attempt to bring theory to action, he works with community organizations and schools to develop curricula that address issues of equity and justice. His work led him to become a member of the Greater Lawndale/Little Village School of Social Justice High School design team, which opened in the Fall of 2005.

May Vang is an Assistant Professor in the department of Curriculum and Instruction at the University of Wisconsin Whitewater. Her research areas include bilingualism and teacher education. Her work focuses on Hmong bilingualism and the socio-cultural impact it has on Hmong identity.

Verónica N. Vélez is Associate Professor and Founding Director of the Education and Social Justice Minor at Western Washington University (WWU). Her research focuses on migrant mother activism, community-based participatory action research, popular education, and the use of geographic information systems (GIS) technologies to explore the spatial dimensions of educational (in)opportunity. Each of these areas is informed by her interdisciplinary training and expertise in Critical Race Theory in education, radical cartography, and Chicana feminist epistemologies.

Paul Warmington is an associate professor in Sociology of Education at the Centre for Education Studies, University of Warwick, UK. Paul has taught and researched in further and higher education for over twenty years. His research interests are in education and social justice, drawing on critical theories of race and class. Paul is an active member of the British Educational Research Association and sits on the editorial boards for *Educational Review* and *Race Ethnicity and Education*. His most recent book is *Black British Intellectuals and Education: Multiculturalism's Hidden History*, published by Routledge.

PART I

Introduction

1

CRITICAL RACE THEORY, RACIAL JUSTICE, AND EDUCATION

Understanding Critical Race Research Methods and Methodologies

Jessica T. DeCuir-Gunby, Thandeka K. Chapman, and Paul A. Schutz

Although there has been substantial Critical Race Theory (CRT) research in education over the last 20-plus years, focusing on a variety of areas, more forms of critical race research in education are needed to interrogate the complexities of race and racism in education. We are currently experiencing a variety of race-related issues within education that disproportionately impact People of Color. For instance, there is increasing underfunding of public schools (e.g. slashing of state budgets, redirecting of school funding through voucher systems and charter schools, etc.). There are continued attacks on multicultural education/initiatives and ethnic studies. Within higher education, affirmative action policies are actively being eradicated. Anti-immigrant sentiments, especially towards people of Latinx descent, are on the rise. White nationalism is growing in acceptance within social and political arenas. All of these issues will detrimentally impact People of Color socially, emotionally, politically, and/or financially for generations. Thus, there is an urgency for more CRT research in education focusing on such topics as well as other topics that address racial justice. Despite this growing urgency around the need for more research into racial justice and education, there is a lack of discussion regarding the use of different research methods and methodologies used to seek racial justice. Thus, our aim in this edited book is to discuss and analyze the different methods and methodologies, including qualitative, quantitative, and mixed methods used by researchers to investigate educational research problems from a CRT perspective.

Critical Race Theory and Research Methods

Although a few special journal issues (Dixson, Chapman & Hill, 2005; Lynn, Yosso, Solórzano, & Parker 2002; Parker, 2015) and a handful of books

(Hopson & Dixson, 2013; Lynn & Dixson 2013; Parker, 1998) have explored race-based research methods and methodologies, there have been few systematic efforts to discuss and analyze how scholars use different research methods and methodologies to examine educational problems from a CRT framework (DeCuir & Dixson, 2004). These published works also reveal the extensive use of qualitative methods in CRT research. In fact, the majority of CRT research in education has utilized qualitative methodological approaches (Hopson & Dixson, 2013; Lynn, Yosso, Solórzano, & Parker 2002; Parker, 1998).

Despite, the majority of CRT research taking a qualitative approach, CRT research is beginning to embrace other methodological approaches. Researchers are increasingly using quantitative approaches. In fact, a recent special issue of *Race Ethnicity and Education* discussed the emergence of *QuantCrit* or Quantitative Critical Race Theory in the field (see Garcia, Lopez, & Vélez, 2018). Also, CRT researchers are increasingly using mixed-methods research, the combining of quantitative and qualitative approaches within one study (see DeCuir-Gunby & Walker-DeVose, 2013). This departure from CRT's qualitative roots has not been without some debate. There are many researchers that feel that quantitative approaches are antithetical to critical frameworks in that quantitative methods are rooted in positivism/post-positivism which embraces assumptions of one truth while qualitative research assumes there are multiple truths (Zuberi & Bonilla-Silva, 2008). However, others feel as though quantitative and mixed methods approaches can be compatible with a CRT framework, as long as the researchers remain true to the tenets of CRT and work to address racial justice (Gillborn, Warmington, & Demack, 2018). Yet, many scholars would agree that the complicated nature of education problems requires varied methodological approaches.

Thus, in general, the objectives of this edited volume are (1) to analyze the research methods and methodologies that have been developed by researchers to investigate educational problems from a critical race theoretical perspective; and (2) to examine the epistemological and ontological issues associated with the transactions among research methods, methodologies, and in this case, critical race theoretical perspectives. This edited book features a number of scholars from a variety of disciplines (i.e. Teacher Education and Policy, School Finance and Policy, and Education Psychology) who use various research methods (e.g. qualitative, quantitative, mixed methods, historical, and archival research) to explore issues of equity and access in the field of education. These scholars discuss their current research approaches using CRT as well as present new models of conducting research within a CRT framework.

Critical Race Theory (CRT) was created as a critique of the slow progress of racial reform within the United States legal arena. It centers around the idea that racism is a permanent fixture of society and focuses on racial power (Bell, 1993). As indicated by Crenshaw, Gotanda, Peller, and Thomas (1995), CRT seeks to understand the creation and maintenance of White Supremacy and how it subordinates People of Color. CRT also seeks to better understand how to change the relationship between race and the law (Matsuda, Lawrence, Delgado, & Crenshaw, 1993).

Although CRT began within the legal realm, it has expanded to many disciplines including the field of education. Ladson-Billings and Tate's (1995) seminal article, "Toward a Critical Race Theory of Education," introduced CRT as an essential framework for examining race and racism in education. Since the publication of Ladson-Billings and Tate's (1995) germinal article, thousands of articles, chapters, and books using a CRT framework have been written, demonstrating the growing importance of CRT in the study of educational problems (Howard & Navarro, 2016). Dixson and Rousseau (2005) provided the initial review of CRT research in education, a ten-year retrospective, and found that most CRT research in education focused on voice, restrictive and expansive views of equality, and colorblindness. Ten years later, Ledesma and Calderón (2015), conducted a review and found that CRT research within K-12 has largely centered around the topics of (1) curriculum and pedagogy; (2) teaching and learning (e.g. teacher attitudes); (3) schooling in general (e.g. climate); and (4) policy, school finance, and community engagement, while the research in higher education has focused on the topics of (1) colorblindness (e.g. language in diversity policies); (2) admissions policies; and (3) campus racial climates (e.g. student and faculty perspectives including racial microaggressions). A review by McCoy and Rodricks (2015) in higher education had similar findings. Within the body of research of CRT in education, researchers have explored instantiations of race and racism through the tenets provided by Ladson-Billings and Tate (1995) as well as other articulations of the theory (Gillborn, 2006; Solórzano & Delgado Bernal 2001; Solórzano & Yosso, 2001; Tate, 1997). Those scholars who use CRT understand the following principles:

- *The Centrality of race and racism.* Race remains the dominant and consistent, yet sometimes elusive, factor that influences laws, policies, relationships, and practices in education.
- *U.S. society is based upon property rights.* This proposition postulates that it is essential to examine social inequities, particularly educational inequities, from the understanding that racism is systemic and Whiteness has value.
- *Intersectionality of race and racism with other forms of subordination.* Racism is intricately woven within all aspects of society and actively interacts with all forms of subordination.
- *Challenge to dominant ideology.* A major goal of CRT is to question and challenge the status quo or majoritarian perspective. CRT promotes skepticism towards how the law operates in terms of neutrality, objectivity, and colorblindness (being uninfluenced by race).
- *Myth of meritocracy.* This principle questions the existence of meritocracy or the idea that advancement in society only occurs because of hard work and ability.

- *Commitment to social justice.* CRT is a liberatory, transformative and emancipatory theory that focuses on racial justice (Peller, 1990). The ultimate goal of CRT is to end racial oppression and other forms of oppression through systemic change.
- *Centrality of experiential knowledge.* CRT analyses highlight the importance of voice and focuses on the experiences of People of Color.
- *Transdisciplinary perspective.* In utilizing CRT, there is a focus on a contextual yet historical interpretation of the law. It is essential to apply a CRT analysis taking context into perspective.
- *Crosses epistemological understandings of race.* CRT stresses the importance of connecting with other disciplines in order to address racism because of its complexity and intricateness.
- *Reinterpretation of civil rights outcomes.* CRT examines the social and political outcomes of civil rights law to explain current institutional and structural components of racism.

Different research methods in CRT allow scholars to more specifically highlight particular structures, events, behaviors, and outcomes, in different aspects of education, through the lens of CRT. As the field of CRT in education becomes more open to the use of different research methods, scholars are able to use the tenets of CRT to analyze different types of data to attack inequity and injustice in education. In no way do we negate the powerful use of storytelling that remains at the heart of CRT. Indeed, what different methods provide to the field of education research are new ways to understand the myriad inflections of race and racism in society—a new way to uncover and process stories that have yet to be told and stories that hold so much complexity that they require multiple tellings.

Book Structure: Critical Race Methods and Methodologies in Context

The chapters in this book provide readers with examples that show how scholars use various methods and methodologies to construct new ways to interrogate race and racism through CRT. As editors, we asked the authors to explain what some may see as difficult to explain—how they, as the primary tools in the research process, design, implement, and evaluate a critical race methodology in their work. We asked the authors to address their writing tasks, not as "how-to" text-book authors, but through the mode of self-reflection and as generators of new knowledge. As such, not only do the authors share intricate frameworks for research, but also the complexities, seen and unforeseen, of conducting CRT research. To provide readers with a familiar structure, this book is organized under traditional expressions of research methods and methodologies. However, in addition to methodological approaches, the chapters

in each section feature a variety of education contexts, epistemological conflu-
ences, and research challenges.

In the section following this, *Critical Race Archival and Historical Analysis,* the
authors focus on inquiries of critical race research methods and methodologies in relations to document analysis including archival and historical analysis.
Document Analysis is a foundational approach in critical race research, often
utilized by legal scholars. The scholars in this section demonstrate a variety of
ways in which they utilize document analysis in their research. In Chapter 2,
Jamel K. Donnor addresses the importance of history and the legal foundation
of CRT by focusing on *Brown v. Board of Education* and its impact on White
antipathy to school desegregation. Similarly, in Chapter 3, Jerome E. Morris
and Benjamin D. Parker draw upon historiographic methods to discuss how
CRT can be used to examine historical documents and archival records in
education. The last chapter in this section, Chapter 4 by Sonja L. Lanehart,
uses document analysis to review the seminal journals in the field of linguistics,
focusing on intersectionality, and demonstrates how Black women have been
ignored in linguistics research.

The next section of the book, *Critical Race Qualitative Methods,* features
chapters that are centered on qualitative research methods. Specifically, this
section features chapters that challenge traditional qualitative approaches, critiques researchers own implementations of traditional approaches, and provides novel ways to conduct qualitative research involving CRT. In Chapter 5,
Bryan McKinley Jones Brayboy and Jeremiah Chin create a counter-narrative
regarding the protagonist Henry Sampson and his experiences in tribal communities and education that is analyzed using the combination of CRT and
Critical Indigenous Research Methodologies (CIRM). In Chapter 6, Adrienne D.
Dixson, ArCasia James, and Brittany L. Frieson examine the intersection of CRT
and *Participatory Action Research* (PAR) as well discussing the challenges of utilizing such approaches in education reform research. In Chapter 7, David Stovall
combines CRT, *Jazz Methodology,* and *Youth Participant Action Research* (YPAR)
in his discussion of the development of a neighborhood school, focusing on the
development of his own member-checking and data triangulation processes as
well as the critique of traditional qualitative research processes. In Chapter 8,
Theodorea Regina Berry and Elizabeth J. Bowers Cook explore the combining
of intersectionality and *Narrative Analysis,* focusing on how narrative analysis and
CRT, particularly counter-storytelling, are compatible. In Chapter 9, Thandeka K.
Chapman, Nicholas D. Hartlep, Mary Vang, Talonda Lipsey-Brown, and Tatiana
Joseph discuss *Team-Based Approaches* to conducting CRT research, focusing on
the importance of researcher positionality, researcher-participant reciprocity, and
general research complexity of team-based research. In the last chapter of this
section, Chapter 10, Dolores Delgado Bernal, Lindsay Pérez Huber, and María C.
Malagón present a discussion of *Critical Race Feminist Methodology,* the combining of CRT and Chicana feminist thought, in education research through the

discussion of research with undocumented women, young Chicanas, and community-engaged partnerships.

Section IV, *Critical Race Quantitative and Mixed Methodologies*, provides a variety of discussions on how to utilize quantitative and mixed-methods approaches within CRT scholarship. As previously discussed, CRT research has been largely dominated by qualitative approaches. However, more CRT researchers are embracing quantitative and mixed-methods approaches. Within this volume, we present various perspectives on how to utilize quantitative and mixed-methods approaches within CRT frameworks. In Chapter 11, Claire E. Crawford, Sean Demack, David Gillborn, and Paul Warmington explain the use of quantitative methods in examining race equity in education while providing a discussion of *QuantCrit*, a critique of the theoretical foundations of quantitative methods through a CRT lens. Similarly, in Chapter 12, Alejandro Covarrubias, Pedro E. Nava, Argelia Lara, Rebeca Burciaga, and Daniel G. Solórzano explicate *Critical Race Quantitative Intersectionality* (CRQI) through their exploration of Whiteness and White supremacy with a case study on academic experiences in California's San Joaquin Valley. Verónica N. Vélez and Daniel G. Solórzano, in Chapter 13, examine *Critical Race Spatial Analysis* (CRSA), the combination of geographic information systems (GIS) and spatial analysis from a critical race lens, and discuss how it can be used as *Critical Race Praxis* through the analysis of real-world case studies. In Chapter 14, the last chapter in this section, Jessica T. DeCuir-Gunby and Paul A. Schutz explain *Critical Race Mixed Methodology* (CRMM), the combining of CRT and mixed-methods research, through their discussion of designing a research study on African American women college students and racial microaggressions.

The last section, *Future Directions in Critical Race Methods and Methodologies*, focuses on the ways in which the methods presented in this text can be extended as well as expanded upon. In Chapter 15, the final chapter, Thandeka K. Chapman, Jessica T. DeCuir-Gunby, and Paul A. Schutz take a thematic approach to discussing the chapters, and re-articulate how the chapters adhere to the tenets of CRT.

Conclusion

We, the editors, decided to create this collection after questioning the quality of research methods associated with the current directions of CRT research. We wanted to design a text that would help educate the field about the importance of utilizing appropriate research methods when engaging in CRT research in education. Thus, this collection was created in order to provide guidance to researchers that are new to critical race research or need a refresher on the topic. However, this book was not designed to tell readers everything they needed to know regarding CRT or research methods. Instead, the goal of this text was to illustrate how seasoned scholars engage in, as well as grapple with, the methodological and epistemological issues associated with the study of CRT in education. It is our hope that with this book, we are elevating the importance of the much needed discourse regarding CRT and research methods, as well as cultivating the next generation of CRT scholars in education.

References

Bell, D. (1993). *Faces at the bottom of the well: The permanence of racism.* NY: Basic Books.

Crenshaw, K., Gotanda, N., Peller, G., & Thomas, K. (Eds.) (1995). *Critical race theory: The key writings that formed the movement.* New York: The New Press.

DeCuir, J. T., & Dixson, A. D. (2004). So when it comes out, they aren't that surprised that it is there: Using critical race theory as a tool of analysis of race and racism in education. *Educational Researcher, 33*(5), 26–31.

DeCuir-Gunby, J. T. & Walker-DeVose, D. C. (2013). Expanding the counterstory: The potential for critical race mixed methods studies in education. In M. Lynn & A.D. Dixson (Eds.), *Handbook of critical race theory in education* (pp. 248–259). New York: Routledge.

Dixson, A. D., Chapman, T. K., & Hill, D. A. (2005). Extending the portraiture methodology. *Qualitative Inquiry, 11*(1), 16–26.

Dixson, A. D., & Rousseau, C. K. (2005). And we are still not saved: Critical race theory in education ten years later. *Race Ethnicity and Education, 8*(1), 7–27.

Garcia, N. M., Lopez, N., & Vélez, V. N. (2018). QuantCrit: Rectifying methods through critical race theory. *Race Ethnicity and Education, 21*(2), 149–157.

Gillborn, D. (2006). Critical race theory and education: Racism and anti-racism in educational theory and praxis. *Discourse: Studies in the Cultural Politics of Education, 27*(1), 11–32.

Gillborn, D., Warmington, P., & Demack, S. (2018). QuantCrit: Education, policy, 'big data' and principles for a critical race theory of statistics. *Race Ethnicity and Education, 21*(2), 158–179.

Hopson, R. K., & Dixson, A. D. (Eds.) (2013). *Race, ethnography and education.* New York: Routledge.

Howard, T. C. & Navarro, O. (2016). Critical race theory 20 years later: Where do we go from here? *Urban Education, 51*(3), 253–273.

Ladson-Billings, G., & Tate, W. (1995). Toward a critical race theory of education. *Teachers College Record, 97*(1), 47–67.

Ledesma, M. C., & Calderón, D. (2015). Critical race theory in education: A review of past literature and a look to the future. *Qualitative Inquiry, 21*(3), 206–222.

Lynn, M., & Dixson, A. D. (Eds.) (2013). *Handbook of critical race theory in education.* New York: Routledge.

Lynn, M., Yosso, T. J., Solórzano, D. G., & Parker, L. (2002). Critical race theory and education: Qualitative research in the new millennium. *Qualitative Inquiry, 8*(1), 3–6.

Matsuda, M. Lawrence, C. Delgado, R., & Crenshaw, K. (Eds.) (1993). *Words that wound: Critical race theory, assaultive speech, and the First Amendment.* Boulder, CO: Westview.

McCoy, D. L., & Rodricks, D. J. (2015). Critical race theory in higher education: 20 Years of theoretical and research innovations. *ASHE Higher Education Report, 41*(3), 16–33; 55–71.

Parker, L. (1998). "Race is race ain't": An exploration of the utility of critical race theory in qualitative research in education. *International Journal of Qualitative Studies in Education*, *11*(1), 43–55.

Parker, L. (2015). Critical race theory in education and qualitative inquiry: What each has to offer each other now? *Qualitative Inquiry*, *21*(3), 199–205.

Peller, G. (1990). Race consciousness. *Duke Law Journal*, (4) 758–847.

Solórzano, D. G., & Delgado Bernal, D. (2001). Examining transformational resistance through a critical race and LatCrit theory framework: Chicana and Chicano students in an urban context. *Urban Education*, *36*(3), 308–342.

Solórzano, D. G., & Yosso, T. J. (2002). Critical race methodology: Counter-story-telling as an analytical framework for educational research. *Qualitative Inquiry*, *8*(1), 23–44.

Tate, W. F., IV (1997). Chapter 4: Critical race theory and education: History, theory, and implications. *Review of Research in Education*, *22*(1), 195–247.

Zuberi, T. & Bonilla-Silva, E. (2008). Toward a definition of White logic and White methods. In T. Zuberi & E. Bonilla-Silva (Eds.), *White logic, White method: Racism and methodology* (pp. 3–27). Lanham, MD: Rowman & Littlefield.

PART II

Critical Race Archival and Historical Analysis

2

UNDERSTANDING THE WHY OF WHITENESS

Negrophobia, Segregation, and the Legacy of White Resistance to Black Education in Mississippi

Jamel K. Donnor

During its introductory phase to the education field, a majority of the critical race scholarship rightfully relied on voice, counter-narrative, and counter-storytelling to articulate the unequal experiences of students of color and its durable ties to White racism.[1] This *more* critical explanation on the "workings of White racism" and race-based inequity was essential to the articulation of a more sophisticated understanding of the continuing significance of race in education. As explained by Ladson-Billings and Tate (1995), "[i]f racism were merely isolated, unrelated, individual acts, we would expect to see at least a few examples of educational excellence and equity together in the nation's public schools. Instead, those places where African Americans do experience educational success tend to be outside of the public schools" (p. 55). While much has transpired socially and politically in the United States since Ladson-Billings and Tate's 1995 germinal article *Toward a Critical Race Theory in Education*, the bulk of the present-day critical race scholarship in education remains anchored to the aforementioned analytical constructs and methodological tools (Dixson & Rousseau Anderson 2017; Donnor & Ladson-Billings, 2017).

In reviewing the critical race literature in education over the past 20 years, Dixson and Rousseau Anderson (2017) found that the primary application of critical race theory (CRT) in education *still* involves the utilization of voice to highlight the "importance of the personal and community experience of people of color as sources of knowledge" (p. 34). The aforementioned findings are consistent with their 2005 review of the critical race scholarship in education, which also identified voice as the "most frequently applied idea from CRT . . ." (p. 35). More recently, Donnor and Ladson-Billings (2017) noted that "[o]ne of the common mistakes we see in those who claim to be using CRT is in 'telling a story' that fails to engage larger legal and social principles" (p. 202). A particularly glaring omission within the current education critical race scholarship is the lack of a theorizing of race that incorporates history and the legal literature, along with a discussion of the legacy effects of White racism on Black people's present-day learning opportunities. According to Donnor and Ladson-Billings (2017),

> [b]eyond referencing the law review articles containing the specific CRT analytical construct one is using to examine race and inequality within his or her particular area of education, a majority of the critical race scholarship in the field of education lack the capacity to connect the contemporary moment to the past or to articulate a 'dynamic understanding of the temporal, institutional, and disciplinary emergence CRT provides for engaging today . . .'.
>
> *(Crenshaw, 2011, p. 1261)*

Stated differently, history and case law are not only foundational components, intellectual resources, and indicia of scholarly rigor, but also essential tools for developing of equitable policy solutions in the present moment.

My purpose in this chapter is to attend to the previously discussed shortcomings within the contemporary education critical race scholarship by discussing the legacy of White racism on the learning opportunities of Black students in modern-day Mississippi. In addition to utilizing the hallmarks of CRT (i.e., history and case law), I include the legal literature to highlight the evolutionary and strategically delayed functions inherent within White racism. As the state that "stood most firm in its resistance to the [Black] civil rights movement and federal efforts to enforce racial equality" (Andrews, 2004, p. 3) in the 1950s and 1960s, Mississippi remains a central site for understanding the dynamic relationship between race, the law, public policy, and the intergenerational impact of White opposition on African American advancement in public education. For example, in *Indigo Williams, et al. v. Phil Bryant, et al.*, 2017, the petitioners contend that the State of Mississippi has "failed to live up to obligations it incurred in 1870 upon its readmission to the United States" (p. 1) after the Civil War. According to the complaint, "[s]ince 1890, when Mississippi rewrote its Constitution in order to reestablish white supremacy, Mississippi has violated the terms of its readmission. As a result, Black students in Mississippi still do not receive an education equal to that received by white students" (p. 2). Indeed, as the "birthplace of the first significant organization of segregationist resistance [e.g., Citizens' Councils] . . . and the first to use state tax dollars to organize an investigative agency committed to preserving [W]hite supremacy" through the State Sovereignty Commission (Crespino, 2007, p. 5), White Mississippians' adversarial stance toward Black education *still* persists.[2]

Organization of Chapter

This chapter is comprised of three sections. The first section presents a historical overview of White Mississippians' attitudes toward Black public education.

The reason for this review is threefold. The first reason as already mentioned is to adhere to CRT's central tenet of historical context. The second reason for the review of White Mississippians' reaction to Black education is to situate contemporary Black legal challenges within a historical continuum of White antipathy dating to Reconstruction, while the third reason is to highlight the correlational linkages and operational constructs of White racism on the present-day learning opportunities of African American students in the State of Mississippi. In the second section of this chapter I discuss *Cowan v. Bolivar County Board of Education* as a way to illustrate the foregoing. A school desegregation lawsuit filed a decade after *Brown v. Board of Education* 1955 (i.e., *Brown II*) in Bolivar County, Mississippi. The plaintiffs in *Cowan v. Bolivar County Board of Education* originally contended that the school district operated a racially *de jure* public education system by maintaining "six Caucasian schools and only four African American schools" (*Cowan v. Bolivar County Board of Education*, 2012, p. 2)." *Cowan* is noteworthy for two reasons. First, the case provides insight into the use of litigation as an ineffective tool for obtaining education equality. Second, and equally significant, *Cowan* is the quintessential example of how the legacy of White racism continues to impact Black people's present-day fortunes to learn. The third and final section of this chapter explains the importance of history and the legal literature to the CRT scholarship in education.

Black Education and Negrophobia in Mississippi: A Historical Overview

Since Reconstruction, Whites in Mississippi have engaged in the systematic disfranchisement of African Americans within the Magnolia State (Donnor, 2017). Guided by a strict doctrine of White supremacy promulgating a doxa of Black inferiority, Black criminality, and an insatiable desire to engage in interracial sex with White women (i.e., miscegenation), White Mississippians have been at the forefront of resistance to "inevitable social change for more than a century" (Silver, 1964, p. 3), utilizing a panoply of "legal" devices and extralegal tactics, such as poll taxes, secret ballots, and lynching, to limit Black political participation and social advancement since 1890. White Mississippians, since the state's readmission into the Union after the Civil War, have intentionally underfunded its public education system in order to: (1) maintain a subservient Black population, and (2) fortify their dominance through racial segregation (Anderson, 1988; Bartley, 1999; Bolton, 2005; Mabry, 1938; Parker, 1987; Perman, 2001; Span, 2009; Silver, 1964; Stavis, 1987). According to historian Charles C. Bolton (2005),

> the shortcomings that permeated Mississippi's public education system could be traced to the effort to establish a dual school system . . . In Mississippi, one of the poorest states in the Union, the state succeeded only

in creating a mediocre school system for [W]hites and an unbelievably impoverished school system for [B]lacks.

(p. 4)

Indeed, with the passage of time, Mississippi's *de jure* public school system became the "most treasured part of the segregated world for [W]hites in the state" (Bolton, 2005, p. xvi). As the aforementioned illustrates, only a sound understanding of history, the law, and public policy can illuminate the complexity and various spaces that race operates within to simultaneously structure and adversely impact the learning opportunities of African American students. In fact, with the U.S. Supreme Court's 1954 verdict in *Brown v. Board of Education* offering African Americans a modicum of franchisement since Reconstruction, public schools were instantly transformed into the existential line in the sand and civilizational rubicon for White people during the mid-20th century (Finely, 2008; Lowndes, 2008; Poole, 2006; Scheurich & Young, 1997; Ward, 2011). In other words, because of its inextricable ties to housing, employment, and social status, Whites in the South, especially in Mississippi, "believed that racial mixing in the classroom would also lead to mixing outside of class, and even to interracial dating or marriage" (Patterson, 2001, p. xviii), and "[l]osing the battle to preserve segregated schools would make it impossible to prevent social equality" (Bolton, 2005, p. xvii). In short, Black education in Mississippi since its inception has been governed by an ethos of Negrophobia.

"On the brain in [many] White men" (Hayes, 1869) since the 16th century, Negrophobia refers to the politically motivated and culturally informed sense of fear held by a majority of White people that their overall well-being will cease to exist if African Americans are accorded a semblance of social, political, legal, and material equality (Armour, 1997; Hayes, 1869; Robin, 2004). Appearing to be reasonable at first glance, Negrophobia by its legal definition is "uniquely insidious . . . [because] . . . it takes the merely typical and contingent, and presents it as truth and morality, objectively construed" (Armour, 1997, p. 26). As a result, White racism under the auspices of Negrophobia assumes a veneer of rationality, because the standard to which it is evaluated is contingent upon whether laws, social policies, and institutional practices can be made to cohere with a set of commonly held beliefs, including stereotypes, which have *some* judicial basis and/or a modicum of scientific grounding (Armour, 1997). Take for example the commonly held belief regarding the purported relationship between race and human intelligence. Despite "seemingly possessing a clear and well-defined meaning for millions of people . . . no one really knows what intelligence is" (Montagu, 1975, p. 1). According to distinguished anthropologist Ashley Montagu, the quality of an individual's experiences more than their genetics is "fundamentally important for the development of the problem-solving behavior we call intelligence or thinking . . ." (1975, p. 191). For Montagu,

[j]ust as the differences in cultural development between different societies may be explained by the differences in the history of their experience, so may the differences in intelligence between individuals be explained, for the most part, by the history of their experience; the parenthetic "for the most part" allowing for any genetic factors that may be involved.

(p. 191)

Regarding the law, particularly in self-defense cases against Black victims, White defendants "often exploit the racial fears of [White] jurors in asserting the reasonableness of their fear of supposed assailants who are Black" (Armour, 1997, p. 4). According to Armour, Negrophobes can readily point to popular news media portrayals and mainstream survey data indicating a disproportionality of African American criminality compared to White people to foreground the reasonableness of their racial fears and racial animus. Thus, the "[r]easonable racist's case hinges on whether he can establish that typical beliefs are reasonable beliefs" (Armour, 1997, p. 22). As such, typical beliefs "in the courts and everyday life . . . carry the presumption of accuracy" (p. 27). Hence, the alleged reasonableness and rationality of Negrophobia as discussed through the use of a legal analysis illustrates how racially informed proclivities and (pre)dispositions become infused with governing institutions to normalize White racism.

With regards to Black education in Mississippi, White people's reactions to African Americans' quest for an education since Reconstruction has varied from "tacit approval to outright hostility" (Span, 2009, p. 84). For many White Mississippians, publicly funded education for the former slaves constituted "both the perceived and real loss of economic, political, social, and psychological control they had maintained over African Americans—in one form or another—before the [Civil] war" (Span, 2009, p. 102). In fact, with the newfound reality that by 1868 Mississippi's Black population was the state's voting majority "the purpose of schools for African Americans assumed even greater significance" (Span, 2009, 11). According to education historian Christopher M. Span, the "type of schooling black children in Mississippi would receive not only determined the status and opportunities for future generations of African Americans, but also, indubitably, the future way of life for white Mississippians as well" (2009, p. 12). In essence, a well-funded and organized public school system for Black people in Mississippi would result in the death of White supremacy and the proprietary attributes associated with Whiteness (Harris, 1995; Donnor, 2013). Resultantly, White Mississippians post-Reconstruction have continued to ensure that the public education initiatives and learning opportunities of Black Mississippians fail (Span, 2009). The case of *Cowan v. Bolivar County Board of Education* is the latest example of the intergenerational impact of White racism on the present-day educational fortunes of Black students in Mississippi. In utilizing *Cowan* as a case study, the methodological goal is to highlight "the persistence of the past" (Donnor, 2017) by showing how race-neutral policies, such as choice, are deployed by Whites to ensure the maintenance of historically derived advantages—both structurally and psychologically.

Brown, Cowan v. Bolivar County Board of Education, and the Continuing Impact of Negrophobia

As already mentioned, *Cowan v. Bolivar County Board of Education* is a school desegregation lawsuit that was filed a decade after *Brown v. Board of Education 1955* (i.e., *Brown II*) in Bolivar County, Mississippi where the petitioners in *Cowan* contended that the Bolivar County School Board operated a racially *de jure* public education system by maintaining "six Caucasian schools and only four African American schools" (*Cowan v. Bolivar County Board of Education*, 2012, p. 2). Having evaded the Supreme Court's "all deliberate speed" dictum from *Brown II*, as well as a lower federal court-ordered rezoning plan and dual residency policy for more than 50 years, the U.S. District Court for the Northern District of Mississippi Delta Division, on May 13, 2016, declared that the Bolivar County Board of Education had "failed to meet this obligation as it concerns the high schools and middle schools" (*Cowan v. Bolivar County Board of Education*, 914 F. Supp. 2d 801, p. 95) in the district. The primary reason for the Bolivar County School Board's successful evasion of *Brown II* is due to its decision to implement a school desegregation policy platform emphasizing freedom of choice.

A federally approved method for assigning students in school districts under desegregation court orders, freedom of choice, posits that "all schools in the system [under court orders] are open to any eligible pupil without regard to race or residence" (U.S. Commission on Civil Rights, 1966, p. 9). In contrast to pupil placement assignments, whereby "each pupil is judged by established criteria and assigned to the school determined to be appropriate" (U.S. Commission on Civil Rights, 1966, p. 9) according to standardized test scores or "morals, community welfare, and health" (Walker, 2009, p. 39), choice assignment plans

> usually provide either that a pupil in a grade reached by the [desegregation] plan has a choice of attending any school in the system or that he may attend any school within a geographic attendance area, subject in either case to limitations of space.
>
> *(U.S. Commission on Civil Rights, 1966, p. 12)*

Because of its emphasis on individual preferences and the supposed absence of external influences, the choice method of school desegregation at first glance appears to be innocuous.

To the contrary however, school choice policies are rife with inconsistencies, paradoxes, and opportunities for circumvention (i.e., tactics of White racism). For example, despite being "permanently enjoined from discriminating on the basis of race and color" and ordered to take "affirmative action to disestablish all school segregation and eliminate the effects of the dual school system" (*Cowan v. Bolivar County Board of Education*, 914 F. Supp. 2d 801, 1969, p. 1) since 1969, the Bolivar County Board of Education, renamed Cleveland after former president Grover Cleveland, as of 2016, still had one middle school that was identified as all White and one middle school that was identified as all Black. Similarly, the Cleveland School District had one predominately White high school and an all-Black high school (*Cowan v. Bolivar County Board of Education*, 914 F. Supp. 2d 801, 2016). This racial marking is particularly troubling given: (1) the district's overall size, (2) the total student population, and (3) the distance between schools. According to the U.S. Census Bureau (2010), Bolivar County, Mississippi, has a total population of 34,145 residents, of which 33.5% are White and 64.2% are African American, and a total student population of 3,652, of which 2,435, or 66.6%, are Black or African American, and 1053, or 28.8%, are White (Holt, 1995; Mississippi Department of Education, 2016). While there are "12 private schools within a 50-mile radius" (*Cowan v. Bolivar County Board of Education*, 914 F. Supp. 2d 801, 2016, p. 25) of the school district, the fact that East Side High remains overwhelmingly Black, with a total student body population of 368 out of 369, and Cleveland High remains predominantly White, with 298 Black students out of 624 (Mississippi Department of Education, 2016), despite being 1.2 miles apart from each other, suggests something other than freedom of choice is at work. Again, it is only by engaging in a legal analysis as the preceding demonstrates that one is better positioned to comprehend how colorblind policy can legalize racial discrimination and racialize the life chances of African Americans over time.

I contend that there are three reasons for East Side High School's predominantly African American student population. The first reason is East Side High's historical reputation as a "Black high school" due, in part, to political gerrymandering, while the second reason, and a proxy for the preceding, as well as the absence of permanent rigorous academic courses, and the nonexistence of a Title I Program at Cleveland High (*Cowan v. Bolivar County Board of Education*, 2013, Doc# 21–1; *Cowan v. Bolivar County Board of Education*, 2014, Doc #79). The third and most significant reason for the continued racial marking of the Cleveland County's two high schools high is the district's overreliance on magnet schools. Originally developed as a strategy for achieving racial integration and improving education quality by providing families in a school district under desegregation orders the opportunity to enroll their children in a specialized public school that offers a unique curriculum or a distinct mode of teaching (i.e., choice), the magnet school program in Cleveland, Mississippi is acutely responsible for maintaining racial segregation because it "turned nearly every one of its all-black schools into a magnet school" (*Cowan v. Bolivar County Board of Education*, 2011, Doc # 6, p. 15). For example, students who are geographically zoned for Cleveland High can take International Baccalaureate courses at East

Side High School without having to enroll in the latter (*Cowan v. Bolivar County Board of Education*, 914 F. Supp. 2d 801, 2016). Also, while East Side High School and Cleveland High School both offered "Honors English I, II, and III, *only* the latter had Advanced Placement (AP) English IV, Biology, Macroeconomics, Physics I and Physics II, Spanish III and Spanish IV, and Saxon Advanced Algebra and Geometry" (*Cowan v. Bolivar County Board of Education*, 2011, Doc# 22–1, p. 13, 16, 18). Historically speaking, the more things changed, the more they stayed the same.

Conclusion-Where Does CRT Go From Here?

> . . . looking back over the decades, I wonder whether the long desegregation effort
> was an unintended but nonetheless contributing cause of current statistical dispari-
> ties that some critics angrily attribute to the continuing effects of racism.
>
> Derrick Bell, 2004, p. 180, *Silent Covenants: Brown v. Board*
> *of Education and the Unfulfilled Hopes for Racial Reform*

In assessing the durability of school choice policies this chapter highlights the long-term strategic goal of White segregationists in Mississippi. More moderate and measured than other demonstrative tactics of White racism (i.e., interposition and massive resistance), freedom of choice as a policy strategy proved more impactful because of its technical emphasis on individual preferences, and the omission of race as an explicit decision-making criterion. In other words, the Cleveland School Board's long-term commitment to promoting school choice over immediate integration not only allowed the vestiges of *de jure* segregation to crystallize, but the associated racial disparities to accumulate intergenerationally.

The goal for the CRT scholars in education moving forward is not simply to articulate the continuity of White racism in education through voice, counter-storytelling, and counter-narrative although important. Instead, the critical race scholarship in education must offer a more nuanced conception of White racism while simultaneously accounting for public declarations supporting racial diversity, along with global and national repudiations of contemporary forms of White nationalism. As constructs that account "ideal factors", voice, counter-storytelling, and counter-narrative "only partially explain how race and racism work" (Delgado, 1989, p. 2280). By using history as both a starting point and roadmap to navigate the contested terrain of race and White racism over time and geographical space, CRT scholars in education will not only learn that most Whites prefer policies that are devoid of explicit mention of race (i.e., color-blind), which meets a key conceptual objective. History, in conjunction with the legal literature, accounts for "material factors" (Delgado, 1989, p. 2280), such as socioeconomic competition and electoral politics, which inform the veracity of White racism. Also, history reveals that most Whites harbor a Negrophobic stance toward policy efforts designed to ameliorate the deleterious effects associated with White racism, which is the reason why substantive social change is never obtained. Finally, history in conjunction with the legal literature shows that White opposition to Black academic advancement is not always hostile, but rather permanent (Bell, 1992).

Notes

1 By White racism, I am specifically referring to: (1) the culturally sanctioned, accepted, and enforced beliefs that regardless of intent defend and advance the historically derived political, legal, social, and material advantages White people have accrued at the expense of the collective advancement of African Americans (Wellman, 1993); and (2) how White people use society's governing institutions (i.e., education, law, and public policy) to entrench the aforementioned advantages and subordinate Black people.
2 According to historian Joseph Crespino (2007), the ascribed characteristics of White Mississippian opposition to African American equality during the 1950s and 1960s became the "cornerstone" of contemporary political conservatism in the United States.

References

Anderson, J. D. (1988). *The education of Blacks in the South, 1860–1935.* Chapel Hill, NC: The University of North Carolina Press.

Andrews, K. T. (2004). *Freedom is a constant struggle: The Mississippi civil rights movement and its legacy.* Chicago: The University of Chicago Press.

Armour, J. D. (1997). *Negrophobia and reasonable racism: The hidden costs of being Black in America.* New York: New York University Press.

Bartley, N. V. (1999). *The rise of massive resistance: Race and politics in the South during the 1950s.* Baton Rouge, LA: Louisiana State University Press.

Bell, D. (1992). *Faces at the bottom of the well: The permanence of racism.* New York: Basic Books.

Bell, D. (2004). *Silent covenants: Brown v. Board of Education and the unfulfilled hopes for racial reform.* New York: Oxford University Press.

Bolton, C. C. (2005). *The hardest deal of all: The battle over school integration in Mississippi, 1870–1980.* Jackson, MS: University of Mississippi Press.

Brown v. Board of Education of Topeka, 347 U.S. 483 (1954).

Brown v. Board of Education of Topeka, 349 U.S. 294 (1955).

Cowan v. Bolivar County Board of Education, 914 F. Supp. 2d 801 (N.D. Miss. 2012).

Crenshaw, K. W. (2011). Twenty years of critical race theory: Looking back to move forward. *Connecticut Law Review, 43*(5), 1253–1352.

Crespino, J. (2007). *In search of another country: Mississippi and the conservative counterrevolution.* Princeton, NJ: Princeton University Press.

Delgado, R. (1989). Two ways to think about race: Reflections on the id, the ego, and other reformist theories of equal protection. *The Georgetown Law Journal, 89*(7), 2279–2296.

Dixson, A. D., & Rousseau Anderson, C. K. (2017). And we are STILL not saved: 20 years of CRT and education. In A. D. Dixson, C. K. Rousseau Anderson & J. K. Donnor (Eds) (2nd ed.). *Critical race theory in education: All God's children got a song* (pp. 32–54). New York: Routledge.

Donnor, J. K. (2013). Education as the property of Whites: African Americans' continued quest for good schools. In M. Lynn & A. D. Dixson (Eds.), *Handbook of critical race theory in education* (pp. 195–203). New York: Routledge.

Donnor, J. K. (2017). *Cowan*, whiteness, resistance to *Brown*, and the persistence of the past. *Peabody Journal of Education, 93*(1), 23–37.

Donnor, J. K., & Ladson-Billings (2017). Critical race theory and the postracial imaginary. In N. K. Denzin & Y. S. Lincoln (Eds.) (5th ed.). *The Sage handbook of qualitative research* (pp. 195–213). Thousand Oaks, CA: Sage Publications.

DuBois, W. E. B. (1999). *Dark water: Voices from within the veil*. Mineola, NY: Dover Publications.

Finely, K. M. (2008). *Delaying the dream: Southern senators and the fight against civil rights, 1938–1965*. Baton Rouge, LA: Louisiana State University Press.

Harris, C. I. (1995). Whiteness as property. In K. Crenshaw, N. Gotanda, G. Peller, & K. Thomas (Eds.), *Critical race theory: The key writings that formed the movement* (pp. 292–302). New York: The New Press.

Hayes, J. R. (1869). *Negrophobia "On the Brain": In White men or an essay upon the origin and progress both mental and physical of the Negro race, and the use to be made of him by politicians in the United States*. Washington, DC: Powell, Ginck & Co.

Holt, T. C. (1995). Marking: Race, race-making, and the writing of history. *The American Historical Review, 100*(1), 1–20.

Indigo Williams, et al. v. Phil Bryant, et al., 3:17-cv-404 (2017).

Parker, F. T. (1987). Protest, politics, and litigation: Political and social change in Mississippi, 1965 to present. *Mississippi Law Journal, 57*, 677–704.

Perman, M. (2001). *Struggle for mastery: Disfranchisement in the South, 1888–1908*. Chapel Hill, NC: The University of North Carolina Press.

Ladson-Billings, G., & Tate, W. F. (1995). Toward a critical race theory of education. *Teachers College Record, 97*(1) 47–65.

Lowndes, J. E. (2008). *From the New Deal to the New Right: Race and the Southern origins of modern conservatism*. New Haven, CT: Yale University Press.

Mabry, W. A. (1938). Disfranchisement of the Negro in Mississippi. *The Journal of Southern History, 4*(3), 318–333.

Mississippi Department of Education. (2016). *Cleveland School District: District level data, 2016*. Retrieved from http://reports.mde.k12.ms.us/data/

Montagu, A. (1975). Intelligence, IQ, and race. In A. Montagu (Ed). *Race and IQ: Expanded edition*. New York: Oxford University Press.

Patterson, J. T. (2001). *Brown v. Board of Education: A civil rights milestone and its troubled legacy*. New York: Oxford University Press.

Poole, M. (2006). *The segregated origins of Social Security: African Americans and the welfare state*. Chapel Hill, NC: The University of North Carolina Press.

Robin, C. (2004). *Fear: The history of a political idea*. New York: Oxford University Press.

Scheurich, J. J., & Young, M. D. (1997). Coloring epistemologies: Are our research epistemologies racially biased? *Educational Researcher, 26*(4), 4–16.

Silver, J. W. (1964). Mississippi: The closed society. *The Journal of Southern History, 30*(1), 3–34.

Span, C. M. (2009). *From cotton fields to schoolhouse: African American education in Mississippi, 1862–1875*. Chapel Hill, NC: The University of North Carolina Press.

Stavis, M. (1987). A century of struggle for Black enfranchisement in Mississippi: From the Civil War to the Congressional challenge of 1965—and beyond. *Mississippi Law Journal, 57*, 591–676.

U.S. Commission on Civil Rights. (1966). *Survey of school desegregation in the Southern and border states, 1965–1966*. Washington, DC: U.S. Government Printing Office.

Walker, A. (2009). *The ghost of Jim Crow: How Southern moderates used Brown v. Board of Education to stall civil rights*. New York: Oxford University Press.

Ward, J. M. (2011). *Defending White democracy: The making of a segregationist movement and the remaking of racial politics, 1936–1965*. Chapel Hill, NC: The University of North Carolina Press.

Wellman, D. T. (1993). *Portraits of white racism* (2nd ed.). New York: Cambridge University Press.

3

CRT IN EDUCATION

Historical/Archival Analyses

Jerome E. Morris and Benjamin D. Parker

One of the basic assumptions of Critical Race Theory is that history matters (Zamudio, Russell, Rios, & Bridgeman, 2011). For researchers within the theoretical tradition of CRT, that means any attempt made to investigate the world with an eye toward racial inequalities will inevitably lead to considerations of the past. These considerations are important because they provide varied perspectives to be distilled, interpreted, represented, and applied. The reconstructed product termed "history" is not the Truth, but rather the conclusions drawn from the resources employed, and the researcher's interpretation of those resources. It is an approximation, tailored to a specific audience, and colored by an agenda, positionality, and the lens through which researchers choose to view the research (White, 1973; Karier, 1967/1986). When viewed through the lens of CRT, the stories told carry the weight of liberation and fly in the face of marginalization and deficit representations of historically marginalized racial and ethnic groups. This chapter highlights the form and function of historical documents and archival records as they relate to CRT and educational research.

The difference between documents and records is distinct and meaningful, making operational definitions necessary. According to Lincoln and Guba (1985), records represent formal transactions and business dealings, while documents are informal texts created for personal use. This difference is significant as it also indicates where researchers might find such resources. While official educational records might be maintained by individual school districts or located in state archives, historical documents pertaining to education and communities may be held in personal collections, with local historical preservation bodies, scattered across libraries and university collections, or held in the "remembrances" by the people.

Oral history interviews and material artifacts also represent the kinds of historical documentary evidence that should be of interest to CRT scholars. Oral history interviews, particularly those of participants from marginalized communities in which physical artifacts and data might have been destroyed, lost, or not considered "valuable" at the time, can provide a perspective that contributes another layer to understanding historical phenomena and their consequences. Whereas material artifacts are important as they are symbolic and substantive representations of both "master" and counter-narratives, they demonstrate aspects of culture that often go untheorized. Deconstructing the evocative nature of visual data can allow researchers to enrich their work through the process of making meaning from abstractions and interactions found in the relative oral and documentary evidence. Archival research involves the analysis of historically rare and valuable documents that are generally held within a repository or among "special collections" of related items. Artifacts, on the other hand, are tangible items that may or not be a part of archival documents. Artifacts have to be understood within a particular context; otherwise, they remain meaningless. Archival documents, artifacts, and oral history interviews contribute to CRT researchers' efforts to uncover the counter-narratives of historically marginalized racial and ethnic groups, in addition to telling the stories.

CRT and Education

When CRT is applied to the field of education, its aim is to root out the systemic inequalities and inequities levied upon marginalized groups and harbored and reproduced by schooling structures (Roithmayr, 1999; Zamudio et al., 2011). Activated in part through the research process itself (Zamudio et al., 2011), the racist structures of U.S. social, political, and educational systems are destabilized through the critical examination of historical phenomena, policies, and practices. As a result, even the traditional educational research methods themselves are implicated as mechanisms of reification for racial inequalities and marginalization (Solórzano & Yosso, 2002). Appropriately, CRT provides both a theoretical framework as well as a methodological instrument for collecting and understanding the perspectives of marginalized groups (Greene, 2013; Ladson-Billings & Tate, 1995; Zamudio et al., 2011). The goal is to conduct education research that, "foregrounds race and racism in all aspects of the research process" (Solórzano & Yosso, 2002, p. 24). To engage in this type of thoughtful and conscious research, researchers must begin squarely with the questions they are asking of themselves, of the resources, of the process, and of the product with regard to their connections to race, racism, inequality, and inequity.

The Researcher

A researcher should ask, "Who am I and why does it matter?" For one, it matters because the researcher is a variable in the research process. The understanding of the subject, conceptions of CRT, and conclusions are shaped in part by the researcher's identity and ways of seeing the world (i.e., epistemology). While historical analyses may seem clinical, and are often presented as straightforward, the tools used to tell history mostly consists of familiarizing oneself with archives and published scholarship in the form of books and articles (Alridge, 2015; White, 1973). And the historian brings another tool into the analysis: his or her own identity. As Alridge further elaborates: "As historians of education we inevitably bring our own subjectivities to our work and thus cannot attain absolute objectivity; we are creatures of the time in which we live, and therefore our work will always be influenced by our context . . . historians can adhere to traditional notions of objectivity, but those notions do not limit them" (Alridge, 2015, p. 124).

Thus, in selecting CRT as the theoretical lens through which to view historical data regarding education, this chapter's authors, as critical race scholars, engaged their research from a critical historical perspective. That began first and foremost with embracing the "critical." Critical historians apply frameworks like CRT to examine and contest the standing record, identify the power structures that determine "winners" and "losers," and consider new ways to conduct meaningful and impactful research (Alridge, 2015). In practice, this means recognizing the researcher's influence on the questions posed and looking for alternative ways to ask questions that will, in turn, establish alternative answers, and thus alternative historical narratives. The following provides a brief illustration of how the authors' identities and positionalities shaped the construction of narrative through textual evidence.

As a researcher whose scholarship includes a focus on how public school desegregation has shaped African-American schools and communities (Morris, 2009, 2008, 2004, 2001), the first author has had to interrogate not only his identities as an African-American male, but also his experiences as someone who grew up in a predominantly Black and urban community in the U.S. South. More than three decades after the Supreme Court's decision in *Brown v. Board of Education*, the public schools he attended in Birmingham remained predominantly Black and overwhelmingly poor; *Brown*'s promise of quality education for Black children had still not been realized. This reflexivity (Hammersley & Atkinson, 1996) has allowed him to develop the kind of nuanced understanding of how social and educational policies such as desegregation have shaped the experiences of African-American students, families, and educators in such a way that is rarely captured in the sociological, educational, and historical literature.

For example, in his research study of a how a St. Louis, Missouri desegregation plan impacted the connections between schools and African-American families, students, and communities, Morris (2001, 2009) demonstrated how 21 Black educators (across an African-American neighborhood school, a predominantly White suburban school, and a magnet school) embraced a "critical race perspective" in terms of how the plan was implemented. Of these 21 Black educators, 17 were female, 13 were classroom teachers, 3 were teaching assistants, 2 were principals (male and female), 1 was an interim principal, and 2 were instructional coordinators. Resonating with CRT, a key purpose was to illuminate the voices of Black educators, a group of professionals who had been summarily dismissed in conversations and policies regarding the education of African-American children. Their stories were as equally important as those which had been published or the perspectives of other stakeholders such as civic and business leaders, attorneys, judges, etc. Throughout the research process, however, it was imperative that systematic research approaches were adhered to such as member checking, the triangulation of multiple data sources, and the constant comparison of data. Thus, the quest to research and understand phenomena requires that the researcher develop a critical analysis of his or her own identities within the overall research process.

Similarly, in his study of the ideological imposition of educational iconography, the second author had to reconcile his identities as a White, male researcher with the source of racial discrimination under investigation. In examining how three Black students (one female and two males) and three White teachers (two females and one male) interpreted Eurocentric symbols of White dominance found on urban school buildings, he outlined his own relationship to the space and his understanding of it. To do so, it was necessary for him to deconstruct how his own identity markers situated him in relation to the phenomenon, participants, research site, and data. Consequently, this prompted him to consider the extent to which his presence engendered or inhibited the documentary evidence made available. In curating source materials, he relied on both insider and outsider positions to diversify and substantiate the co-constructed narrative through triangulation, the collective use of multiple independent sources of data or methods for the purpose of establishing a validated and corroborated understanding of the phenomenon under investigation (Patton, 1999).

Researchers do not exist in a vacuum. They bring their own epistemological perspectives—ways of knowing—into how they decide on certain questions to investigate, the framing of researchable questions, interactions with participants, data collection and analysis, and interpretations and conclusions. How researchers' experiences and identities, which shape their ideological views and epistemologies, are composed cannot be dismissed as a nonessential component of the research process (Scheurich & Young, 1997). Researchers' epistemologies arise from individuals' and groups' social histories (Banks 1993; Connolly & Troyna, 1998; Gordon, 1990; Stanfield, 1985, 1993). Within the scope of the second author's research project, participants included former students of his, and he was forced to be conscious of the need to not fall back into the role of teacher, and to allow the participants to expound on their experiences and relationships to the space under investigation.

Social scientists often argue the primacy of approaching the analysis of phenomenon from "objective" perspectives, so as not to "bias" the data analysis and interpretations. Arguments for objectivity, in many ways, are synonymous to status quo research because of the potential to marginalize voices and perspectives from non-dominant backgrounds. Researchers' experiences and identities cannot be wholly separated from their ideological experiences. Epistemologically racist interpretations, analyses, and conclusions result when privileged and dominant group researchers' experiences and identities diverge greatly from those individuals and groups they research—but exclude the indigenous *meaningfully* from the overall research process.

While a key responsibility of the archivist is to position the records chronologically and categorically, the researcher's responsibility is to make sense of these records and to tell a cohesive story based on his/her collection of sources. The story to tell as a researcher, therefore, stands at the intersection of the researcher and his or her source material. Without the materials, it is just an opinion. Without the researchers it is just data. The researcher's responsibility is to situate the data, through a CRT lens, within a broader racial, historical, economic, and sociopolitical context. Consistent with the aim of CRT, it is important to make sure that the archival data and the subsequent stories are uniquely sensitive to the experiences and realities of those at the "bottom of the well" in a racial and social class hierarchy (Bell, 1992).

The Resources

When explicating historical records and documents—with an awareness of the centrality of race and racism within a particular social and political context—what researchers don't find can be equally as telling as what they do find. For example, while the long history of racial oppression in America can be well documented through primary and secondary sources, more-modern social and political shifts began to drive more-overt practices of racism underground (Bonilla-Silva, 2006), and began to tout the notion that the United States had entered a post-racial era with the election of Barack Obama as the first African-American President (Morris & Woodruff, 2015). As overt racism became less socially acceptable, symbolism substituted for substance, and policies and practices that aimed to sustain inequalities appeared subtle. Yet, the 2016 national election of Donald Trump to the U.S. presidency represented a seismic shift that encouraged the overt display of a White nationalist agenda as witnessed in Charlottesville, Virginia. Thus, CRT researchers must consider historical records and documents within the broader racial and political climate of the time.

In some cases, the documentary evidence is missing and what needs to be considered by the researcher is why certain records are unavailable and what implications that has on the research at hand. "Past processes have generated surviving structures—documents, images, memories—that allow us to reconstruct in our minds . . . what happened" (Gaddis, 2002). Conversely, the absence of surviving structures that portray the violence of marginalization are not evidence of its non-existence but rather tributes to the machine of oppression. Therefore, for critical researchers, it is imperative to question and consider the record, recorder, and repository for their contributions to the master narrative confronted or the counter-narrative they seek to develop.

In this sense, oral history and people's stories (as data) become useful for buttressing the limited records that exist. Moreover, the role of CRT researchers might include creating documents from that oral history. But how do critical researchers know which oral histories to include in the broader effort to create documents and documentary evidence? Researchers with an interest in examining archival and other data are often taught to consult books, articles, newspapers, interviews, individuals' personal collections, etc. But relying on such data sources is not sufficient because of the great likelihood that these might not include perspectives from the marginalized. Critical Race Theory archival research might entail seeking out people from communities that provide insights and stories about people that one might not normally encounter. For example, Foster's (1990) notion of "community nomination" provides a way of thinking about how to select participants. In her research on Black teachers, Foster describes "community nomination" as a process of relying on Black people who are experts in the area to inform how oral history researchers choose certain people to include in research projects. Accessing communities, thus, is an important part of the process of creating rich historical documents for future analyses. But who gets to access communities, particularly across race, gender, and social class?

Even the concept of primary and secondary sources should be critically examined when conducting educational research within CRT. Primary sources in the form of historical documents are those that were created during the period under investigation while secondary sources analyze primary sources and are created after the fact (Barton, 2005). In effect, surviving historical documentary primary sources that come to be recognized as master texts often align with a master narrative that reifies the power and influence of White male privilege. The preservation of historical primary sources from marginalized communities is not as robust due to the sociopolitical structures that perpetuated notions of cultural deficiencies and devalued the histories and legacies of the people and places involved.

The Process

How can historical context help critical researchers understand their source materials? As historiography makes evident, history is not without bias (Gaddis, 2002). For that reason, even seemingly benign documents are expressive of a position, a perspective, and a contextual imprint that is inextricably linked to the origins of the source. The work of the researcher is not to simply collect a pile of similarly themed artifacts and present them as fact. Instead, the work is in the weaving together of reliable sources to establish a collective narrative that acts as an evidentiary pillar for the argument being made or the question(s) being answered. Critical historians of race and education need to "[f]orge a new narrative which documents racism as a contemporary phenomenon" (Zamudio et al., 2011, p. 120). The record of the past is not frozen, nor should it be when it comes to understanding the present and considering the future. Historical documents and records can be deceptive as the constructed narrative that builds around these artifacts itself begins to seem historical. Particularly when talking about racism, the researcher must remain cognizant of the perpetuity of offenses and how the past has continued to shape the future. Framing past transgressions as isolated markers of racism confounds the permanence of oppression upon which CRT builds. Statements such as, "I didn't own slaves," or the notion of a post-racial America are examples of efforts to dismiss the existing legacies of racism by relegating them to the past and ignoring the entrenchment of structures that reify racial inequalities. So, in keeping with the foundational work of scholars like Carter G. Woodson, researchers should produce scholarship that contests inaccurate portrayals of race, recognizes and meets the needs of oppressed groups and individuals, and becomes concerned with the work of racial equality (Alridge, 2015).

The Historical Narrative

The end result of a CRT-informed research study that relies heavily on historical documentary, archival data, and oral history is ultimately a counter-narrative. Solórzano and Yosso (2002) have defined the counter-narrative or counter-story as a "method of telling the stories of those people whose experiences are not often told (i.e., those on the margins of society) . . . a tool for exposing, analyzing, and challenging the majoritarian stories of racial privilege" (p. 32). In this sense, when researchers incorporate sources of data that have traditionally not been a part of the historical record, they elevate the voices of those on the racial margins by giving value to their perspectives and experiences. The following demonstrates the application of a CRT framework to historical policy analysis.

Recognizing how most narratives of *Brown v. Board of Education* primarily focused on integrated schooling as the ultimate objective in Black people's quest for quality schooling, Morris (2008), offered a counter-narrative that asserted that the push by Black people for quality schooling during the segregation era was not uniformly about integration, but instead, was a part of multiple ideologies within the African-American community of which integration represented only one. The analytic review profiled a group of scholars (mostly African American) who had gone beyond truncated and deficit representations of all-Black schools during legalized segregation (e.g., Cecelski, 1994; Dougherty, 2004; Jones, 1981; Morris & Morris, 2002; Noblit & Dempsey, 1996; Siddle Walker, 1996). For the most part, they were challenging representations in the historical literature that primarily focused on the fiscal inequalities between segregated Black and White schools, thereby conflating the quality of the schools with the absence or presence of fiscal resources. Collectively, they highlighted how Black schools and the educators within them played a critical role in shaping African-American identity, culture, and achievement in a White-dominated society. This counter-narrative scholarship raised poignant questions concerning (1) the efficacy of desegregation as the primary means to implement *Brown*, (2) how desegregation policies ignored the sociocultural and historical contexts of Black schooling, and (3) *Brown*'s second—but often ignored—promise of quality schooling for low-income Black children.

Rather than disconnecting historical research from contemporary sociological scholarship on the representation of predominantly Black schools, Morris further noted how contemporary views of Black schooling in many ways reproduced the dominant historical narrative of Black education during legalized segregation. Based on extensive and intensive sociological research in the urban South and Midwest, he described how two predominantly African-American schools— one located in Atlanta, Georgia, and the other in St. Louis, Missouri—defied the disasters portrayed in the media about urban and contemporary predominantly African-American schools. Contrary to the pervasive and contemporary view of urban schools as inept, the schools were renowned for connecting with African-American families and nearby respective Black communities, and for educating primarily low-income African-American students who attended the schools (Morris, 2009, 2004). Methodologically, his research approach focused on schools that personified "health" rather than pathology, in order to put forth new models for African-American education. The research process included ethnographic interviews with parents, teachers, and school district leaders, but also oral history interviews with African-American community members and the analysis of historical documents and artifacts from "community-based" African-American historians.

Conclusion

The purpose of this chapter was to illustrate how a CRT framework can inform all phases of historical research, focusing on the process from collection to dissemination, the resources, the researcher, and the historical narrative. The authors provided examples of how this unfolded in their research studies. As with any research, researchers' identities, epistemologies, and interpretation of data are important, specifically in the way historical documents, artifacts, and other sources become interpreted. As critical race theorists continue to push boundaries in order to bring forth the voices of racially marginalized groups on key issues around race, class, power, and education, it is also important to include archival resources such as historical documents and artifacts that emanate, not only from traditional repositories such as libraries, university collections, and historical preservation groups, but from community-based and local historians and within the "remembrances" by those on the margins of society.

References

Alridge, D. P. (2015). The ideas and craft of the critical historian of education. In Ana M. Martínez-Alemán, Brian Pusser, and Estela Mara Bensimon (Eds.), *Critical approaches to the study of higher education: A practical introduction* (pp. 103–129). Baltimore, MD: Johns Hopkins University Press.

Banks, J. A. (1993). Multicultural education: Development, dimensions, and challenges. *The Phi Delta Kappan, 75*(1), 22–28.

Barton, K. C. (2005). Primary sources in history: Breaking through the myths. *The Phi Delta Kappan, 86*(10), 745–753.

Bell, D. (1992). *Faces at the bottom of the well: The permanence of racism.* New York: Basic Books.

Bonilla-Silva, E. (2006). *Racism without racists: Color-blind racism and the persistence of racial inequality in the United States* (2nd ed.). Boulder, CO: Rowman & Littlefield.

Cecelski, D. S. (1994). *Along freedom road: Hyde County, North Carolina, and the fate of Black schools in the South.* Chapel Hill: University of North Carolina Press.

Connolly, P., & Troyna, B. (1998). *Researching racism in education.* Buckingham, UK: Open University Press.

Dougherty, J. (2004). *More than one struggle: The evolution of Black school reform in Milwaukee.* Chapel Hill: University of North Carolina Press.

Foster, M. (1990). The politics of race: Through African American teachers' eyes. *Journal of Education, 172*(3), 123–141.

Gaddis, J. L. (2002). *The landscape of history: How historians map the past.* Oxford: Oxford University Press.

Gordon, B. M. (1990). The necessity of African-American epistemology for educational theory and practice. *The Journal of Education, 172*(3), 88–106.

Greene, S. (2013). *Race, community, and urban schools: Partnering with African American families.* New York: Teacher's College Press.

Hammersley, M., & Atkinson, P. (Eds.). (1996). *Ethnography: Principles in practice* (2nd ed.). New York: Routledge.

Jones, F. (1981). *A traditional model of educational excellence.* Washington, DC: Howard University Press.

Karier, C. J. (1986 [1967]). *The individual, education, and society: A history of American educational ideas.* Urbana-Champaign: University of Illinois Press.

Ladson-Billings, G., & Tate, W. (1995). Toward a critical race theory of education. *Teachers College Record, 97*(1), 47–68.

Lincoln, Y. S., & Guba, E. G. (1985). *Naturalistic inquiry.* Newbury Park, CA: Sage.

Morris, J. E. (2009). *Troubling the waters: Fulfilling the promise of quality public schooling for Black children.* New York: Teachers College Press.

Morris, J. E. (2008). Research, ideology, and the *Brown* decision: Counter-narratives to the historical and contemporary representation of predominantly Black schooling. *Teachers College Record, 110*(4), 713–732.

Morris, J. E. (2004). Can anything good come from Nazareth? Race, class, and African American schooling and community in the urban South and Midwest. *American Educational Research Journal, 41*(1), 69–112.

Morris, J. E. (2001). Forgotten voices of African-American educators: Critical race perspectives on the implementation of a desegregation plan. *Educational Policy, 15*(4), 575–600.

Morris, J. E., & Woodruff, S. E. (2015). Adolescents' Perceptions of Opportunities in the U.S. South: Postracial Mirage or Reality in the New Black Mecca? *Peabody Journal of Education, 90*(3), 404–425.

Morris, V. G., & Morris, C. L. (2002). *The price they paid: Desegregation in an African American community.* New York: Teachers College Press.

Noblit, G., & Dempsey, V. (1996). *The social construction of virtue: The moral life of schools.* Albany: State University of New York Press.

Patton, M. Q. (1999). Enhancing the quality and credibility of qualitative analysis. *Health Services Research, 34*(5 Pt. 2), 1189.

Roithmayr, D. (1999). Introduction to critical race theory in educational research and praxis. In L. Parker, D. Deyhle, & S. Villenas (Eds.),. *Race is . . . race isn't: Critical race theory and qualitative studies in education.* Boulder, CO: Westview Press.

Scheurich, J. J., & Young, M. D. (1997). Coloring epistemologies: Are our research epistemologies racially biased? *Educational Researcher, 26*(4), 4–16.

Siddle Walker, E. V. (1996). *Their highest potential: An African American school community in the segregated South.* Chapel Hill: University of North Carolina Press.

Solórzano, D. G., & Yosso, T. J. (2002). Critical race methodology: Counter-storytelling as an analytical framework for education research. *Qualitative Inquiry, 8*(1), 23–44.

Stanfield, J. H. II (1993). Epistemological considerations. In J. H. Stanfield II, & R. M. Dennis (Eds.), *Race and ethnicity in research methods* (pp. 6–36). Thousand Oaks, CA: Sage.

Stanfield, J. H. II (1985). The ethnocentric basis of social science knowledge production. *Review of Research in Education, 12*, 387–415.

White, H. (1973). *Metahistory: The historical imagination in nineteenth-century Europe.* Baltimore: Johns Hopkins University Press.

Zamudio, M., Russell, C., Rios, F., & Bridgeman, J. (2011). *Critical race theory matters: Education and ideology.* New York: Routledge.

4

CAN YOU HEAR (AND SEE) ME NOW?

Race-ing American Language Variationist/ Change and Sociolinguistic Research Methodologies

Sonja L. Lanehart

I am an African American, Christian, cis-female, heterosexual, middle-class, college-educated, Black feminist, Houstonian Texan, and abled woman who is a mother, wife, daughter, social justice advocate, scholar, teacher, sponsor (Hewlett, Peraino, Sherbin, & Sumberg, 2010), and mentor. These are my salient identities, varying in their saliency from moment to moment and pointing to my subjectivities. I value my race/ethnicity, Christianity, womanhood, personal relationships, and affiliations within my sociocultural and historical contexts as an African slave descendant of involuntary minorities (Ogbu, 1978) living in the "not post-racial" U.S.

As a language and identity scholar using the frameworks of Critical Race Theory (CRT), Black feminism, and intersectionality theory for my method-ologies and multi-methods for more complex and inclusive narratives, I thrive when pushing boundaries and opening new spaces and places for people like me. In the case of this project, I conducted a survey of the entirety of one jour-nal using a CRT (Delgado and Stefancic, 2001), Black feminist (Collins, 1990), intersectionality lens (Crenshaw, 1991; DeCuir-Gunby and Schutz, 2014). The goals of this chapter are to: (1) critique the status quo of (a) American language variation/change and sociolinguistic (ALVCS) research as well as researchers as "White, heterosexual, and male" (WHAM), and (b) African American Language research as "African American, heterosexual, and male" (AAHAM); and (2) using CRT, intersectionality, and Black feminism as methodologies to demonstrate the need for more inclusive, critical, and intersectional ALVCS research addressing more complex questions around language and identity as well as interrogating researcher identities and their subjectivities – especially as it involves African Americans in general and African American women in particular.

Houston, We Have a Problem

In ALVCS research, African American women have often been ignored, made invisible, and overlooked as both research participants and researchers. These omissions are examples of the permanence of racism and sexism, or misogynoir: the hatred of Black[1] women (Bailey, 2010). Much research on language uses in African American communities has long focused on young, urban AAHAMs as the "authentic" users of African American Language (AAL)[2] or, specifically, African American Vernacular Language (AAVL), which is a sub-variety of AAL representing the everyday, informal speech used by and among African Americans. I can only assume that, given their omission as participants in AAL research, African American women have been viewed as either inauthentic, the same as African American men, or simply irrelevant. As such, I made a commitment to African American women's lives and African American Women's Language (AAWL) because, as an African American woman, I saw the multiplicative effects of racism and sexism, on the quality and quantity of research on language use in African American communities, and because this omission has consequential implications beyond ALVCS research.

ALVCS researchers seem to have difficulty going beyond two speaker/demographic variables from the "norm" of "WHAM." White, heterosexual, cis-females; White, gay, cis-males; and AAHAMs are acceptable; however, given their omission, African American, LGBTQ women and girls are not acceptable, demonstrating daily that "all the women are White and all the Blacks are men" (Hull, Bell Scott, & Smith, 1982). Even though AAL is the most studied language variety in the United States, these studies too often exclude more than half the population of AAL speakers. However, still, some of us are brave (Hull, et al., 1982).

To demonstrate the pall of Whiteness in ALVCS research, I critique the research methods and methodologies in ALVCS, specifically the demographics of the participants, the demographics of the researchers, and the obfuscation of data. My data set comes from the feature articles published in the venerable journal *American Speech* (*AmSp*) from its first issue in 1925 to 2017. It has been a publication of the American Dialect Society (ADS), which was founded in 1889, since 1969, and has been published by Duke University Press since 2000.

Full disclosure: I am a lifetime member of ADS. I became aware of the organization as an undergraduate student studying in the English Language and Linguistics Program at the University of Texas at Austin. I dreamt of being published in *AmSp* because it epitomized the ALVCS research, specifically dialectology, I aspired to do. I have attended ADS annual meetings since being introduced to them by my doctoral advisor and dissertation chair at the University of Michigan, Richard W. Bailey, a well-respected senior scholar in English language and linguistics research. I served briefly as the Book Reviews Editor of *AmSp* and most recently as a member of the ADS Executive Council. In all that time and interaction with ADS, I have too often been the only person of color (POC) and one of the few women in the room. Suffice it to say, despite my fondness for my ideal of the journal and the organization as opposed to the reality, ADS essentially has been a "good ol' White boys" network. In its history, it has had only one POC as its president: John Baugh, a distinguished Black male scholar in Linguistics, Anthropology, and Education at Stanford University at the time. ADS has only had six White women as president in its nearly 130-year history, four of whom served after 2004. In 2018, the ADS Executive Council selected a White woman as Executive Secretary after decades of service by a White male. I say this because who is in the room has a lot to do with what questions are asked and what decisions are made about those who are not allowed in the room (Lanehart, 2017).

Researching African American Language and Speech Communities

After the Ebonics Controversy of 1996–1997, the number of publications on AAL increased greatly. Although several publications were aimed at explaining the Ebonics issue (e.g., Baugh, 2000), others provided a new forum for discussing past research on AAL (e.g., Baugh, 1999; Rickford, 1999; Smitherman, 2000); expanded the conversation (e.g., Alim, 2004a, 2004b, 2006; Alim & Baugh, 2007; DeBose, 2005; Morgan, 2002; Smitherman, 2006); followed untraditional groups in the African American community (Green, 2011; Jacobs-Huey, 2006; Lanehart, 2002, 2009); provided a primer on AAL (Green, 2002; Rickford & Rickford, 2000), or broadened conversations about AAL (Lanehart, 2015a, 2015b) and the intersection of language and race in general (Alim, Rickford, & Ball, 2016; Alim & Smitherman, 2012). However, underneath traditional research on AAL is the narrow emphasis on viewing AAL as a language spoken mostly by and among AAHAM youths. There is little regard or recognition that language used in African American communities includes all demographics – children, men, women; working class, middle class, upper class; educated, uneducated; literate, illiterate; Southerners, Northerners, Midwesterners, etc. – and all stylistic varieties. Although one can now find language research on African American groups other than young AAHAMs, it is still a problematic issue and runs to the heart of the question: Who uses AAL? The notion that AAL is simply a street language or only part of a very specific AAHAM subculture is so ingrained it is difficult to break some researchers out of that mindset.

Since linguists know that all segments of African American communities speak AAL, ALVCS needs research and researchers exploring these segments so that when we use "AAL" it is not an elision for "AAL of men and boys." There are still very few books addressing the issue of AAWL or simply speech communication and discourses of African American women (see Etter-Lewis, 1993; Houston & Davis, 2001; Hudson, 2001; Jacobs-Huey, 2006; Lanehart, 2002,

2009, 2015a). This gap in the research literature exposes the lack of and need for more Black-identified and allied language and discourse scholars in the room and CRT, intersectionality, and Black feminist lenses on the research that is conducted, as well as on the researchers themselves. According to Crenshaw (1991, p. 1244), there are three ways of conceptualizing intersectionality: structural, political, and representational. Structural intersectionality proposes that strategies based solely on the experiences of women who do not share the same class or race backgrounds will be of limited help to women who face different obstacles because of race and class (Crenshaw, 1991, p. 1246). This was, and is, a divide that exists within the feminist movement and led groups of women of color to emerge as separate from White women's groups. Black women, Latinas, etc. have many shared struggles with White women, but they also have many more dissimilar struggles because society is not only sexist, but it is also racist and classist. Hence, the feminist movement is not big or inclusive enough for women of color, those living in poverty, and other marginalized groups. As Crenshaw (1991, p. 1250) asserts, women of color occupy positions both physically and culturally marginalized within dominant society, so methodologies must be targeted directly to them in order to reach them.

Beyond Two Degrees of Separation: Intersectionality, CRT, and Diversity in ALVCS Research

The term "intersectionality theory" gained prominence in the 1990s when sociologist Patricia Hill Collins (1990) integrated the idea as part of her discussion on Black feminist thought, making research about Black women more complex and less connected to White feminist research than before. Collins's work included women of color in her theoretical perspective and accounted for the exponential salience, hence, intersection of race, gender, class, and sexuality. According to Crenshaw (1991, p. 1252), political intersectionality proposes that women of color are situated within at least two subordinated groups that frequently pursue conflicting political agendas. The need to split one's political energies between two, sometimes opposing, groups is a dimension of intersectional disempowerment that White women seldom confront. Because women of color experience racism in ways distinct from men of color and sexism in ways not always parallel to White women, antiracism and feminism are limited, even on their own terms. Sexual stratification theory posits that women are stratified sexually by race. As a result, traditional ALVCS studies on AAL, AAHAMs, and AAVL have been more favored than African American women and AAWL because, for some, AAHAMs have been seen as the true arbiters of AAVL. Only more recent research has focused on African American women (e.g., Jacobs-Huey, 2006; Lanehart, 2002, 2009; Troutman, 2001; Morgan, 1991, 1996, 1999). This seems unconscionable given that both African American men and women use language, but women are typically early primary carriers of culture and history through childrearing. To negate or subordinate the existence and experience of one is contrary to the nature of sociolinguistics: the study of language within sociocultural and historical contexts.

The failure of feminism to interrogate race means the resistance strategies of feminism will often replicate and reinforce the subordination of POCs, and the failure of antiracism to interrogate patriarchy means that antiracism will frequently reproduce the subordination of women (Crenshaw, 1991, p. 1252). Likewise, race-based priorities function to obscure the issues of women of color whereas feminist concerns often suppress minority experiences. In ALVCS research, women's language is dominated by White, middle-class, women's language and discourse. The field looks to Robin Lakoff, Jennifer Coates, Deborah Tannen, and other White women who focus on White women as the arbiters of women's language for all women. The languages of women of color are not the same as White, middle-class, women's languages and not the same as AAHAMs' language.

According to Crenshaw (1991, p. 1283), representational intersectionality purports that race and gender converge so the concerns of minority women fall into the void between concerns about women's issues and concerns about racism. Debates over representation continually elide the intersection of race and gender in the popular culture's construction of images of women of color. Accordingly, an analysis of what may be termed "representational intersectionality" would include recognition of both how these images are produced through a confluence of prevalent narratives of race and gender and how contemporary critiques of racist and sexist representation marginalize women of color (Crenshaw, 1991, p. 1283).

Thus, from an intersectional analysis I argue that: (1) racial and sexual subordination are mutually reinforcing; (2) Black women are commonly marginalized by a politics of race alone or gender alone; and (3) a scholarly response to each form of subordination must, at the same time be, a scholarly response to both (Crenshaw, 1991, p. 1283). In addition to a Black feminist intersectionality lens, a CRT framework reveals what is endemic to ALVCS research: (1) the permanence of racism, since racism will always be present in ALVCS research as long as WHAMs rule the roost; (2) interest convergence, since this revolution of inclusion and diversity will not happen without Whites perceiving more benefits for themselves; (3) essentialism, since AAVL is the prevalent emphasis of AAL research and that AAL is AAHAM; and (4) colorblindness, since neoliberalism is prevalent in sociolinguistics.

The Survey Says ...

In Lanehart (2017), I argued that it matters who is in the room making decisions for those who are not in the room, who is doing the research on whom, and who is asking the questions. As I indicated at the beginning of this chapter, subjectivities guide research, Supreme Court decisions, tenure and promotion cases, hiring decisions, and journal publications. The survey I conducted of *AmSp* using a CRT, intersectionality, Black feminist lens provides further evidence.

Table 4.1 shows the survey of literature data I collected for all 92 volumes available of *AmSp* since 1925–2017. The "Years" Column refers to the publication years of the volumes and issues. The "Volumes" and "Issues" columns refer to the corresponding volumes and issues for the years presented. The table is delineated based on the volume issues in order to provide more comparable periods of time than volumes or years would otherwise provide. The "Feature Articles" column refers to the total number of feature articles published in the corresponding years/volumes/issues. Although there have been and are other types of articles published in *AmSp*, such as book reviews, a Teaching section, Among New Words section, responses, bibliographies, indexes, notes from the editor, or the like, I chose to focus on the feature articles. Keep in mind that the feature articles, especially in the early volumes, vary greatly in length.

Early volumes contained many more articles, usually six to eight, than later volumes, usually two to four. They also contained many more issues, usually 12 issues per volume until 1927 and six issues per volume from 1927 to 1932, compared to later the standard four issues per volume beginning in 1933. The "POC Articles" column refers to the total number of feature articles in the years/volumes/issues/ articles that acknowledge POCs specifically as part of their sample participants or

TABLE 4.1 *American Speech* feature articles that include or focus on POCs

Years	Volumes	Issues	Feature Articles	POCs included in Articles	Percentage of POCs in Articles
1925–1928	1–4.2	32	191	10	5.2%
1929–1935	4.3–10	34	283	19	6.7%
1936–1944	11–19	36	225	10	4.4%
1945–1953	20–28	37	210	10	4.8%
1954–1961	29–36	33	163	6	3.7%
1962–1969	37–44	32	169	6	3.6%
1970–1977	45–52	32	116	17	14.7%
1978–1985	53–60	32	125	16	12.8%
1986–1993	61–68	32	124	29	23.4%
1994–2001*	69–76	32	169	52	30.8%
2002–2009	77–84	32	111	35	31.5%
2010–2018	85–93.2	34	111	37	33.3%
Totals:					
93 years	93 volumes	398 issues	1997 articles	247 POC articles	12.4% POC articles

* Includes volumes 75.3 and 75.4 in 2000 which were special issues for the 75th diamond anniversary of *American Speech*. The two issues included 65 (31 and 34, respectively) short articles, each from a different scholar. In those 65 articles, seven were written by POCs, 4 and 3, respectively.

data collection section of the articles, since the title does not usually provide that information. Groups included in the POC category are African Americans, Latinx Americans, Native Americans, and Asian Americans and Pacific Islanders. If the researcher noted "Negro," "African American," "Black," "African," "Gullah," "Mexican American," "Hispanic," "Japanese," "Native American," and the like in the methodology section or data tables or literature review, then it is counted as including POCs in some way in the article. The "Percentage" column represents the percentage of feature articles in the years/volumes/issues/articles specifically including POCs as part of their sample participants or data collection. The total number of feature articles in the "POC Articles" column for each row is divided by the total number of feature articles listed in each row of the "Feature Articles" column for the percentage of articles including POCs.

From 1925 to 1970, the inclusion of POCs was negligible and not representative of POC populations in the United States specifically or North America generally, but the percentage did increase considerably in the 21st century. In the 21st century, the inclusion of POCs is seemingly more representative with their proportion of the population in the United States specifically and North America generally. I say "seemingly" because some things the data obscure are made evident using a CRT, intersectionality, Black feminist lens.

First, I found it astounding how often the methods and methodologies sections were not delineated or discussed in much detail in the feature articles. Since ALVCS is social science research, most studies involve empirical data – which supposes a methods and methodologies section that outlines what was done, how it was done, and why it was done in the way it was done. In ALVCS research, that especially should include demographic, or speaker, variables and who collected the data. However, in far too many instances, the researcher does not provide this information. Feature articles from 1925–1950s including reference to POCs as part of the sample participants or data collection only did so as studying vocabulary, slang, folk songs, proverbs, names, humor, or as the language used in literature by White authors as representations of AAL. Even though the articles' titles imply they include Black people, they really do not. They include aspects of linguistic data about Black people, but without actually having to interact with Black people. Again, Whiteness makes this acceptable because Whiteness defines which stories are valuable and how they should be expressed and interpreted.

Second, the way POCs and/or their languages are referred to is problematic because POCs did not get to tell their own stories, especially in the early years of the journal. Although one would expect "Negro" as a common term of reference for Blacks without a negative connotation, other racist terms are used for POCs. For example, volume 4.4 in 1929 includes a feature article entitled "Bamboo English" in reference to language in the Philippine Islands. In a 1932 article in volume 7.6, Dutch Guiana is referred to as "Bush-Negro Speech." Native Americans are referred to as "the Red Man" in a 1965 article in volume 31.1. "Negro" gives way to "Black" in the early 1970s, along with the problematic terminology for POCs in the journal's earlier history. Using a CRT lens, the journal's problematic language serves to highlight and reinforce the hegemony of Whiteness, the permanence of racism, and the need for counterstories. It tells POCs that stories are being told from the master's narrative and that counterstorytelling is necessary and was inevitable with the civil rights movement and the more recent #BlackLivesMatter and #SayHerName. Although offensive terminology is not used, it is part of the history of the journal and ALVCS, and highlights who gets to tell their stories and have the right to name themselves. As such, it is not something to ignore or deny since history has a way of repeating itself and is, often times, re-imagined with rose-colored glasses by those in power.

Third, and one of the most problematic aspects of the *AmSp* feature articles, the unmarked term, that is, the "normal" meaning or referent – the one that can go without saying – is WHAM. In the majority of feature articles in *AmSp* – which include titles such as "Folk Sayings from *Indiana*" in volume 14.4 (1939), "*Campus* Slang" in volume 39.2 (1964), "Studies of *American* Pronunciation since 1945" in volume 52.3/4 (1977), "The Changing Language of *American Catholicism*" in volume 52.2 (1979), or "Dahntahn *Pittsburgh*" in volume 77.2 (2002) – POCs are not included in the sample population or data collected, despite the titles which appear to be inclusive of all Americans or all "X" people in a state, city, or institution. Unless there is some indication in the title that only White people are included – which hardly ever happens – wouldn't it be normal to think that everyone is included? That would be a mistake. Not only are POCs not included, in many cases POCs are not even acknowledged to exist, hence there is no mention of their exclusion. POCs are not a part of the United States or North America if one subscribes to the omissions in these articles. POCs are sociolinguistically invisible because they are socially and humanly invisible in everyday society. But, then again, that is how POCs have often been treated in research – unless it is to see the "exotic" or look through the White gaze. CRT's critique of liberalism reveals their neoliberal colorblindness. That is to say, "of course POCs are included because they really are 'Americans' or speak 'Pittsburghese' or go to college, but there was no need to be more specific because it is implied." However, further investigation reveals POCs are not included.

Fourth, it is not until 1984 that an article about Black people is first/solo-authored by a Black person: John Baugh's "Steady" in volume 59.1. Several articles were published before this in *AmSp* that in some way dealt with Black language – sometimes in derogatory and superficial ways as indicated in the second point above – but it took almost 60 years of the journal's existence to publish a feature, first/solo-authored article by a Black scholar on any subject and, of course, that author was a Black male. The first Black woman to publish a feature article as first/sole author in *AmSp* was Kean Gibson in volume 63.3 in 1988 on Guyanese and Jamaican Creoles. As Table 4.2 indicates, the 1980s coincide with an increase in the percentage of feature articles at least including POCs or Black people specifically that are more representative of the percentage of the population in the

TABLE 4.2 *American Speech* feature articles first, or sole-authored by POCs

Years	Volumes	Issues	All Feature Articles	POC Authors	Percentage POC Authors
1925–1928	1–4.2	32	191	0	0.0%
1929–1935	4.3–10	34	283	0	0.0%
1936–1944	11–19	36	225	0	0.0%
1945–1953	20–28	37	210	0	0.0%
1954–1961	29–36	33	163	0	0.0%
1962–1969	37–44	32	169	0	0.0%
1970–1977	45–52	32	116	1	0.9%
1978–1985	53–60	32	125	3	2.4%
1986–1993	61–68	32	124	12	9.7%
1994–2001★	69–76	32	169	17	10.1%
2002–2009	77–84	32	111	7	6.3%
2010–2018	85–93.2	34	111	9	8.1%
Totals:					
93 years	93 volumes	398 issues	1997 articles	49 POC authors	2.5% POC authored

★ Includes volumes 75.3 and 75.4 in 2000 which were special issues for the 75th diamond anniversary of *American Speech*. The two issues included 65 (31 and 34, respectively) short articles, each from a different scholar, with a total of seven POC authored articles.

United States specifically and North America generally. This indicates it took 60 years for a POC to tell a story from the perspective of a POC and have the opportunity for counterstories. Unfortunately, as a product of the times, the story told excluded Black women as a source of AAL and privileged AAHAMs – the racial equivalent of excluding Black people as American, I would propose.

Fifth, it is apparently more acceptable for White people to research POCs than actual POCs. Table 4.3 shows that, of the 247 feature articles including POCs, 80.2 percent are by White authors and only 19.8 percent are by POC authors. From 1925 until 1970, no feature articles were authored by POCs about POCs.

The 49 POC authored articles by 28 different POC authors in the history of the journal have only been published since 1984: twenty Black-identified authors, ten males and ten females; nine Asian/Pacific Islander-identified authors, three males (all Japanese from a 1996 special issue in honor of Professor Takesi Sibata) and six females; and two Latino-identified authors. None of the feature articles about Native American language were published by a Native American-identified author. None of the feature articles including Spanish language were written by a POC with the exception of one full-length article in volume 58.1 from 1983 and another which appeared in the 75th Diamond Anniversary double issues in 2000 that only included short articles (see Table 4.4). As expected, men of color outnumber women of color in feature articles published.

TABLE 4.3 *American Speech* feature articles with POC data authored by Whites compared to POCs

Years	Total Feature Articles	POC Data Included	White Authored	Percentage White Authored with POC data	POC Authored	Percentage POC Authored with POC data
1925–1928	191	10	10	100.0%	0	0.0%
1929–1935	283	19	19	100.0%	0	0.0%
1936–1944	225	10	10	100.0%	0	0.0%
1945–1953	210	10	10	100.0%	0	0.0%
1954–1961	163	6	6	100.0%	0	0.0%
1962–1969	169	6	6	100.0%	0	0.0%
1970–1977	116	17	16	94.1%	1	5.9%
1978–1985	125	16	13	81.3%	3	18.7%
1986–1993	124	29	17	58.6%	12	41.4%
1994–2001★	169	52	35	67.3%	17	32.7%
2002–2009	111	35	28	80.0%	7	20.0%
2010–2018 Totals:	111	37	28	75.7%	9	24.3%
93	1997	247	198	80.2%	49	19.8%

★ Includes volumes 75.3 and 75.4 in 2000 which were special issues for the 75th diamond anniversary of *American Speech*. The two issues included 65 (31 and 34, respectively) short articles, each from a different scholar, with a total of seven POC-authored articles and four White authors.

TABLE 4.4 *American Speech* feature articles by POCs

POC	Black		Latinx		Asian		POCs Total	
Sex	F	M	F	M	F	M	F	M
1970–1979	0	0	0	0	1	0	1	0
1980–1989	1	9	0	1	0	0	1	10
1990–1999	3	7	0	0	0	3★	3	10
2000–2009+	8	6	0	1	0	0	8	7
2010–2018	1	3	0	0	5	0	6	3
Totals	**13**	**25**	**0**	**2**	**6**	**3**	**19**	**30**

★These authors are all from a 1996 (71.2) special issue dedicated to a Japanese scholar
+Includes the 75th anniversary double issues of short articles

Conclusions: Where Do We Go from Here?

The goals of this chapter were, first, to critique the status quo in ALVCS research and researchers with respect to race and gender and, second, make a case for more inclusive, critical, and intersectional ALVCS research addressing more complex questions around language and identity, as well as interrogating researcher identities and their subjectivities by using CRT, intersectionality, and Black feminist methodologies. As the survey of *AmSp* revealed, most of the participants and researchers are WHAMs. Even when they are not WHAMs, they are male POCs. When POCs and women of color, that is to say not WHAMs, engage in research and research their own communities, it is not only more representative of humanity but also broadens our understanding of all of humanity from multiple perspectives.

I started this chapter with my salient identities and subjectivities. I believe all researchers need to not only be cognizant of their subjectivities, but they also need to articulate them and the impact they have on their research methods and methodologies. ALVCS researchers need to understand that their identities impact the questions they ask, the methodologies they use, and their interpretation of the data. I know some on the U.S. Supreme Court do not believe their WHAM identities impact their world-view or interpretation of the U.S. Constitution or even inform their legal theories – but they do. Ironically, they do believe this is the case if the Justice is not WHAM. Hence, the all-too-familiar situation of POC scholars being told they are too close to their subject (i.e., subjective) to study it, but WHAM and White, heterosexual, cis-females can research anything because they, alone, are/can be "objective".

I cannot stress enough the importance of diversifying all fields of study. ALVCS research and other fields continue to substantiate the permanence of racism and, when that is not working or is scrutinized, then it is about interest convergence. All of this leads to the need for counterstories that identify, illuminate, and critique neoliberalism, racism, sexism, etc. Opportunities to write pieces such as this help shine a spotlight on the issues using a CRT, intersectionality, Black feminist lens. Doing so means moving beyond the false quantitative-qualitative binary, the Black-White binary, and the lack of human diversity and intersecting and intersectional identities that make social science research complex, fluid, and colorful. In addition, I would suggest further engaging in interdisciplinary research that allows use of Black feminist theory and CRT in a study of ALVCS since individuals and communities exist in those areas that are more complex than simplistic, territorial myopia allow.

What do I suggest? Tell our own counterstories. Use our own tools (Lorde, 1984). Say it like it is. Can you hear (see) me now? You will.

Notes

1 I use the term "Black" to refer to the socially constructed racial classification of those who are of dark-skinned African ancestry (although it is not indicative of one's skin color) and "African American" to refer to the ethnic group of Americans who are African slave descendants or who have African ancestry.
2 I use the term "African American Language" to refer to all variations of language use in African American communities, recognizing that there are many variations within the umbrella term, including Gullah, Standard African American Language, and African American Vernacular Language as well as varieties that reflect differences in age/

generation, sex, gender, sexuality, social and socioeconomic class, region, education, religion, and other affiliations and identities that intersect with one's ethnicity/race and nationality (Lanehart and Malik, 2015, p. 3). I simply define African American Language as language spoken by or among African Americans. (see Mufwene, 2001). That is not to say non-Blacks cannot speak it or use it, just as those who are not Japanese can still learn or acquire and use Japanese (e.g., my son is learning Japanese and wants to live there someday). Likewise, it does not mean that *all* African Americans speak AAL because not all African Americans, just like not all people of Japanese descent or Mexican descent, speak their heritage languages. Like any variety, AAL is part of a community and socioculture and history (Lanehart, 2015b, pp. 866–67).

References

Alim, H. S. (2004a). Hip hop nation language. In E. Finegan & J. R. Rickford (Eds.), *Language in the U.S.A.: Themes for the twenty-first century* (pp. 387–409). Cambridge, UK: Cambridge University Press.

Alim, H. S. (2004b). *You know my steez: An ethnographic and sociolinguistic study of styleshifting in a Black American speech community.* Durham, NC: Duke University Press.

Alim, H. S. (2006). *Roc the mic right: The language of hip hop culture.* London, UK: Routledge.

Alim, H. S., & Baugh, J. (2007). *Talkin Black talk: Language, education, and social change.* New York, NY: Teacher's College Press.

Alim, H. S., Rickford, J.R., & Ball, A. F. (Eds.). (2016). *Raciolinguistics: How language shapes our ideas about race.* Oxford, UK and New York, NY: Oxford University Press.

Alim, H. S., & Smitherman, G. (2012). *Articulate while Black: Barack Obama, language and race in the United States.* Oxford, UK and New York, NY: Oxford University Press.

Bailey, M. (2010). They aren't talking about me. . . *The Crunk Feminist Collective, 14.* Retrieved from http://www.crunkfeministcollective.com/2010/03/14/they-arent-talking-about-me.

Baugh, J. (1999). *Out of the mouths of slaves: African American Language and educational malpractice.* Austin, TX: University of Texas Press.

Baugh, J. (2000). *Beyond Ebonics: Linguistic pride and racial prejudice.* Oxford, UK and New York, NY: Oxford University Press.

Collins, P. H. (1990). *Black feminist thought: Knowledge, consciousness, and the politics of empowerment.* New York, NY: Routledge.

Crenshaw, K. (1991). Mapping the margins: Intersectionality, identity politics, and violence against women of color. *Stanford Law Review, 43(6),* 1241–99.

DeBose, C. E. (2005). *The sociology of African American Language: A language planning perspective.* New York, NY: Palgrave Macmillan.

DeCuir-Gunby, J. T., & Schutz, P.A. (2014). Researching race within educational psychology contexts. *Educational Psychologist, 49(4),* 244–60.

Delgado, R., & Stefancic, J. (2001). *Critical race theory: An introduction.* New York, NY: NYU Press.

Etter-Lewis, G. (1993). *My soul is my own: Oral narratives of African American women in the professions.* New York, NY: Routledge.

Green, L. J. (2002). *African American English: A linguistic introduction.* Cambridge, UK: Cambridge University Press.

Green, L. J. (2011). *Language and the African American child.* Cambridge, UK: Cambridge University Press.

Hewlett, S. A., Peraino, K., Sherbin, L., & Sumberg, K. (2010). *The sponsor effect: Breaking through the last glass ceiling.* Boston, MA: Harvard Business Review.

Houston, M., & Davis, O. I. (2001). *Centering ourselves: African American feminist and womanist studies of discourse.* Cresskill, NJ: Hampton Press.

Hudson, B. H. (2001). *African American female speech communities: Varieties of talk.* Westport, CT: Praeger Publishers.

Hull, A., Bell Scott, P., & Smith, B. (Eds.). (1982). *All the women are White, all the Blacks are men, but some of us are brave: Black women's studies.* New York, NY: The Feminist Press.

Jacobs-Huey, L. (2006). *From the kitchen to the parlor: Language and becoming in African American women's hair care.* Oxford, UK: Oxford University Press.

Lanehart, S. L. (2002). *Sista, speak! Black women kinfolk talk about language and literacy.* Austin, TX: University of Texas Press.

Lanehart, S. L. (Ed.). (2009). *African American women's language: Discourse, education, and identity.* Newcastle upon Tyne, UK: Cambridge Scholars Publishing.

Lanehart, S. L. (Ed.). (2015a). *The Oxford handbook of African American Language.* Oxford, UK and New York, NY: Oxford University Press.

Lanehart, S. L. (2015b). African American language and identity: Contradictions and conundrums. In S. Lanehart (Ed.), *The Oxford handbook of African American Language* (pp. 1–19). Oxford, UK and New York, NY: Oxford University Press.

Lanehart, S. L. (2017). Being in the room. In M. Harris, S. L. Sellers, O. Clerge, & F. W. Gooding, Jr. (Eds.), *Stories from the front of the room: How higher education faculty of color overcome challenges and thrive in the academy* (pp. 83–85). Lanham, MD: Rowman and Littlefield.

Lanehart, S. L, & Malik, A. M. (2015). Language use in African American communities: An introduction. In S. Lanehart (Ed.), *The Oxford handbook of African American Language* (pp. 863–80). Oxford, UK and New York, NY: Oxford University Press.

Lorde, A. (1984). The master's tools will never dismantle the master's house." In A. Lorde (Ed.), *Sister outsider: Essays and speeches* (pp. 110–114). Berkeley, CA: Crossing Press.

Morgan, M. (1991). Indirectness and interpretation in African American women's discourse. *Pragmatics, 1(4),* 421–51.

Morgan, M. (1996). Conversational signifying: Grammar and indirectness among African American women. In E. Ochs, E. Schegloff, & S. Thompson (Eds.), *Interaction and Grammar* (pp. 405–33). Cambridge, UK: Cambridge University Press.

Morgan, M. (1999). No woman no cry: Claiming African American women's place. In M. Bucholtz, A. C. Lang, & L. A. Sutton (Eds.), *Reinventing identities: The gendered self in discourse* (pp. 27–45). Oxford, UK and New York, NY: Oxford University Press.

Morgan, M. (2002). Language, discourse, and power in African American culture. Cambridge, UK: Cambridge University Press.

Mufwene, S. (2001). What is African American English? In S. Lanehart (Ed.), *Sociocultural and historical contexts of African American English* (pp. 21–51). Amsterdam, NL: John Benjamins.

Ogbu, J. U. 1978. *Minority education and caste: The American system in cross-cultural perspective.* Cambridge, MA: Academic Press.

Rickford, J. R. (1999). *African American Vernacular English: Features, evolution, educational implications.* Oxford, UK: Basil Blackwell.

Rickford, J. R., & Rickford, R. J. (2000). *Spoken Soul: The story of Black English.* New York, NY: Wiley & Sons.

Smitherman, G. (2000). *Talkin that talk: Language, culture and education in African America.* New York, NY: Routledge.

Smitherman, G. (2006). *Word from the mother: Language and African Americans.* New York, NY: Routledge.

Troutman, D. (2001). African American women: Talking that talk. In S. L. Lanehart (Ed.), *Sociocultural and historical contexts of African American English* (pp. 211–38). Amsterdam, NL: John Benjamins Publishing.

PART III
Critical Race Qualitative Methods

5

A MATCH MADE IN HEAVEN

Tribal Critical Race Theory and Critical Indigenous Research Methodologies

Bryan McKinley Jones Brayboy and Jeremiah Chin

As academics, we are often faced with questions of how and why we engage in research, but as scholars of color the answer to both questions is rooted in the same story. For us, research begins with experience and commitment to justice, which necessarily means combating, subverting, or examining relationships of power. This starts with White supremacy and colonization. In this chapter, we connect Critical Race Theory (CRT) and Critical Indigenous Research Methodologies (CIRM) as two intersecting ways of ensuring research looks to those who have been marginalized or hurt by it in the past, as an emancipatory project that forefronts community relationships and interests (Brayboy, Gough, Leonard, Roehl, & Solyom, 2011). Rather than offering a conventional chapter, we draw on the tradition of CRT and offer our contribution as a counter story.

Counter storytelling subverts dominant paradigms or epistemologies, and presents new solutions or policies that disrupt the status quo (Delgado, 1989). However, using counter narratives is not a decision made lightly, since doing so creates significant responsibility. As R. A. Williams reminds us, for Indigenous peoples:

> [t]o be a Storyteller, then, is to assume the awesome burden of remembrance for a people, and to perform this paramount role with laughter and tears, joy and sadness, melancholy and passion, as the occasion demands. The Storyteller never wholly belongs to himself or herself. The Storyteller is the one who sacrifices everything in the tellings and retellings of the stories belonging to the tribe".

(1996, xi)

Counter stories serve many purposes. First, they expose structures as simultaneously oppressive, marginalizing, and enabling. Second, they present stories of possibility and can serve to build much needed community or local capacity. In short, they are not stories of dispossession or victimry; they are narratives of how people see structures, combat them-when necessary—and utilize them—when possible—to create better lives for themselves and others. Counter stories are not apologia; they recognize that communities are besieged and people from these communities may participate in these sieges. Structures and policies may enhance and enable these foci of destruction, but counter narratives re-center purpose and possibility.

Third, counter stories disrupt taken-for-granted beliefs about the world. Because counter narratives are often grounded in fine detail they make the invisible visible. Scholars like Derrick Bell (1987, 1995), Richard Delgado (1989), and Patricia Williams (1991) remind us that stories are critical tools for many in academia who seek to speak truth to power as they ground questions of ideologies and social structure in lived experience. Counter narratives are told by oppressed peoples to challenge dominant ideologies and encourage us to imagine a social world different from the one(s) we currently inhabit. Counter stories "enrich imagination and teach that by combining elements from the story and current reality, we may construct a new world richer than either alone" (Delgado 1989, 2314). Derrick Bell (1987) argues that counter narratives often use fictional stories, "to explore situations that are real enough but, in their many and contradictory dimensions, defy understanding" (7). Bell's story of The Space Traders, for example, tells of aliens visiting earth offering gold, a clean environment, and alternative fuels in exchange for Black people—a bargain the U.S. accepts. Bell crafted the story to "convince a resisting [law school] class that the patterns of sacrificing black rights to further white interests, so present in American history, pose a continuing threat" (Bell 1995, 902), illuminating the trend sacrificing Black rights, health, and wellbeing for White prosperity through slavery, the end of Reconstruction, mass incarceration, and diminishment of civil rights in the 20th and 21st centuries. Counter stories may be fictional, but above all they highlight the social, historical, and structural dimensions of racism, colonization, patriarchy, and other oppressions in a relatable, allegorical, or insightful narrative.

Creating counter stories is therefore about realizing the potential of thick, rich data of our everyday lives to enrich the theoretical, empirical, and scholarly insights offered by academic writing. In part, counter storytelling is autoethnographic; many of the characters and events are drawn from aspects of our personalities, our personal experiences, stories told by our parents, friends, mentors, and others. Characters in the story similarly mirror people from our own lives, as re-presentations or composites of people we have known or encountered, microaggressions we have faced, and advice we have been given. Importantly though, the counter story is written from the perspective of a marginalized person, relating the entrenched nature of race and/or colonization in ordinary or extraordinary life events. Rather than write a lengthy empirical description, the use of counter stories supplements academic analyses by relating concepts conversationally, helping us think about ways to talk about complex topics. For our counter story in this chapter, we choose to highlight the ordinary, looking at a day in the life of Dr. Henry Sampson, an established Indigenous professor at Desert University (DU), attempting to navigate theories and practices of research at a major university with connections to Indigenous people. Sampson grapples with these questions with his former students Dr. Lola Pons and Dr. Jerome Jackson, to integrate Dr. Sampson's understanding of Critical Indigenous Research Methodologies through engaged research. Sampson's exploration of CIRM highlights the four Rs of research as embedded in praxis: responsibility, reciprocity, respect, and relationality (Brayboy et al., 2011; Kirkness & Barnhardt, 2001).

A Match Made in Heaven

An electronic voice chirped from Henry Sampson's car speakers: "You are on the fastest route." So much for finding a way around the mile of brake lights in front of him. After eight years as a professor at Desert University, Sampson had spoiled himself by investing in a fast car, but these days the only accelerating was merging on to the stop and go traffic. Traffic was only a problem when Henry was in a rush. With the semester just starting, Henry's days were full of meetings; phone calls, video calls, and the occasional face to face with students or colleagues. These early morning hours were the best time to get writing done before scheduled appointments, but today traffic was not cooperating. "Siri, what's on my calendar for today?" Henry's car pinged and replied with stilted electronic optimism: "Ok, Henry, I found eight appointments for today. At 9 A.M. . . . ." Sampson sighed as the list of appointments faded into the background. Hopefully traffic will clear in time to do some writing, but at least the slow down would let him breathe and think about the day. All these meetings were about juggling his different responsibilities, teaching, mentoring, administrating, parenting. Maybe he needed to schedule breathing and sleeping too, some days it didn't feel like he had time for either. He tried to remind himself that being busy was a good thing; his mother always told him "people with too much free time are up to no good."

In the minutes it took to go over his schedule, Henry wondered if he had moved more than five feet on the freeway. He hadn't moved any closer to getting writing done, but considering how far he had come from his first job at Mountain State University, he was glad to be stuck in traffic. For as much as Henry echoed the theories of Bourdieu and Passeron (1990), urging his students not to have "genesis amnesia" or forgetting how we got here through the "naïve illusion that things have always been as they are" (9), maybe Henry needed to spend more time thinking about how he got here: as a tenured, full-professor, with full responsibilities, a fast car, and nowhere to go. In his first academic job before tenure, he was still stretched across different responsibilities with more pressure to write. Luckily, his students and programs he helped build gave him the inspiration he needed, but often not in ways they intended.

Part of what drew him to Desert University was what pushed him from Mountain State, when a right-wing legal think tank tried to dismantle a teacher training program designed to serve Native students and teachers by embedding the program in Native communities and epistemologies. In the early years of the Native Teacher Training Program (NTTP) that Henry and his team founded, Mountain State University received a letter indicating intent to sue the University and all responsible parties because the NTTP was an "unconstitutionally race-based" program which excluded White people from participating. At first Henry tried not to laugh at the challenge; it was ridiculous that a program rooted in trust responsibilities and guarantees to Native people for education funded through federal monies would be that easily challenged, but the university was scared and not willing to fight. Henry wasn't a lawyer, but he knew that the University had no legal concerns in a suit over NTTP. Over the ensuing months Henry was pulled in to countless extra meetings to convince the university's office of legal counsel that federal Indian law protected the program.

Luckily, he knew where to look. Beginning with Vine Deloria Jr.'s foundational discussions on federal Indian law (1969), moving into modern legal histories (Pevar, 2012), Henry outlined the key feature that the University missed: funding was not solely based on race, but rooted in federal, legal obligations to Tribes and Native peoples. Even if there was a racial component, Henry drew on Critical Race Theory (CRT) to unpack how programs serving people of color are constitutionally valid, crucial restorations and responses to histories of oppression, especially in education (Ladson-Billings & Tate, 1995). Between the legal histories of CRT and federal Indian law, Henry found a key work from another Native scholar that found the synergy he was looking for: Tribal Critical Race Theory (TribalCrit) (Brayboy, 2005). Building on CRT's foundational notion that racism is permanent and endemic, TribalCrit adds that colonization is endemic, particularly in education of Native peoples.

Even with all the work he put in to educating the institution, support for NTTP waned at the University. Surely not for lack of success, Henry still received e-mails and texts from the many students that went through the program as students or even student-workers for NTTP. And, the university collected the overhead on the millions of dollars of grants that came with the grants. Before he left Mountain State, Henry would never forget the University's half-hearted attempt to change his mind, offering him a salary bump because of his work with NTTP, even after the university defunded the program. "I think the University benefits tremendously from our relationships with the community, and Native people all together. I mean just look at everything you've done for us!" his department chair said, laughing. Henry knew they meant it sincerely, but he still winced, thinking back on all he had put in for the University. It had strengthened his resolve to move on.

TribalCrit so effectively highlights the pervasive social and cultural effects of colonization in education, but when the institution is still deeply invested in the colonial, racist structures, it makes the praxis springing from the theory less effective. About as effective as his speedster in this traffic. Henry's ruminations would only carry him so far, and now forty-five minutes into his commute, he was starting to grow restless. He was almost to his exit on what should be a fifteen-minute drive, when traffic began to clear and he was finally able to use the over-priced gas he had pumped into his expensive car. From 5 mph to 50 in the two seconds it took to go down the off-ramp, only to stop and wait through the stop lights all the way to the office.

Stalking with Stories

Traffic had set back Henry's day, but that wasn't going to stop him from getting some writing time. He breathed a sigh of relief when he got to his empty office suite. *Nobody has to even know I'm here!* he smiled to himself as he slipped into his office and quickly closed the door. Henry turned on his music and clicked on his latest article ready to write. Out of the corner of his eye, Henry noticed his door had cracked open. Peering over his glasses he noticed a large purple blob filling the gap in his doorway. "Hey Jerome." He didn't need to see the face to know that Jerome was trying to creep into his office. "How'd you know it was me?" Jerome asked incredulously as he opened the door. Henry laughed and waved Jerome into the office. At 6'7" it was hard not to notice Jerome anywhere he went, and he didn't help the fact by wearing the brightest possible colors. Leaning against the doorway in his yellow baseball cap, bright purple t-shirt and Nantucket red pants, Jerome asked, "you got a minute Dr. S?" "For you, I got five." Henry said, chuckling as he minimized the Word document. Writing wasn't on the agenda today. Henry had known Jerome since he started as a student researcher as a freshman in college. Now more than a decade later, Henry had chaired Jerome's dissertation and hired him on as a postdoctoral fellow. Henry knew Jerome well enough to know this was going to be more than a minute.

Jerome took off his hat as he sat in the chair across from Henry. "I know you've got the meeting today with Lola and the Tribal Education Department, and I'm trying to figure out why this hasn't been done sooner. I mean, not you, but on a university level. Desert U is built on these people's lands, and it's good that there's a partnership with the community, but I don't know if the university really takes that seriously. We have institutions that are attempting to transform higher education, but there's little institutional or practical memory in the histories of the institutions themselves. Higher education in the United States was built on Indigenous lands, using enslaved labor, and funded with the slave trade. Like Craig Steven Wilder says, 'the fate of the American college had been intertwined from the beginning with the social project of dispossessing Indian people' (2013, p. 150). Think about Desert State or land grant schools in the west, they're sitting on land seizures and dispossession, and Ivy League schools are largely funded with the labor or buying/selling of enslaved peoples. Even as schools celebrate their hundredth, hundred and fiftieth anniversaries, that doesn't become part of the conversation. So even as we are building with local communities, where's the public recognition of that history?"

Henry leaned forward in his chair as he finished cleaning his glasses, Henry's secret strategy to give him time to think. "I'm picking up what you're putting down," Henry said with a smile, using one of Jerome's favorite catch phrases. "I think you already know the answer, and it's in the story of the University. I grew up in a storytelling family and community, where I learned the most important trait of stories: listening. Stories are more than just stories; they carry messages with them. They outline our theories of life and living, moral and ethical behavior, and pathways to living the 'right way.' In many ways, they do the work that Keith Basso suggests when he notes that stories 'stalk' (1996). By this, he is specifically referencing the moral, ethical, and theoretical work that stories do. Stories guide us. They teach. Whether historical or fictional, stories from people who have been pushed out, or whose stories are suppressed play a vital role in uncovering the larger story of power. They show how race and colonization are ubiquitous, but hide behind commonsense to make them look like they're nowhere. So you tell me, why don't universities talk about where they came from?"

"You're just tryin' to get me to say genesis amnesia again, so you're right, it's genesis amnesia. They forget how and why processes and practices were instituted in the first place and so they no longer question why they have remained that way. The status quo becomes accepted and remains unchallenged. The origin story of the institution is ignored, except for mostly White men and women who get the paintings in old corners of the building with a small plaque with their name and how many years they were in power. And yeah, it's part of hegemony too. Like Gramsci explained, we have a taken-for-granted set of beliefs that society, and its structures, are set up in some neutral manner when really it is set up to benefit those in power who have the most resources. All this talk of academic freedom and market places of ideas at a university obfuscate—you like how I used your word there, obfuscate?" Jerome said as he leaned back in his chair and put his hat back on. "It's about getting those who have the least power—the ones Gramsci refers to as the 'subordinate' group—buy into and perpetuate their own subordination (2014). I get that. But is telling a story enough, on its own? It's like Crenshaw says about CRT, it's not just about understanding the 'vexed bond' between race and the law, it's about changing it (1995, xiii)."

"Right," Henry replied. "Those who control the discourse impose their own ideologies and subjective beliefs as legitimate. In the process, they engage in what Bottomore calls symbolic force, concealing their power in driving the agenda (1990). Exposing power is a huge step, and I don't want you to jump over that, it's no small thing I mean, look at what Georgetown is doing. It's not just telling the story about how the University benefits from slavery, it's actively granting admissions preference to the descendants of those who were enslaved (Domonoske, 2016). That's going beyond some blanket talk to include some action, and even consider some responsibility to the community as well. Remember, as researchers we are storytellers, but we are storytellers who in our research process engage in a process with communities that go with the four Rs of research: responsibility, reciprocity, respect, and relationality. Making this kind of change, I think gets at that first R, with making the University responsible to the descendants of those who were sold by Georgetown, ensuring they get better access to the resources the University provides."

"Man, Listen," Jerome drawled, taking his hat back off and leaning forward in his chair. "That's some empty-ass action. I'm sorry. All that's doing is giving legacy admission status to a select few who can actually trace their histories back to the people who were documented by the University's slave trade. I mean we are talking about a university that bought and sold people, on land it took from other people. I think the responsibility point is nice, and I think it's important to get all them good R's into the conversation, but they're not even engaging in the relational or reciprocal nature of the whole enterprise. What about financial aid or any kind of, I'm gonna add an R for you, reparations?"

"So we have to get our own institution to do better" Henry chided, "I think your fifth R is great, but also embedded in the reciprocity, respect, and relationality that I don't know if Georgetown is getting at. But here, with Desert U and our partnership with the Tribe, we're looking to change all that. It's not just about remembering the beginning, but it's saying we have to begin again. We have to make universities engage in capacity-enhancing strategies. That's why it's all about nation building, to me. This is what Brayboy talks about in TribalCrit: the liminal status of Native peoples, and the way racial power and colonization are made legal, obligate the University to do more, and do it better (2005)." Henry was happily on a roll, forgetting his writing until his computer pulled him back to his own responsibilities as the calendar chimed. "We have to get back to this, in writing too! But right now, I've got to run to pick up Lola and get to the Tribal Education Director," Henry said calmly as he unplugged his computer from the dock and put it into his bag. "My bad Dr. S! I should have guessed from the way you're suited and booted that it's a big meeting day," Jerome teased. Everyone in the office could tell Henry had a big meeting when he wore a full suit to the office, especially on these hot desert days. Jerome left Henry to pack up, "We still on for our phone call?" "Of course," Henry replied as he walked out the door and back to his car.

Driven to Success

Henry smiled when he finally got to use the gas pedal as he pulled out of the parking lot to pick up Lola. She had been part of Henry's team almost as long as he had been a professor. Now, a few years after earning her Ph.D., she was an assistant professor at Desert University and continuing the work they started years ago. As Henry pulled up to the coffee shop he easily spotted Lola standing outside waiting for him. Even with dark hair hiding her face as she looked down at her phone, it wasn't hard to notice her professional attire outside the relaxed storefront, looking more like a business owner than customer. "Well hello Dr. Pons, those are some very nice tall shoes you have on," Henry teased as she put her bag in the back seat and climbed into his car. Her fashion sense reflected her personality, serious without being overly formal. Lola was self-conscious about her height, but it never stopped her from wearing high heels and towering over Henry. "First, good morning, you look lovely as well Dr. Sampson. Second, ewww!" Lola scrunched up her face in mock disgust as they started their drive.

"I just wanted to go over our agenda before we get to the meeting so we are clear," Lola said, readying to write. Henry loved new gadgets, but he appreciated Lola's low-tech approach. "What do we want to accomplish in this meeting with the Tribe's education director?" Henry took a moment to think and enjoy accelerating on the open road to the reservation. Once they were cruising slightly over the speed limit, Henry started to talk: "I think it has to be the other way around. What does the Tribe need from us? We spend so much time telling the University how things need to be done, we can't forget we're going into these communities who have researchers come in all the time to listen and take."

"H," as Lola was fond of calling Sampson, "don't even get me started. We know the history, you remember the chapters in my dissertation I spent writing about researchers and my own positionality as a non-Native person. From Deloria's beautiful dismantling of anthropologists appropriating Native knowledges (1969) to Linda Tuhiwai Smith's gorgeous discussions of decolonizing methodologies (2012) or Shawn Wilson's personal *Research Is Ceremony* (2009)—you want me to keep going?" Henry frowned and smiled at the same time, pleased with his own work as a teacher and teller of bad jokes. "You missed Arthur C. Parker, don't forget he was the O.G." (1916). "So, you did read my dissertation; some days I worry." Lola replied with thick sarcasm. "I know what you are saying about responsibility and establishing a respectful relationship with the Tribe, but what do we have to offer this nation? When we meet with leaders, there's a common focus on education that their citizens can bring home, and help their community. But what can the University offer beyond a diploma?" Henry laughed quietly at Lola's sarcasm. "What's wrong with a diploma?" he replied, knowing he could bait Lola into an answer.

Lola sighed, "I see what you're doing, but fine. I can talk. I'm thinking of Lani Guinier's writing on democratic merit. At the individual level, this calls for a rethinking of merit as investment-based, where individuals are admitted for their potential contributions to a larger democratic project rather than performance on some standardized exam (Guinier, 2016). The current use of 'merit' narrowly considers past accomplishments—test scores and grades—and this mostly benefits those from economically advantaged backgrounds. Democratic merit focuses on how individuals will contribute in the future. This means recognizing, investing in, and building capacity for students to become leaders and give back to their communities, creating sustainable healthy relationships with those communities." As Lola paused to take a sip of her coffee, Henry finished her thought: "Of course, democracy and merit haven't always worked out for us Native folks. Colonization, assimilation, and genocide are all projects of elected officials in democracy. That's why we look to capacity building, self-determination, and self-education (Brayboy, Solyom, & Castagno, 2014)." "Thanks for putting the bow on it," Lola replied as she finished her coffee. "But that's my question, what capacity building are we offering? What do we bring to the table to make this a real partnership?"

"It sounds overly simple, but we offer everything we can," Henry said as they exited the freeway. "Engaging in this work comes with responsibilities. Not only do they encourage us to think about the present and imagine a different future; they also require us to remember and honor the pain and struggles of those who have come before us. It's our responsibility in university, as researchers and storytellers, to be in a reciprocal relationship with those involved in the narrative. When we engage in this work we do so with respect and with a full understanding of what is at stake. We are offering diplomas, but also a meaningful partnership that should continue beyond a cohort of students and into the community, for generations ahead." Henry put the car into park and turned to see Lola grinning, with a blank notepad and no agenda. "You were just trying to get me warmed up for the meeting, weren't you?" he asked, with fake indignation. "Maybe I was, and maybe I wasn't. Either way, we're here." Lola climbed out the car as Henry put his sunglasses away, turning off his car to the familiar ping of his phone reminding him to get to his next meeting.

Closing Calls

After a long day of meetings and a fundraising event, Henry's calendar was at his favorite part: picking up his boys from soccer practice. The fundraiser let Henry flex his social skills and shake a lot of hands, with the hope that the relationships he formed there would mean something for the peoples he worked for. He and his team spent the days working in the name of DU, an institution he gladly, and often proudly, served. The real goal was making sure he got funding and support for programs, students, and communities he served. Jerome, Lola, and so many others were products of that work, and he couldn't help but feel proud of their accomplishments and humbled by their drive, foresight, and brilliance. As he approached the soccer fields, his phone started to buzz again through his car speakers.

Without looking, he knew who it was. "Hello Dr. Pons, how can I help you?" he said with feigned formality. "How do you always know it's me?" "Just psychic, I think," he replied coyly. Check-ins were common, Lola usually asking for clarification or direction, but Henry knew it was about keeping a strong relationship and helping him to stay in the loop. "H, I've got Jerome here on speaker." "Sup, Dr. S. How's Tracy Chapman?" Jerome joked. Henry knew Lola was giving Jerome the same puzzled look he had, "What?" "You know, you've got a fast car?" Jerome said in a deadpan. "I can hear Lola rolling her eyes from here. The drive is good, what are y'all still doing in the office? It's late!"

"H, I need you to settle one question. We're finalizing the proposal for DU to fund a community-based grant project, for the Tribe to fund their education projects going forward. Jerome and I are trying to think of how we tie Institutional Review Boards (IRBs), Tribal IRBs, and DU's cultural review process together. Since we're emphasizing self-determination, we want to make it as hands off as possible, but still keep these boundaries in place since . . ." as Lola trailed off, Jerome jumped in, "since you can't trust an institution to do nothing for nobody. We should be as engaged as is necessary to the projects the Tribe is promoting, but it's still a colonial institution, and it's the university's money. If they change in a couple years, and they try to manipulate, appropriate, or just straight up steal the benefits that are supposed to come from this grant, we were talking how it's best to have methodical safeguards in place."

"Y'all are thinking steps ahead. We have to start with CIRM, to get at all them good R's, as you say Jerome. Responsibility, reciprocity, relationality, and respect are the foundations of what we do, but at the end of the day, we are also in a society where racism and colonization are endemic, working for institutions and processes that have never been friendly to us as Native folk, or Black folk, or Brown folk, any of us. So, focus on the Tribe's IRB and power of review, to make sure the respect and responsibility are grounded in the Tribe's sovereignty, but keep the University's IRB and cultural review involved to get the reciprocity and relationship between the Tribe's institutions and DU."

"H, that's all we needed. Give Berry and Lowrie all of my love." Lola joked. "Yeah thanks, Dr. S, let's get this done, I got kids to feed, y'all take care." Henry laughed as the line went silent. He admired the dedication his colleagues put in to this project, here they all were sacrificing personal time to work late. Henry wistfully imagined a time when he wouldn't be bound to the all-day calendar and could spend more quality time doing all the other things that made him happy, with space to write or spend time with his teenage boys, even if they weren't too interested in spending time with him these days. Henry relished the ending of the day to spend time with his family, even though he knew once they were all going to bed he would have to slip away to his home office to try and get that last bit of writing and e-mails done before the whole thing started over again tomorrow.

Conclusion

Counter storytelling, for us, is about building on lived experience to start thinking about what's possible. In this story, we theorize how policy should be created on the possibilities of people, with structures to contribute to the betterment of the community and society. This is where benevolence, hope, and possibility come together. We build policies with the idea of assisting others, create structures to unlock their power, and look to the possibilities of what those people can become.

In this chapter's counter story, we explore the day-to-day implications of Critical Indigenous Research Methodologies and TribalCrit in practice with a day in the life of Dr. Henry Sampson, and his former students Dr. Lola Pons and Dr. Jerome Jackson. We structure it in story form to highlight how storytelling can shift analyses beyond an examination; they usually question those structures and often offer ways to disrupt and rebuild these structures. CIRM becomes central both to the story as a framing for engaging in research, but also in imagining how we might create community partnerships from inside the institution. Each character is engaged in mutually respectful conversations, building on established relationships that earn familiarity, and hold each other accountable to principles and a common goal: creating beneficial programs, policies, and practices for Indigenous communities and communities of color. Through counter narratives, we move beyond the idea of reporting the existence and mechanisms of oppression, which reify structures that have led, in part to the struggles for historically disenfranchised communities. Instead we re-think the common-sense purpose of the academy—admission and graduation—and discuss what it means for an institution to go beyond these taken-for-granted phenomena. Our aim is to transcend the specifics, while providing context that can travel through storytelling and open up the discussion for reimagining university partnerships through CIRM. Counter stories have potential to display dialogue, conversation and the genesis of ideas as they are formed by collaboration and context. This is different than the usual monologues that academic research and writing has traditionally enforced where the author/ researcher is removed from voice, made invisible, obscuring perspective, positionality privilege, and power—or as Jerome might say, "All them good Ps."

References

Basso, K. H. (1996). *Wisdom sits in places: Landscape and language among the Western Apache.* Albuquerque: University of New Mexico Press.

Bell, D. (1987). *And we are not saved: The elusive quest for racial justice.* New York: Basic Books.

Bell, D. (1995). Who's afraid of critical race theory? *University of Illinois Law Review, 1995*(4), 893–910.

Bottomore, T. (1990 [1977]) Foreword. In. P. Bourdieu & J.-C. Passeron, *Reproduction in education, society, and culture.* New York: Sage.

Bourdieu, P., & Passeron, J. C. (1990 [1977]). *Reproduction in education, society and culture* (Vol. 4). New York: Sage.

Brayboy, B. M. J. (2005). Toward a tribal critical race theory in education. *The Urban Review, 37*(5), 425–446.

Brayboy, B. M. J., Gough, H. R., Leonard, B., Roehl, R. F., & Solyom, J. A. (2011). Reclaiming scholarship: Critical Indigenous research methodologies. In S. D. Lapan, M. T. Quartaroli, and F. J. Reimer (Eds.), Qualitative research: An introduction to methods and design (423–450). New York: John Wiley & Sons.

Brayboy, B. M. J., Solyom, J. A., & Castagno, A. E. (2014). Looking into the hearts of Native peoples: Nation building as an institutional orientation for graduate education. *American Journal of Education, 120*(4), 575–596.

Crenshaw, K. (1995). Introduction. In K. Crenshaw, N. Gotanda, G. Peller, & K. Thomas (Eds.), *Critical race theory: The key writings that formed the movement.* New York: The New Press, xiii–xxxii.

Delgado, R. (1989). Storytelling for oppositionists and others: A plea for narrative. *Michigan Law Review, 87*(8), 2411–2441.

Deloria, V. (1969). *Custer died for your sins: An Indian manifesto.* Norman, OK: University of Oklahoma Press.

Domonoske, C. (2016, September 1). Georgetown will offer an edge in admissions to descendants of slaves. *NPR.* Retrieved from http://www.npr.org/sections/the two-way/2016/09/01/492223040/georgetown-will-offer-an-edge-in-admissions-to-descendants-of-slaves.

Gramsci, A. (2014) *Selections from the Prison Notebooks* (G. N. Smith & Q. Hoare, Trans.). New York: International Publishers.

Guinier, L. (2016). Tyranny of the meritocracy: Democratizing higher education in America. Boston, MA: Beacon Press.

Kirkness, V. & Barnhardt, R. (2001). First nations and higher education: The four R's— respect, relevance, reciprocity, responsibility. *Journal of American Indian Education, 30*(3), 1–15.

Ladson-Billings, G., & Tate, W. F. (1995). Toward a critical race theory of education. *Teachers college record, 97*(1), 47–68.

Parker, A.C. (1916). The social elements of the Indian problem. *American Journal of Sociology,* 22, 252–267.

Pevar, S. (2012). *The rights of Indians and tribes.* Oxford: Oxford University Press.

Smith, L.T. (2012). *Decolonizing methodologies; research and Indigenous peoples* (2nd. Ed.). New York: Zed Books.

Wilder, C. S. (2013). *Ebony and ivy: Race, slavery, and the troubled history of America's universities.* New York: Bloomsbury Press.

Williams, P. J. (1991). *The alchemy of race and rights.* Cambridge, MA: Harvard University Press.

Williams, R. A. (1996) Foreword. In R. Delgado, *The Rodrigo Chronicles: Conversations about America and Race* (pp. xi-xv). New York: NYU Press.

Wilson, S. (2009). *Research is ceremony: Indigenous research methods.* Black Point, NS: Fernwood Publishing.

6

TAKING IT TO THE STREETS

Critical Race Theory, Participatory Research and Social Justice

Adrienne D. Dixson, ArCasia James, and Brittany L. Frieson

Public protests against public policy, state and federal legislation, and politicians, while not unique to the socio-political and socio-historical landscape of the United States, appear to have become more frequent over the last decade, and certainly more widely attended since the last presidential election. On college campuses, protests about administrative decisions, lack of diversity and overall campus climate relative to diversity, have also been a normative aspect of college life, at least since the 1960s when college students were particularly active in anti-war and civil rights demonstrations. Recently, students of color across the U.S. have protested the lack of diversity among both students and faculty, and campus climates that they have all described as racially hostile (e.g., #BeingBlackatIllinois) (Stamm, 2015). At the K-12 level, students have engaged in protests against education reform (Dixson, Buras, & Jeffers, 2015) and police brutality in their cities (Serpick, 2015). Making sense of not only the meaning of protests, but also the contexts that have led to student-protests, is an obvious question for Critical Race Theory (CRT) scholars to examine.

In education, scholars have become increasingly more interested in using CRT as both an analytical framework and a research methodology. CRT scholars in education have theorized on CRT methodology in education (Lynn & Dixson, 2012) and the relationship of other methodologies to CRT (Chapman, 2007; Dixson, Chapman, & Hill, 2003). In this chapter, we also examine the relationship of CRT to methodology, specifically, we examine the relationship between CRT and Participatory Action Research (PAR). In many ways, the connection between CRT and PAR is implicit in that CRT scholars, as articulated in the very foundation of CRT, actively work with those "on the bottom" (Bell, 1995, Matsuda, 1987) to challenge, disrupt, re-orient, and fight to eradicate oppression. Thus, for us as CRT scholars who are oriented to working with communities, PAR may be a methodology that helps us think and act more carefully about how we engage in research. We offer reflections on our own experiences as CRT scholars, an established CRT scholar and two emerging CRT scholars, who have conducted scholarly inquiry that attempts to center, privilege, and affirm the voices and perspectives of the communities within which they work. These communities are geographic, scholarly, and professional, that have been marginalized, distorted and/or rendered invisible through and by traditional scholarship. We have learned through our projects to adjust our lens, perspectives, beliefs, and practices as researchers, given our commitments as CRT scholars in education. We will share these narratives and offer recommendations that reflect what we have learned as researchers.

Critical Race Theory and Participatory Action Research

To support our perspective on race research that reflects the social justice and social change origins of CRT, we provide a brief conceptual genealogy of both CRT and PAR in this section. Shortly after the creation of CRT in legal studies, Gloria Ladson-Billings and William Tate (1995) argued for the usefulness of CRT in education, citing the urgent need for a more robust explanation of enduring racial inequity in education; their contribution inspired ample, related research. Refined and organized into eight operational constructs that Dixson and Rousseau (2006) define as: (1) Whiteness as property; (2) Intersectionality; (3) Critique of liberalism and colorblindness; (4) Interest-Convergence; (5) Racial Realism; (6) Restrictive versus Expansive notions of equality; (7) Voice/Counter-story; and (8) Social Change, CRT has grown into a major theoretical orientation within and beyond the field of law and education. As far as how CRT might inform education research, Lynn, Yosso, Solórzano, & Parker (2002) contend that CRT illuminates and clarifies lines of qualitative research inquiry. Thereafter, CRT has continued to offer a fruitful site for developing research methods and methodologies in education (Chapman, 2007; Dixson, 2015; Parker & Lynn, 2002; Solórzano & Yosso, 2002).

Committed to social improvement as determined by marginalized and oppressed groups, particularly along lines of race, socio-economic status, and gender, PAR aims to disrupt the dichotomy routinely constructed between researcher and participant (Fals-Borda & Rahman, 1991; Noffke & Somekh, 2009). Recognizing that research plays a sizable role in preserving and disrupting power in society, PAR meaningfully engages people who are not traditionally trained researchers in the research process (Noffke & Somekh, 2009). These individuals drive research foci and questions by identifying their concerns and adapting methods and methodologies to create solutions and work toward social justice (Reason & Bradbury, 2008). As a way to undercut positivist notions of knowledge and bring experiential epistemologies to the fore of human learning (Maguire, 1987), this aspect of PAR well serves CRT, as experiential knowledge plays an integral role in examining the salience of race and racial oppression (Bell, 1987; Bell, 1992). Analyses from this perspective will be instructive for the purposes of our multi-vocal chapter since experiential knowledge plays a vital part in our separate research projects, and largely dictates how we cultivate our own research orientations.

As PAR works toward expanding critical consciousness, self-determined life improvement, and structural change in society (Maguire, 1987), it also functions as an alternative inquiry method to oppose misrepresentations of people of color by their oppressors (Akom, 2011; Smith, 1999). Hall (1981) notes PAR's central focus on community transformation and its centering of exploited and oppressed groups as a thoroughly political act. PAR's international roots draw from subaltern struggles across South America, East Africa, and South Asia (Akom, 2011; Fals-Borda & Rahman, 1991; Park, Brydon-Miller, Hall, & Jackson, 1993). For educational purposes, much PAR literature (Brydon-Miller, 1997; Brydon Miller & Maguire, 2009; Maguire, 1987; Noffke, 1994; Ozanne & Saatcioglu, 2008) acknowledges its US roots as growing out of Myles Horton's Highlander Folk School in the Appalachia region of Tennessee in the 1930s, where marginalized residents engaged in labor organizing, civil rights activist training, and environmental justice.

Integrating themes from action research (Noffke, 1989) and participatory research (Brydon-Miller, 1997), PAR builds from both and continues to expand, per methodological and theoretical developments around youth (Cammarota and Fine, 2008), Black youth (Akom, 2011), and indigenous groups (Tuck, 2009). Researchers apply many of these approaches in P-20 educational contexts and aim to engage students, their families, and communities. However, PAR stands to benefit from more sophisticated theorizations of race (Bell, 2006), a task with which CRT is apt to assist. Thus, our multi-vocal chapter joins Maria Torre (2009) and Antwi Akom (2011), two scholars who have meaningfully blended key insights from both PAR and CRT, in this small, but growing, line of inquiry.

Way Down Yonder in New Orleans

Since 2007, I, Adrienne, have been engaged in a long-term research project focused on education reform in post-Katrina New Orleans. I originally conceptualized the project to examine culturally relevant pedagogy within the context of the trauma of Hurricane Katrina, a trauma that presumably both teachers and students would have experienced. Having been a teacher in New Orleans in the 1990s and having local and familial ties to New Orleans and southern Louisiana, I believed that gaining access to schools, classrooms, teachers, students, parents, and community members would give me insight on how teachers use the collective tragedy of Hurricane Katrina and the rebuilding process in New Orleans, in their teaching.

Over the last decade, I have attended scores of meetings on the "rebuilding" of New Orleans and its public education system. Eventually, I began helping both groups and individuals document and publish scholarly articles on the impact of the reforms on students and parents (Dixson et al., 2015). I view my experience as becoming a "reluctant" scholar-activist. To be clear, I was not opposed to activist scholarship; however, prior to this project, and despite identifying as a Critical Race Theorist, I did not intend for this project to be the platform for my scholarly activism, nor did I imagine that I would be engaged in efforts to oppose education reform. I began my project interested in how teachers and students were making sense of the post-Katrina tragedy. Yet, given my scholarly lens and perspective on race and education, I could not ignore what I viewed then in 2007, and what has and is manifesting now in 2017, as a clear pattern of racialized educational inequity in the post-Katrina educational landscape in New Orleans. Thus, I felt compelled to do what I tell all my students: "Use your skills for good, not evil."

My engagement as a scholar-activist has been critical in supporting communities and constituencies in New Orleans as they desire to document both the actions by education reformers and peoples organizing efforts and resistance to those actions and policies. I provided expert testimony at the NAACP (National Association for the Advancement of Colored People) hearing in New Orleans on charter schools; served as the education expert on education reform at the National Association of Black Journalists national conference in New Orleans and have provided research support for a constituency of New Orleans parents who testified at a senate hearing on charter schools in Washington, DC. In this way, I believe this phase of my scholarship and scholarly productivity is in keeping with one of the fundamental tenets of CRT: social change. I view this work as my CRT research praxis (Yamamoto, 1997).

Yamamoto (1997) describes CRT praxis as:

> Critical race praxis combines critical, pragmatic and socio-legal analysis with political lawyering and community organizing to practice justice by and for racialized communities. Its central idea is that racial justice requires anti-subordination practice. In addition to ideas and ideals, justice is something experienced through practice. . .critical race praxis requires an understanding of justice in terms of both method—experience- rethinking-translation-engagement—and norm—first principles of anti-subordination and rectification of injustice. It requires, in appropriate instances, using, critiquing, and moving beyond notions of legal justice pragmatically to heal disabling intergroup wounds and forge intergroup alliances. It also requires, for race theorists, enhanced attention to theory translation and deeper engagement with frontline practice; and for political lawyers and community activists, increased attention to a critical rethinking of what race is, how civil rights are conceived, and why law sometimes operates as a discursive power strategy.
>
> *(p. 829)*

Related to educational research, this notion of CRT praxis describes in large part how we view PAR, through a CRT lens, and its relationship to education research for social justice. Specifically, as CRT scholars who engage PAR, we should always be engaged in this process of understanding racial and social justice in education through "experience-rethinking-translation-engagement." This process of reflection and action, requires CRT researchers to view our projects as partnerships where our work is in the service of working with communities to engage in a critical rethinking of what race is, how educational equity is conceived, and why education policy and practice operate to confer or withhold equitable education opportunities and outcomes.

An Educational Historian's Efforts to Draw on PAR through a CRT Frame

Recasting much of what we think we know is my task as a burgeoning educational historian. This requires me, ArCasia, to enter projects carefully so that current conceptions of the past do not color my research findings ahistorically. In my current dissertation project, I am relying on oral history interviews with African Americans who, as primary and secondary students, desegregated secondary schools in Waco, Texas, after the Supreme Court rendered *de jure separate but equal* segregation policies unconstitutional after the *Brown v. Board of Education* (1954) case. Centering these oral history narratives signifies a departure from more conventional historical research methods, a departure I hope speaks more genuinely to and better represents former students' experiences.

Revisiting these moments with the individuals who were most directly affected by the *Brown* ruling represents an attempt to draw on both PAR and CRT, two approaches designed to supplant White dominance and widespread reliance on sanitized interpretations of the past. Trusting direct actors to identify significant research questions and provide "a counter-hegemonic edge to action research" (Brydon-Miller & Maguire, 2009, p. 79) in this historical transformation reflects PAR principles. In a similar vein, privileging participants' counter-narratives situates my study within the CRT tradition, wherein they guide me in engaging counter-storytelling analytically, and debunking the deficit historiographies framing how we understand African Americans in history (Solórzano & Yosso, 2002).

As an essential tool for demystifying many of the ways in which popular rhetoric encourages us to conceive of the *Brown* decision as one of forward progress, CRT affords the opportunity to rethink this interpretation from the perspective of those "on the bottom" long subject to subjugation (Matsuda, 1987). Lawrence (1992) notes that CRT offers strategies for opposing subaltern positionality by centering fundamental dignity and equity within human rights. Often, such revision complicates or contests notions long held about victorious historic events.

The meeting of PAR and CRT in historical work does present productive challenges. In endeavoring to incorporate these two orientations, I must take a number of, at times conflicting, considerations into account. There is much of the past that does not stand to be held to contemporary standards—to do so forces the present to bear on the past in disingenuous, inauthentic, and distracting ways that do not help demystify events of the past. However, my investigations stand to be enriched through the process of lens shifting that requires me to maintain a sensitivity to race and the incorporation of participants in revelatory ways. CRT has taught me to ask where and in which ways has race helped determine one's lot in life. How does recognizing racism as a permanent feature throughout US history help clarify the relationship of the past to how we understand it today?

In my historical work, I have to practice caution to not carry my conceptualizations of the present into my rediscovery of the past, which can be difficult at times. Particularly, in my interviews with individuals who are at present living and excavating their memories from and reflections of the past, my work pushes beyond the boundaries of traditional standards held by historians regarding what constitutes legitimate historical work. In an effort to convey the past validly through perspectives of silenced groups, I aim to offer analyses which center and interrogate subjectivities infrequently privileged in the literature. I seek to demonstrate some ways in which CRT can provide a productive site of examination for education historians, revealing the compatibility of CRT and history, if done carefully in a manner that upholds experiential knowledge and the veracity and value of counter-hegemonic truth-telling. For me, the benefits outweigh the costs, and the clarity I seek and am afforded in interpreting the past through a lens deeply sensitive to race in work I do centering African Americans is well worth the disciplinary challenges.

History in general, and African-American history in particular, is marred by mischaracterizations of the past that deny the long legacy of Black agency, acumen, resistance, and self-determination. By shedding a more complex, truthful light on African Americans' past efforts, CRT and PAR help combat this issue by providing tools to privilege and affirm Black perspectives and experiences. These insights are urgently needed within the disciplines of history and education, and, perhaps equally, in primary and secondary school curricula and textbooks (Anyon, 1979; Brown & Brown, 2010a; Brown & Brown, 2010b; Loewen, 2008; Loewen, 2013; Paxton, 1999). History is a shared enterprise that ought to be probed, critiqued, and reconfigured in generative ways that expose the inadequacies of dominant narratives.

Critical Racial Incidents: A PAR Study on African-American Teacher Burnout

My interest in African-American teacher burnout increased during the early years of my career, experiencing dissatisfaction within my role as a teacher, Brittany. As the search for literature on teacher burnout continued, specifically with African-American teachers, articles on classroom management, differentiation, and excess amounts of grading were found. These articles did not address my experience with teacher burnout and the decision was made to embark on a personal journey that investigated the stories of my colleagues' lived experiences with teacher burnout. The inspiration to "take it to the streets" emerged from the gap in the literature about critical racial incidents and teacher burnout. PAR was an appropriate methodological approach as it provided the space for this work as it values the knowledge of participants as a starting point in the investigation to bring about social change and to challenge institutions of power in addressing social justice issues (Brydon-Miller & Maguire, 2009; Cahill, 2007).

Both Attribution theory and CRT were used as frameworks to investigate the factors that contributed to African-American teacher burnout. Attribution theory essentially answered the question of "why" when referring to event causes and emotional influences, which provided space to investigate the factors that were contributing to teacher burnout (Weiner, 1985). In addition to Attribution theory, CRT was added when the participants' narratives begged for a more critical approach to examine critical racial incidents that were being mentioned in the interviews by my colleagues. Using CRT as a lens to deconstruct critical racial incidents that contributed to the participants' narratives as reasons for wanting to depart from the profession provided a critical angle that Attribution theory simply neglected.

PAR supports the notion of the knowledge of the participants guiding the study and bringing about change within the research process, such as collectively investigating and reflecting upon methods to bring about change (Johnston-Goodstar, 2013). CRT has six main tenets that support indigenous ways of knowing and understanding the world, including counter-storytelling. Stories from African-American teachers on teacher burnout have been excluded from historical accounts or replaced with the opinions of the dominant population (Delgado, 2012). Scholars believe that first-hand narratives of marginalized groups can be used to share the lived experiences of oppressed groups and challenge the dominant discourse, which is why it was crucial to vocalize the stories of African-American teachers directly from the streets (Bell, 1995; Cook & Dixson, 2013; Jackson, Bryan, & Larkin, 2016). The stories shared by African-American teachers who experience burnout aid in understanding not only the stress-related factors, but also the racially charged factors that White teachers do not experience. The stories also seek to rewrite the master narrative about teacher burnout, which assumes that all teachers, regardless of race, experience similar factors that eventually lead to teacher burnout.

The literature review on teacher burnout focuses on emotional exhaustion, stress, and work conditions but noticeably omitted any roles that racism plays in burnout among African-American teachers. More than anything, taking it to the streets and engaging in meaningful conversations with fellow colleagues about the challenges of being an African-American teacher in a White, female-dominated profession added a level of richness to the dialogue more than any piece of literature could have ever vocalized.

Burnout is not a "one-size-fits-all" issue. Race matters, and without the intersection of CRT and PAR, the argument for more conversations in the workplace surrounding African-American teacher burnout could not have been as powerful. Teacher burnout is typically a taboo topic in the field of education, but this project quickly addressed the elephant in the room surrounding race and teacher burnout that the literature previously silenced. Delgado (1989) discusses how counter-narratives promote group solidarity in order for marginalized individuals to know that they are not alone. PAR encouraged both the participants and myself to build a tighter community that placed self-care at the center of our well-being as African-American teachers. All of my participants mentioned that this was the first occasion that their experiences with teacher burnout were shared and how liberating it was to share their story with in-group members who had similar narratives, which is the first step in bringing about social change. Without PAR and involving my colleagues in the research process, the goal of bringing about social change would have presented itself much more difficult to achieve.

Counter-storytelling challenges the status quo and interrupts comforting stock stories (Delgado, 1989). The ease of reading about low salaries and the work-demanding tasks of being a teacher recreates the dominant narrative about White teachers, while, on the other hand, discussing race-related incidents that African-American teachers experience shatters complacency about teacher burnout. Sharing the stories of my participants assists in understanding how African-American teachers become oppressed in educational settings. Although PAR and CRT provided many benefits, there were also challenges that presented themselves noteworthy of discussion. Crafting narratives with my colleagues about their experiences with burnout was a role that was not taken lightly; after all, here we were inserting ourselves into a dialogue that had been previously written without our voices. We wanted our stories to be heard in hopes of resonating with another African-American teacher who shared a similar experience with race-related issues that contributed to burnout.

At the time of the data collection, I was "in the streets" as a practitioner and doing this work was a method of survival. Experiencing teacher burnout was one of the toughest struggles that I had as a teacher, but hearing stories from my colleagues about their struggles was a form of liberation. At the end of the day, the participants, and myself knew that we could depend on one another for support in the streets; and that is something that can never be replicated.

Pulling It All Together: What Does All of This Mean to Researching Race in Education?

Our three different, but complementary narratives illustrate our perspective on how CRT and CRT praxis as articulated by Yamamoto (1997) intersects with PAR. We are not making a claim that there is a "CRT" PAR, rather, we believe that for CRT researchers who engage in qualitative methods, PAR can be a method of choice.

Our narratives all illustrate the challenges we faced in attempting to understand how seemingly objective or race-neutral education policy manifests and impacts communities and people of color differently, often with deleterious effects. For Dixson, what initially began as a project to understand how teachers utilize a natural disaster in their teaching, had to be redesigned to document and understand how education reform dismantled a public education system. For James, a historian, making sense of the impact of *Brown v. Board*, in her hometown in Texas, has pushed her to look beyond traditional historiographic methods as the context and history of educational equity in Waco is wrought with complexity and nuance. Frieson's narrative offers not only a first-person account of teacher burnout, but also includes the voices of other African-American teachers who face challenges that have little do with their students, and more to do with racial microaggressions and often blatant acts of racism.

A final important commonality in our narratives that also reflects the CRT praxis-PAR intersection is the commitment we have to honoring and serving our participants and their communities. While this is not unique to our practices as researchers, it is a mandate for researchers who identify as CRT scholars and an inherent aspect of PAR. That is, inherent within CRT research is this notion of praxis (Yamamoto, 1997). In addition, we argue that qualitative CRT researchers would do well to look to PAR as a methodology that will help facilitate the need for research to be focused on social and racial justice, translate theory for communities, behave ethically and morally within and with the communities within which they work.

References

Akom, A. A. (2011). Black emancipatory action research: integrating a theory of structural racialisation into ethnographic and participatory action research methods. *Ethnography and Education*, *6*(1), 113–131.

Anyon, J. (1979). Ideology and United States history textbooks. *Harvard Educational Review*, *49*(3), 361–386.

Bell, D. A. (1980), Jr. *Brown v. Board of Education* and the interest-convergence dilemma. *Harvard Law Review*, 518–533.

Bell, D. A. (1987). *And we are not saved: The elusive quest for racial reform.* New York, NY: Basic Books.

Bell, D. A. (1992). *Faces at the bottom of the well: The permanence of racism.* New York, NY: Basic Books.

Bell, D. A. (1995). Who's afraid of critical race theory? *University of Illinois Law Review*, *4*, 893–910.

Bell, D. A. (2004). *Silent covenants: Brown vs. Board of Education and the unfulfilled hopes for racial reform.* New York, NY: Oxford University Press. Bell, E. E. (2006). Infusing race into the US discourse on action research. In P. Reason and H. Bradbury (Eds.), *Handbook of action research* (pp. 49–59). London: SAGE.

Brayboy, B. (2005). Toward a tribal critical race theory in education. *The Urban Review*, *37*(5), 425–446.

Brown, A. L., & Brown, K. D. (2010a). Strange fruit indeed: Interrogating contemporary textbook representations of racial violence toward African Americans. *Teachers College Record*, *112*(1), 31–67.

Brown, K. D., & Brown, A. L. (2010b). Silenced memories: An examination of the socio-cultural knowledge on race and racial violence in official school curriculum. *Equity & Excellence in Education, 43*(2), 139–154.

Brown v. Board of Education, 347 U.S. 483 (1954).

Brydon-Miller, M. (1997). Participatory action research: Psychology and social change. *Journal of Social Issues, 53*(4), 657–666.

Brydon-Miller, M. & Maguire, P. (2009). Participatory action research: Contributions to the development of practitioner inquiry in education. *Educational Action Research, 17*(1), 79–93.

Cahill, C. (2007). The personal is political: Developing new subjectivities through partici-patory action research. *Gender, Place & Culture, 14*(3), 267–292.

Cammarota, J., & Fine, M. (2008). Youth participatory action research: A pedagogy for transformational resistance. In J. Cammarota & M. Fine (Eds.), *Revolutionizing education* (pp. 1–11). New York, NY: Routledge.

Cammarota, J., & Fine, M. (Eds.) (2008). *Revolutionizing education: Youth participatory action research in motion.* New York, NY: Routledge.

Chapman, T. K. (2007). Interrogating classroom relationships and events: Using portraiture and critical race theory in education research. *Educational Researcher, 36*(3), 156–162.

Cook, D.A., & Dixson, A.D. (2013). Writing critical race theory and method: A compos-ite counter story on the experiences of Black teachers in New Orleans post Katrina. *International Journal of Qualitative Studies in Education, 26*(10), 1238–1258.

Crenshaw, K. (1989). Demarginalizing the intersection of race and sex: A Black feminist critique of antidiscrimination doctrine, feminist theory and antiracist politics. *University of Chicago Legal Forum, 1*(8), 139–167.

Crenshaw, K. (1991). Mapping the margins: Intersectionality, identity politics, and vio-lence against women of color. *Stanford Law Review,* 43(6), 1241–1299.

Crenshaw, K., Ocen, P. & Nanda, J. (2015). *Black girls matter: Pushed out, overpoliced and underprotected.* New York, NY: African American Policy Forum.

Crenshaw, K. W., Gotanda, N., Peller, G., & Thomas, K. (Eds.) (1995). Critical race theory: Key writings that formed the movement. New York, NY: New York Press.

Delgado, R. (1989). Storytelling for oppositionists and others: A plea for narrative. *Michigan Law Review,* 87, 2411–2441.

Delgado, R. (2012). Precious knowledge: State bans on ethnic studies, book traffick-ers (librotraficantes), and a new type of race trial. *North Carolina Law Review, 91,* 1513–1554.

Dixson, A. (2015). NEPC Review: *Ten years in New Orleans: Public school resurgence and the path ahead.* Boulder, CO: National Education Policy Center. Retrieved from http://nepc.colorado.edu/thinktank/review-NOLA-public-impact.

Dixson, A. D., & Rousseau, C. K. (2006). *Critical race theory in education: All God's children got a song.* New York, NY: Routledge.

Dixson, A. D., Buras, K. L., & Jeffers, E. K. (2015). The color of reform: Race, education reform, and charter schools in post-Katrina New Orleans. *Qualitative Inquiry, 21*(3), 288–299.

Dixson, A. D., Chapman, T. K., & Hill, D. A. (2005). Research as an aesthetic process: Extending the portraiture methodology. *Qualitative Inquiry, 11*(1), 16–26.

Fals-Borda, O., and Rahman, M. A. (1991). *Action and Knowledge: Breaking the Monopoly with Participatory Action-Research.* New York, NY: Apex Press; London: Intermediate Technology Publications.

Ford, C. L., & Airhihenbuwa, C. O. (2010). Critical race theory, race equity, and public health: toward antiracism praxis. *American Journal of Public Health, 100*(S1), S30–S35.

Gilbert, M. (2010). Theorizing digital and urban inequalities: Critical geographies of "race", gender and technological capital. *Information, Communication & Society, 13*(7), 1000–1018.

Hall, B.L. 1981. Participatory research, popular knowledge and power: A personal reflection. *Convergence, 14*(3), 6–19.

Jackson, T.O., Bryan, M.L., & Larkin, M. L. (2016). An analysis of a white preservice teacher's reflection on race and young children within an urban setting. *Urban Education, 51*(1), 60–81.

Johnston-Goodstar, K. (2013). Indigenous youth participatory action research: Re-visioning social justice for social work with indigenous youths. *Social Work, 58*(4), 314–320.

Ladson-Billings, G. (1998). Just what is critical race theory and what's it doing in a nice field like education? *International Journal of Qualitative Studies in Education, 11*(1), 7–24.

Ladson-Billings, G., & Tate, W. (1995). Toward a critical race theory of education. *The Teachers College Record, 97*(1).

Lawrence, C.R. III (1987). The id, the ego, and equal protection: Reckoning with unconscious racism. *Stanford Law Review, 39*(2), 317–388.

Lawrence, C. R. III (1992). The word and the river: Pedagogy as scholarship as struggle. *Southern California Law Review, 65*, 2231.

Loewen, J. W. (2008). *Lies my teacher told me: Everything your American history textbook got wrong.* New York, NY: The New Press.

Loewen, J. W. (2013). *Teaching what really happened: How to avoid the tyranny of textbooks and get students excited about doing history.* New York, NY: Teachers College Press.

Lynn, M. & Dixson, A.D. (2012). *Handbook of Critical Race Theory and Education,* New York, NY: Routledge.

Lynn, M., Yosso, T., Solórzano, D., & Parker, L. (Eds.) (2002). Critical race theory and qualitative research. *Qualitative Inquiry, 8*(1).

Maguire, P. (1987). *Doing participatory research: A feminist approach.* Amherst, MA: The Center for International Education.

Matsuda, M. (1987) Looking to the bottom: Critical legal studies and reparations. *Harvard Civil Rights-Civil Liberties Law Review, 22*, 323–399.

Noffke, S. (1994). Action research: Towards the next generation. *Educational Action Research, 2*(1), 9–21.

Noffke, S. E. & Somekh, B. (Eds.) (2009). *The SAGE handbook of educational action research.* Thousand Oaks, CA: SAGE.

Noffke, S. E., & Stevenson, R. B. (1995). *Educational action research: Becoming practically critical.* New York, NY: Teachers College Press.

Ozanne, J.L., & Saatcioglu, B. (2008). Participatory action research. *Journal of Consumer Research, 35*(3), 423–439.

Park, P., Brydon-Miller, M., Hall, B., & Jackson, T. (Eds.) (1993). *Voices of change: Participatory research in the United States and Canada.* Toronto: OISE Press.

Parker, L., & Lynn, M. (2002). What's race got to do with it? Critical race theory's conflicts with and connections to qualitative research methodology and epistemology. *Qualitative Inquiry, 8*(1), 7–22.

Patton, L. D. (2016). Disrupting postsecondary prose: Toward a critical race theory of higher education. *Urban Education, 51*(3), 315–342.

Paxton, R. J. (1999). A deafening silence: History textbooks and the students who read them. *Review of educational research, 69*(3), 315–339.

Price, P. L. (2010). At the crossroads: Critical race theory and critical geographies of race. *Progress in Human Geography, 34*(2), 147–174.

Reason P., & Bradbury, H. (Eds.) (2008). *The SAGE handbook of action research: Participative inquiry and practice*. Thousand Oaks, CA: SAGE.

Schensul, J. J., & Berg, M. (2004). Youth participatory action research: A transformative approach to service-learning. *Michigan Journal of Community Service Learning, 10*(3).

Serpick, E. (2015, September 24). Why we should call recent Baltimore events an 'uprising.' *The Baltimore Sun*. Retrieved from http://www.baltimoresun.com/news/opin ion/oped/bs-ed-baltimore-uprising-20150924-story.html.

Smith, L.T. 1999. Decolonizing methodologies: Research and indigenous people. New York, NY: Zed Books.

Solórzano, D. G., & Yosso, T. J. (2002). Critical race methodology: Counter-storytelling as an analytical framework for education research. *Qualitative Inquiry, 8*(1), 23–44.

Stamm, C. (2015, January 23). Being Black at Illinois. *News in the archives*. Retrieved from https://archives.library.illinois.edu/slc/black-illinois.

Tate, W. F. (1997). Critical race theory and education: History, theory, and implications. In M. W. Apple (Ed.) *Review of research in education* (Vol. 22, pp. 191–243). Washington, DC: American Educational Research Association.

Torre, M. E. (2009). Participatory action research and critical race theory: Fueling spaces for nos-otras to research. *The Urban Review, 41*(1), 106–120.

Tuck, E. (2009). Re-visioning action: Participatory action research and Indigenous theories of change. *The Urban Review, 41*(1), 47–65.

Weiner, B. (1985). An attributional theory of achievement motivation and emotion. *Psychological Review, 92*(4), 548.

Yamamoto, E. K. (1997). Critical race praxis: Race theory and political lawyering practice in the post-Civil Rights America. *Michigan Law Review, 95(4)*, 821–900.

7

THE COMMITMENT TO BREAK RULES

Critical Race Theory, Jazz Methodology and the Struggle for Justice in Education

David Stovall

The editors of this collection have charged me with the task of writing a chapter about critical race theory (CRT) as jazz methodology. As qualitative methods often reveal a messy and winding road, I try with all I can to center accountability and responsibility in my iteration of community-based research. I emphasize the word "try" because these attempts are not always successful, in that there are missteps and discrepancies along the way. At the same time, I turn to CRT to make sense of a world that deems the punishment, exclusion, and marginalization of people of color to be normal, right, and good. This also requires us to be careful that CRT does not become a "catch-all" term, but instead a constellation of critical theoretical paradigms used to understand the multilayered contexts in which White supremacy/racism operates. Because CRT has never intended to purport a singular approach, the original tenets in legal and educational scholarship are intended to provide a bridge for scholars to understand our lives and our work from an intersectional perspective (Crenshaw, 1991). Because we live lives that simultaneously experience multiple oppressions given particular interpretations of our bodies and social position (e.g. race, class, gender, age, ability, sexual orientation, etc.), I use CRT to make space for scholars and organizers who are thinking and working collectively to change our conditions.

With regards to methodology, the remainder of this account borrows heavily from youth participatory action research (YPAR), critical race methodology, and a methodological approach utilized by Shawn Ginwright (2010) known as jazz methodology. Borrowing from these approaches and the work of earlier scholars who utilize jazz methodology (Calmore 1992; Dixson 2005, 2006, 2007; Oldfather & West 1994), I have used the concept to document my involvement on a high school design team and as a volunteer social studies teacher/collaborator and to document researcher accountability to a community-driven initiative.

Deeply influenced by Ginwright and Adrienne Dixson's take on the construct, I attempt to offer similar critical guideposts for my own research that seeks to "inform and inspire . . . pose new questions, challenge assumptions and move together in an entirely different direction" (Ginwright 2010, 21).

Most familiar in the traditions of YPAR, engaging from the perspective of co-constructor or co-collaborator challenges CRT scholars to work at the intersection of multiple approaches (Cammarota & Fine, 2008; Ibanez-Carrasco & Meiners, 2004; Lynn & Jennings, 2005; Parker & Lynn, 2002; Smith, 2012). By interrupting the traditional research paradigm suggesting "objectivity" or "validity," CRT, like YPAR, critical ethnography, and community-based participatory research, encourages scholars to get "close" to our work. Encapsulated in this approach is the understanding that any work in this vein will sometimes require making tough, uncomfortable decisions that often have the potential to isolate scholars from the groups they work with (Smith, 2012).

Jazz Methodology and CRT

The process of engaging a methodological approach centered in CRT always pushes me to retain the ability to make my research accessible to the people I work with outside of the academy. Many times, the struggle in reading piles of manuscripts, policy papers, and journal articles is to avoid the tragic mistake of adopting "highbrow" language that only makes sense to other academics. As irritating as this was to read as a graduate student, it becomes almost unbearable as a university professor. While I claim my position in the universe of academics who actively refuse to let the academy define their humanity, I take this position understanding the inherent contradictions of secure, long-term employment (tenure) and salaries that offer a living wage. Presenting a process that incorporates the improvisational nature of jazz, Ginwright (2010) incorporates a broad constellation of strategies to capture the depth and breadth of his project. Pairing jazz and methodology as the constructs by which to "move beyond simplistic explanations, descriptions and predictions," his work effortlessly maneuvers musical and textual examples to explain his method of accountability to the youth workers and young people he has encountered in his time with the organization Leadership Excellence (Ginwright 2010, 20). Where my own work may not reach his proscribed goals, I move forward in my process humbly and cautiously.

Similar to Calmore's take on Archie Shepp's "fire music", this chapter takes from a series of instances to create a composite on the ways I incorporate jazz methodology into CRT to create an "oppositional cultural practice" to traditional methodology (Calmore 1992, 2134). As jazz is the composite of African-descended musical forms transmuted through the experiences and musical practices of Black people in the U.S., a jazz methodology for the purpose of this document is the amalgamation of qualitative methods to tell a layered, but comprehensive narrative on the form and function of White supremacy, including the struggle against it.

A process such as this is subjective, as one cannot know something and "not be invested in its meaning or the process of discovery" (Dixson, 2005, 107). Because my intention is not to make the process one that is sanguine with the supposed "objectivity" of mainstream academic research, CRT jazz methodology allows for a space to "analyze, question, and express ideas creatively" (ibid.). Reflecting on her time as a Jazz Studies major in her undergraduate studies, I pull from Dixson's process to tell a story deeply situated in context, nuance, and political economy. Using the jazz concepts of "riffs", solos, and breaks, Dixson makes clear the uses of jazz concepts in her process.

> Although jazz musicians generally perform their solos without accompaniment by other wind instruments, in ensemble playing, riffs and breaks played by the other horn players in the band quite often serve as backdrops for the soloist and often complement what the soloist is playing. Riffs may be played spontaneously or written as part of the composition . . . the creativity of riffs lies not in their originality, as many riffs are lines from famous or commonly recognized melodies, but in their frame of reference and how they add to the aesthetic expression of the composition . . . This can be a playful move on the part of the background and/or the rhythm section. They may use a riff to lighten the tone and timbre of the solo and/ or as a way to engage the audience. It may also serve as an inspiration to the soloist. Breaks serve as a form of rhythmic, melodic, and harmonic relief. The break is a momentary suspension of harmonic, rhythmic, and melodic activity by the rhythm section.
>
> *(Dixson, 2005, 126)*

From her use of these jazz concepts, Dixson amasses that "jazz, as both a musical and cultural concept, is a powerful way to discuss . . . projects that are inherently political and cultural" (ibid., 129). I agree with her assertion that "jazz methodology has important implications for those of us engaged in research and scholarship that takes a critical look at race and racism in education" (ibid.).

For the purpose of this chapter, my use of CRT as jazz methodology comes in the form of the amalgamation of my experiences, processes, and reflections as a member of the design team for the Greater Lawndale/Little Village School of Social Justice (SOJO). Similar to a jazz rhythm section, my experiences at SOJO sometimes requires me to sit in the "break" section of the song and take notes (like the rhythm section in big-band jazz or smaller jazz ensembles like trios, quartets, quintets or sextets) or to "riff" like a soloist in the form of teaching a class at the high school for early college credit. Just like the soloist, I would have to return to the harmony of the song when I am interviewing others who participate in the life of the high school.

In relationship to traditional qualitative methodology, this chapter is not reflective of the conventional longitudinal study or extended case study. However, there are elements that are coherent with both methodologies in that the processes and reflections occur over a nine-year period (2003–2014) with a relatively consistent group of people in the same setting. Many of these people were responsible for reading chapters while in draft form, offering suggestions and corrections, providing accuracy to the document. My own process of member-checking and triangulation, utilizing CRT as jazz methodology to create this account, was critical for me in developing a process that includes a broad collection of participants that were instrumental in creating this account. The process became useful in that it continually pressed me on ways to tell a story that I was part of in a way that is responsible and accountable. Where Institutional Review Boards (IRBs) and Human Subjects Review panels at colleges and universities use the rhetoric of "ethics" primarily to protect themselves from lawsuits, CRT as jazz methodology challenges me to be responsible to the people I care about beyond a contractual agreement to use their commentary.

From documenting community resistance in the initial hunger strike that led to the creation of the high school, to my team-teaching a class at SOJO, this account is the amalgamation of field notes (in design team meetings, classrooms, main offices of community organizations, community settings, homes of teachers, community residents, and design team members, etc.), interviews, informal conversations, and archival research to assemble a puzzle of complex, shifting, and sometimes conflicting pieces. Nevertheless, I was not in the position of the passive observer and was immersed in the process, including extensive conversations with other design team members, teachers, students, public officials, Chicago Public Schools (CPS) representatives, community organizers, and community residents. In the spirit of Ginwright's jazz-influenced approach to methodology, my struggle to create a coherent document is rooted in observation, description, history, and action (2010, 21).

Critical Race Method as Entry Point and Counterstory

Solórzano and Yosso (2002) contend that CRT method seeks to build counterstories that stand in resistance to deficit-based narratives on communities of color. In a place like Chicago, this becomes critically important given a recent history of gun violence in particular communities. As counternarrative, it should be noted that gun violence is not the sum-total of the neighborhoods in which they occur, but is instead deeply impacted by historical disinvestment, dispossession, and displacement of particular communities of color. CRT method, as a tool to interrupt White, mainstream notions of deficit and disposability raises counternarrative as the necessary interruption to "open new windows into the reality of those at the margins of society by showing possibilities beyond the ones they live and demonstrating that they are not alone in their position" (Solórzano & Yosso, 2002, 36).

For my own work, CRT as jazz methodology shifts my understandings to one of documentarian, with a number of responsibilities to community-based struggle. First is the documentation of the process engaged to responsibly record and report the events in question. Second is to provide an example for current and future researchers of the attempt to work in a way that challenges "the perceived wisdom of those at society's center by providing a context to understand and transform established belief systems" (ibid.). Even in the world of qualitative research, there are those that support a process that engages a specific set of conventions that determine "rigor" and "structure". While I am not opposed to structure, I am not wedded to the structures that prove my work to stand as research in the annals of the academy. Instead, like Solózano and Yosso (2002), I am less concerned with proving my worth to an academic discipline rooted in the vestiges of settler colonialism and White supremacy and am more concerned with a process that is thorough and reflective in its understanding of the expressed concerns of communities experiencing and resisting White supremacy.

CRT as Jazz Methodology in Concrete Examples of Pedagogy, Analysis and Implementation

While developing the proposal for SOJO, one of the components inserted into the document that had to be presented to central office of CPS was a section stating the intent of myself and another colleague to teach courses at the high school. The intention of the courses was to provide college access to students traditionally excluded from similar opportunities in traditional high schools. As the students who began as freshmen at SOJO in the fall of 2005 approached their senior year, Rico and myself, along with SOJO faculty and administration began to discuss the possibilities of students attaining early college credit. Utilizing our networks as university professors, we contacted the university while SOJO administration addressed our concerns with CPS. This process was recorded through field notes with the design team in the years 2003–2005. It was also archived in the proposal submitted to CPS. Lastly, it was revisited in the 2008–2009 academic year, as we moved to implement the courses.

The implementation of the course was an attempt to fulfill the original premise of the proposal submitted to CPS. As jazz methodology, this was the assemblage of the band, making a decision to write the composition and playing a series of songs for an album or performance. On the ground, this would include myself and other faculty members being on the SOJO campus five days per week, one period per day, with the addition of any time we used to update the administration on the progress of the course. The course would be the equivalent of two semesters long, in that it ran for the entire school year at SOJO. I received a real challenge in that my class was scheduled for first period (8 a.m.). Remaining accountable to the community-driven initiative, the decision to teach the class on campus allowed for a more tangible connection to the intent of the initial proposal for SOJO.

Utilizing CRT as jazz methodology, I documented a process that did not depend on the conventions of a discipline, but instead allowed space for the narrative to remain at the center of the analysis. As method, I archived the letters of recommendation and logged the field notes from the conversation with UIC and CPS officials. Once both data sets were archived, they were reviewed, taking sections of the notes to create a coherent narrative as presented in this chapter.

Returning to the Rhythm Section

As promised, we secured a day and time to present to researchers at a local university. Unfortunately, due to previous travel arrangements, Professor Mills was unable to attend but let the class know how honored he was that they were using his text to analyze their conditions. Some of the students expressed their nervousness as we approached the university, but I told them not to worry, they were well-prepared and would not have a problem in their presentations. Earlier in the week, with the help of clerical staff, I was able to publicize the event in several departments throughout the College of Education and the College of Liberal Arts and Sciences. The event was well attended by university faculty and staff. Also, in attendance was the Associate Dean who was instrumental in providing the initial matching funds for tuition and supplies for the students.

I provided a brief introduction of the course and how myself and other university colleagues were engaging in a year-long project to provide high school students with early college entrance credit. From there students began to present their group presentations on Mills' *The Racial Contract*. From explaining the premise of the text, they began to explain gentrification, immigration, and health care. Followed by a question and answer session, faculty asked students on how they came to their projects and what were their key discoveries. Students responded soundly to the questions, providing definitive answers that were situated in their research. Many of my colleagues approached me after the presentation, congratulating myself and the students on the projects.

The projects served as jazz methodology by shifting the notion of "expertise". As a facilitator, the responsibility to students serves as the "break" in that my responsibility was to make space for them to demonstrate their expertise. If we think of the multiple presentations to the faculty as a single song, students were able to "riff" off the topic of the racial contract as a grouping of soloists that created a collective song.

Reflexivity and CRT as Jazz Methodology

Throughout the duration of the course students were challenged to address issues of inequality and devised several strategies to address issues and concerns they saw as pertinent to their communities. We were also challenged to investigate policies and practices that directly affected young people in schools (i.e., the Dream Act, teacher pay, immigration, homelessness, school discipline policies, etc.). Standing in the face of recent CPS data where less than 30% of CPS graduating seniors were admitted to four-year colleges and universities, 22 of the 26 graduating seniors (77%) enrolled in the course received admission to four-year institutions.

For many of us who work with communities, families, and young people, we need to recognize the potential disconnects we may have experienced with them. Where we can experience deep and tangible connections with young people in the fight for justice in education, there are other spaces where generational divisions are present. As method, field notes and student journaling became critical in understanding the ways students received the material. With a course for high school seniors that was taught during first period, there were sometimes issues with tardiness and attendance. Instead of viewing this reality as a point of contention, these sites should be viewed as spaces of recognition and accountability. At this moment teachers have the opportunity to create a space where they can learn from their students. In my own classroom, I have numerous technological challenges that my students often correct. Additionally, if I do not understand a term or a position that they are communicating, I ask them to explain or demonstrate how the term is used. This process of "putting me on" was integral to strengthening relationships with my students, allowing me to experience a level of comfort in dealing with my own ignorance in reference to their understandings. The connection to CRT methodology comes forward in the idea of shifting from the position of teacher to co-teacher and learner, in reference to the methodological and pedagogical approaches to the class. By disturbing the methodological approaches that are aimed at excluding communities of color, humility becomes a critical component in reframing the concepts of "expertise" and "researcher". Similar to my earlier interaction with Dixson's meditations on riffs, solos and harmony, I had to sit in the break and let students lead as the soloists. The constant interplay between who occupies the role of facilitator and learner is emblematic of jazz methodology.

Because discussion was an integral component of the course, many of our conversations would focus on their understandings as young people. Because I'm older, our dialogues and reflections allowed me to realize how much the world has changed for young people. Where many concerns remain the same (i.e. food, clothing, shelter, employment, education, self-determination, peace of mind, etc.), there are nuances that deserve some attention. Technology, through access and distribution, conflates and democratizes many dimensions of the world. In the same light, policies aimed at repressing youth have also intensified. Instead of looking this as a disconnect, I used it as a space for solidarity. If our concerns are for self-determination and liberation, we cannot hold on to the sentiment of "things were better in my day." Instead, we must understand the times as different and should embrace the idea that the new understandings of young people have the potential to serve as sights for liberation. The idea is not to privilege, fetish, or romanticize the contributions of young people. Instead, the sentiment is to live in recognition of their contributions. If used properly, our experiences can provide some insight to the questions young people may have concerning their lives. By providing guidance and support through examples, spaces like a college-bridge class have the potential to contribute to the larger project or racial and educational justice. In the same vein, despite their stated likes of the course, they also offered an important critique. They still felt that my teaching was too lecture-driven and did not incorporate enough hands-on, project-based activities. They felt that I had "deep" knowledge of the subject matter, but sometimes I struggled to communicate my points. In the attempt to reframe relevant, justice-centered teaching, willingness to improve on my shortcomings must be the starting point if I have any hope in working towards a justice condition. Similar to the tenets of CRT in education, the commitment to social justice requires dislodging the traditional conventions of disciplines to provide a tangible example of accessible research that is meant to be accessed by the people we care about.

More importantly, I have to be critical of my own teaching, biases, and privilege. No matter how good I may have felt about a particular lesson, my teaching still needs serious work. Throughout the course, there were attendance issues that had to be dealt with. Having a group of seniors during first period presents a set of challenges, especially if they feel as if they don't have a reason to attend. It would be irresponsible not to address the issue—it was one that deserved attention, especially in the process of developing structure and a culture of engagement in the course. To simply teach the students that come to class while ignoring the others is reminiscent of practices engaged in other schools that only teach the students that come. Once I started to talk to students about why they were coming late, I got the range of answers, revealing that some had to work late shifts while others felt that the course wasn't connected to credits that would count towards graduation. Instead of completely blaming the students, I have to take my part in the fact that maybe I didn't communicate the college credit component fully. Because responsibility is shared in the liberatory project of education, blame cannot be placed on students and families absent of accountability from teachers and administrators.

Conclusion: Rethinking and Reimagining Method

Rather than a fixed rubric of methodological tenets and approaches, CRT as jazz methodology, like its contemporaries YPAR, critical ethnography, and feminist methodology, seeks to disrupt, reimagine and abolish the colonial practice of "speaking for" communities in research. The process in doing so, however, is not straightforward as many would like. What I have learned in this process however, is that the goal of CRT as jazz methodology should not be to settle the tensions, but instead to enter them and excavate the contradictions. Similar to pedagogy, if there is a path we take to get us to a space where self-determination to reverse dispossession (that which has been stolen from communities of color in terms of material possessions, access to resources, and knowledge of self) is the norm, CRT as jazz methodology should be considered an operational tool in achieving the aforementioned goals.

In the end, my offering to this collection remains a humble one. I do not pretend to have the answers or proper pathways to engage CRT as jazz methodology in a way that is proscriptive to other projects. Instead, my thinking is that the process should include connections to scholars who have come before me to continue their process of documenting strategies to resist and build against White supremacy, settler colonialism, sexism, heteropatriarchy, ageism, transphobia and ableism. As a documentarian strategy to make sure the story gets out beyond the walls of the ivory tower, I remain thankful for the editor's consideration of my contribution.

References

Calmore, J. O. (1992). Critical race theory, Archie Shepp, and Fire Music: Securing an authentic intellectual life in a multicultural world. *Southern California Law Review,* 65(1), 2129–2230.

Camangian, P. (2011). Subverting the master('s) syllabus. *Monthly Review,* 63(3), 128–135.

Cammarota, J., & Fine, M. (2008) (eds). *Revolutionizing education: Youth participatory action research in motion.* New York: Routledge.

Cammarota, J., & Romero, A. (2014) (eds). *Raza studies: The public option for educational revolution.* Tucson, AZ: University of Arizona.

Crenshaw, K. (1991). Mapping the margins: Intersectionality, identity politics and violence against women of color. *Stanford Law Review,* 43(6), 1241–1299.

Diamond, J. (1999). Guns, germs and steel: The fates of human societies. New York: W.W. Norton.

Dixson, A. (2005) Extending the metaphor: Notions of jazz in portraiture. *Qualitative Inquiry,* 11(1), 106–137.

Dixson, A. (2006) The fire this time: Jazz, research and critical race theory. In Dixson, A. and Rousseau, C. *Critical race theory in education: All God's children got a song.* New York: Routledge.

Dixson, A., & Bloome, D. (2007). Chapter Two: Jazz, Critical Race Theories, and the Discourse Analysis of Literacy Events in Classrooms. *Counterpoints,* 310(1), 29–52.

Ginwright, S. (2010). *Black youth rising: Activism and radical healing in urban America.* New York: Teachers College.

Hill, M.L. (2009). Beats, rhymes and classroom life: Hip-hop pedagogy and the politics of identity. New York: Teachers College.

Ibanez-Carrasco, F., & Meiners, E. (2004). *Public acts: Disruptive readings on making curriculum public.* New York: Routledge.

Klinenberg, E. (2002). *Heatwave: A social autopsy of disaster in Chicago.* London: University of Chicago.

Lynn, M., & Jennings, M. (2005). The house that race built: Critical pedagogy, African-American education, and the re-conceptualization of a critical race pedagogy. *Qualitative Inquiry,* 19(3), 15–32.

Majors, Y. J. (2007). Narrations of cross-cultural encounters as interpretive frames for reading word and world. *Discourse and Society,* 18(4), 497–505.

Mills, C. (1997). *The racial contract.* New York: Cornell.

Oldfather, P., & West, J. (1994). Qualitative research as jazz. *Educational researcher*, 23(8), 22–26.

Parker, L., & Lynn. M. (2002). What's race got to do with it? Critical race theory's conflicts with and connections to qualitative research methodology and epistemology. *Qualitative Inquiry*, 8(1), 7–22.

Smith, L. T. (2012). *Decolonizing methodologies: Research and indigenous peoples*. New York: Zed Books.

Solórzano, D., & Yosso, T. (2002). Critical race methodology: Counter-storytelling as an analytical framework for education research. *Qualitative Inquiry*, 8(1), 23–44.

Tuck E., & Yang, K. W. (2012). Decolonization is not a metaphor. *Decolonization, indigeneity, education and society*, 1(1), 1–40.

8

CRITICAL RACE PERSPECTIVES ON NARRATIVE RESEARCH IN EDUCATION

Centering Intersectionality

Theodorea Regina Berry and Elizabeth J. Bowers Cook

Telling stories of one's experiences can provide important lessons for the future. Stories of education and schooling are not an exception to this point. However, education stories, like all stories, are contextual; social, historical, and political variables and viewpoints position the meanings of stories for both the storyteller and the listener. In their seminal work *Teacher Lore*, Schubert and Ayers (1999) provide stories of teachers' experiences in the classroom. These stories position education as valuable to the social and political order of society. Michele Foster's (1998) exceptionally noteworthy scholarship *Black Teachers on Teaching* is a collection of stories from Black teachers in both social and historical contexts, providing insights on the lived experiences of Black teachers over time. Critical race theory scholars have recognized the significance of story and storytelling from the inception of the movement. In *Critical Race Theory: An Introduction* (2012), an important primer in the field, legal scholars Richard Delgado and Jean Stefancic dedicate an entire chapter to legal storytelling and narrative analysis. Legal scholar Patricia Williams skillfully grounds her work on spirit murder (1987) in narrative. Regina Austin (1992) masterfully weaves narrative in the legal analysis of defiance among Black women activists. Critical race education scholars have engaged in narrative research as a methodological approach for the last 20 years (Chang, 1993; Duncan, 2005; Parker, 1998; Parker & Lynn, 2002; Solórzano, 1998; Solórzano & Yosso, 2001; Solórzano & Yosso, 2002). However, to our knowledge, there is no singular work that specifically addresses narrative research in education with intersectionality, a central tenet of Critical Race Theory (CRT).

In this chapter we focus on the ways in which the centrality of intersectionality can prove to be important for critical race scholarship that utilizes narrative research as a methodological approach. We begin with an overview of narrative research by addressing its historical development, its definitions and types (including counterstory), and narrative research in education. A discussion of CRT, centering intersectionality, follows. We conclude with talking points to address the usefulness of including a CRT perspective in narrative research for education.

Understanding Narrative Research

Narrative has been associated with many definitions and fields of research and requires definition and interpretation. Narrative has a long history within the humanities and the social sciences and "does not fit neatly within the boundaries of any single scholarly field" (Riessman, 1993, p. 1). According to Clandinin and Connelly (2000) this qualitative research design has its roots in in anthropology, history, literature, and sociology, articulating influences from "Geertz and Bateson in anthropology, Polkinghorne in psychology, Coles in psychotherapy, and Czarniawska in organizational theory" (pp. 1–2). Connelly and Clandinin (1990, p. 2) note that "the entire field is commonly referred to as narratology, a term that cuts across" several disciplines within the humanities and social sciences. Narratives are accounts of people's lives, and speak to the telling and retelling of said stories in our own lives, the histories and perspectives that are brought to the table, and the conversation and the lives of those that intersect and connect with us as scholars, as teachers, and as colleagues. Narrative research is an interdisciplinary qualitative research approach that relies on stories *as told by* individuals – the *lives* of individuals as told through their own stories in social and historical context; ". . . narrative is understood as a spoken or written text giving an account of an event/action or series of events/actions, chronologically connected" (Czarniawska, 2004 as cited in Creswell, 2013, p. 70).

The emphasis is on the story, where both *what* and *how* is narrated (Cook, 2017). Narrative can be a "short topical story . . . an extended story about a significant aspect of one's life . . . or a narrative of one's entire life" (Chase, 2005, p. 652). Chase (2005) provides some key points toward identifying narrative. First, she notes that it can be oral or written. This diminishes commonly held notions that narrative must be written to be valid. Second, Chase notes that narrative can be systematically evoked or drawn out during a data collection process such as fieldwork or an interview. Finally, narrative can be heard in a "naturally occurring conversation" (Chase, 2005, p. 652). Polkinghorne (1995) also notes that this methodology involves "noticing the differences and diversity of people's behavior" (p. 11). Narrative inquiry, then, can be both a phenomenon and a method; and central to narrative inquiry are the beliefs that stories give meaning to people's lives, and those stories are treated as data.

Narrative focuses on the use of specific terms (interaction, continuity, situation) and spaces (temporality, sociality, place) (Clandinin & Connelly, 2000).

As such, narrative research methodologically intends to capture the whole-ness of experiences, working against dissecting identities from interactions in the story.

Counterstory as a Type of Narrative Research

CRT scholars "have built on everyday experiences with perspective, viewpoint, and the power of stories and persuasion to come to a deeper understanding of how Americans see race" (Delgado & Stefancic, 2012, p. 44) and use "narrative and storytelling as a means to challenge the existing social construction of race" (Lynn, Jennings, & Hughes, 2013, p. 607) as a means of addressing uniqueness of voices of color. In CRT, narrative is counter-storytelling. Counterstory is a tool for countering the master narrative, commonly held stories, assumptions, and presuppositions (Romeo & Stewart, 1999). DeCuir and Dixson (2004) explained that counter-storytelling provides voice for underrepresented or marginalized groups to challenge the dominant normative discourse, providing alternative and necessary realities to conversations specifically within the context of education.

Understanding Critical Race Theory and Intersectionality

Legal scholars Derrick Bell, Alan Freeman, and Richard Delgado conceptualized critical race theory as an avenue for engaging in a "race-based, systematic critique of legal reasoning and legal institutions themselves" (Harris, 2001, p. xix), daring to place race as central to the law. Delgado and Stefancic (2012) identify the CRT movement as "a collection of activists and scholars interested in studying and transforming the relationship among race, racism, and power" (p. 2). In building a bridge between the applicability of critical race theory in the law to critical race theory in education, William Tate and Gloria Ladson-Billings met as colleagues at the University of Wisconsin-Madison and spent significant time reading and understanding case law so as to understand the legal cases that were being cited in the evolution of critical race theory. Their work was pivotal in connecting the legal argument to the educational pipeline and offering tools/tenets to critique and challenge educational systems and institutions (Bonilla-Silva, 2003; Ladson-Billings & Tate, 1995; Ladson-Billings, 2009; Solórzano & Yosso, 2000).

CRT in education also calls out White privilege and White supremacy, allowing for protest and challenges in the way school administration, policy and funding are managed (Berry & Stovall, 2013; Stovall 2006). In their foundational work, Ladson-Billings and Tate (1995) assert that race is a significant factor affecting educational justice in the United States and therefore continues to repeat the conditions of inequity in education for many students. CRT was and is a movement that requires action – not just to address and destruct systems of oppression – but also to build up and repair that which has been broken.

The aim of CRT is to question the foundational ideas in traditional legal discourse and – in so doing – critique spaces that need to do the hard work of addressing principles of racism on which much of our country was founded, including our entire educational system.

Important to the critique and praxis centered in CRT is the examination of those who are "multiply burdened" (Wing, 1990), those with intersectional identities. Much of the early work (Crenshaw, 1991, 1989; McCall, 2005) appears in the context of the law and, specifically, addresses issues connected to women of color, focusing on the intersections of race and gender. Later work, specifically in the context of education (Berry, 2018; Berry & Stovall, 2013; Cook, 2017; Evans-Winters & Esposito, 2010), addresses the complexities of intersectionality for women and girls of color.

Intersectionality

Intersectionality studies the convergence of multiplicative identities through a lens of power and oppression (Delgado & Stefancic, 2012). Race, gender, class, and religion are social constructs that have independently bred massive discrimination throughout the world. Each person's lived experience is comprised of multiple layers by which they define themselves (Wing, 2003). Interrelated, they have the potential to create "intersecting" forms of oppression and compound biases under traditional systems of power (Cook, 2017).

First articulated by Kimberlé Crenshaw in 1991, it is defined as "the examination of race, sex, class, national origin, and sexual orientation and how their combinations play out in various settings" (Delgado & Stefancic, 2012, p. 51). As human beings we are multifaceted individuals and possess multiple identities. However, most significant to our understanding of intersectionality is the centrality of the interaction of "multiple inequalities" (MacKinnon, 2013, p. 1019). Intersectionality is not simply about the multiple and intersecting identities individuals may possess. It is, however, the ways in which individuals possess multiple and intersecting identities that have been socially constructed as marginalized in U.S. society. Crenshaw (1991) noted that the work of feminist scholars and anti-racists efforts were significant but proceed as though "they are mutually exclusive terrains" (p. 1242). Women of color are no more women than they are bodies of color. Women particularly, are especially subjected to the multiple ways in which their identities become fractured. Crenshaw (1991) goes on to say,

> . . . a category such as race or gender is socially constructed is not to say that that category has no significance in our world. On the contrary, a large and continuing project for subordinated people – and indeed, one of the projects for which postmodern theories have been very helpful- is thinking about the way power has closeted around certain categories and is exercised against others. This project attempts to unveil the processes

of subordination and the various ways those processes are experienced by
people who are subordinated and people who are privileged by them.

(pp. 1296–1297)

Without the acknowledgement of intersectionality, women of color are forced
to choose from a hierarchy of oppressions despite experiencing both racism and
sexism as interlocking (and sometimes conflicting) oppressions.

Crenshaw's work also reminds us that the privileges that women do/ do not
experience through ability, social class, and educational status also impact the way
that they mediate racialized and gendered experiences. Intersectionality allows for
the acknowledgement of the interplay between human, civil and constitutional
rights from the perspective of a raced and gendered body. As such, Crenshaw
(1991) articulates three forms of intersectionality: (1) structural; (2) political; and
(3) representational. Structural intersectionality addresses "the fact that minority
women suffer from the effects of multiple subordination, coupled with institutional expectations based on inappropriate, nonintersectional contexts, shapes
and ultimately limits the opportunities for meaningful invention on their behalf"
(p. 1251). Within the context of education, an example scenario of this phenomenon is when a Black woman faculty member at a university files an EEOC
complaint against her White female department chair on the grounds of sexism
because the department chair makes decisions and provides opportunities that
benefit White male faculty members, and the EEOC office finds no evidence of
discrimination simply because the department chair is a woman. Political intersectionality "highlights the fact that women of color are situated within at least
two subordinated groups that frequently pursue conflicting political agendas"
(pp. 1251–1252). Imagine if the White male athletic director of an NCAA Division I university referred to his Black female basketball players as "nappy-headed
ho's" and these athletes protested but couldn't gain support from Black male
athletes until he referred to the Black male football players as 'young bucks'. Representational intersectionality addresses "how women of color are represented
in cultural imagery" and "include both the ways in which these images are produced through a confluence of prevalent narratives of race and gender, as well as
a recognition of how contemporary critiques of racist and sexist representation
marginalize women of color" (p. 1282). While Hollywood movie production
companies have released several movies that depict White people, and particularly
White women, who find a way to educate Black youth, there are few movies
that depict Black women teachers and fewer that actually depict us engaged in
teaching. In each of these forms of intersectionality, Whiteness and/or maleness
is privileged.

The uniqueness of voice tenant of CRT speaks to the idea of giving voice
through counter-narrative. Offering a story and retelling a truth – allowing for
space that honors the voice of marginalized people. CRT operationalizes this
counter-narrative three different ways: (1) lifts the voices of people of color so that
race and racism are seen from an alternative lens; (2) pushes against ethnocentrism

and one-world views to construct a new reality; and (3) works against silencing oppressed individuals and provides legitimated space for the 'counter' perspective/narrative to be heard (Solórzano & Yosso, 2002; Delgado & Stefancic, 2000; Tate, 1994). The valuing of stories acknowledges that ". . . those who lack material wealth or political power still have access to thought and language, and their development of those tools . . . differs from that of the most privileged" (Matsuda, 1995, p. 65). This tenet of CRT speaks directly to understanding context in the social condition as well as addressing issues of power and privilege that can then be used to highlight disparities in a policy or program and push back against the so-called "neutrality" of race.

These scholars have provided much to consider, to think about, regarding intersectionality. MacKinnon (2013) discusses intersectionality as method, focusing less on what we think and more on the way we think about intersectionality. In positioning intersectionality as method, derailing of traditional and conventional ways of addressing race and gender issues which have, historically, focused on one attribute is necessary. "The conventional framework fails to recognize the dynamics of status and the power hierarchies that create them, reifying sex and race not only along a single axis but also as compartments that ignore the social forces of power that rank and define them relationally within and without" (MacKinnon, 2013, p. 1023). Intersectionality as method demands a praxis that gives voice to the nexus of racialized and gendered experiences.

The Significance of Counter-Storytelling: Intersectional Identities

Critical race scholars understand that the stories of the dominant society oftentimes fail to speak to the lived experiences of people of color. People of color adapt to the master narrative, the commonly held beliefs and presuppositions of the lived experience (Romeo & Stewart, 1999), while engaging in a counterstory deeply connected to multiple and intersecting identities subjugated to oppression such as race, class, and gender. In this way, people of color embody the Du Boisian notion of double-consciousness, experiencing both the master narrative and counterstory, simultaneously. Master narratives have little to no regard for the voices of people of color; counterstories center the experiences and knowledge of people of color as truth.

Women of color possess a double-bind narrative; we must be able to understand and operate the general master narrative as well as the master narrative of White women while living the counterstory of Black/Latino people and, specifically, Black/Latina women. Counter-storytelling from this perspective highlights the nuances of the lived experiences that are designed to debunk myths and challenge misconceptions of oppressed peoples. Counter-storytelling for intersectional identities is a cure for the silencing and/or marginalization for women of color as it challenges essentialization as women and moves to thwart the normalness and ordinariness of racism.

Master Narrative, Counterstory, Intersectionality, and the Narrative Researcher

Particular traditions have been upheld in narrative research.

Table 8.1 depicts the process by which narrative research is, traditionally, conducted. This master narrative proclaims the experience is represented as "talk, text, interaction, and interpretation" (Riessman, 1993, p. 8). As part of this tradition, narrative research yields to Clandinin and Connelly's (2000) terms and spaces. Finally, the process of (1) attending, (2) telling, (3) transcribing, (4) analyzing, and (5) reading is embedded in the canon of narrative research (Riessman, 1993).

As a critical race scholar, it is imperative to engage in this work from the space of identity central to the experiences expressed, focusing on the notion of intersectionality as method. Valuing experiences as knowledge is significant to narrative research positioned for intersectionality. As a critical race scholar engaging with intersectionality, narrative exists at the crossroads of these experiences. An intersectional praxis of narrative research considers the whole-ness of narrative, as both phenomenon and inquiry, positioned with the lived experiences.

Narrative, as both phenomenon and inquiry, must participate in the wholeness of the lived experience. The lived experience does not operate in isolation but rather as intersectional praxis. Table 8.2 depicts the relationship between narrative research as phenomenon (Clandinin and Connelly's use of space, specifically sociality) with intersectionality. Table 8.3 depicts the relationship between narrative research as inquiry (process) and intersectionality.

TABLE 8.1 Traditions of Narrative Research

Representation of Experiences	Terms and Spaces	Process
Talk, Text, Interaction, Interpretation	Terms: personal and social (interaction); past, present and future (continuity); place (situation)	Attending Telling Transcribing Analyzing
	Space: temporality, sociality, place	Reading

TABLE 8.2 Narrative (Phenomenon) and Intersectionality

Multiple Inequalities/Intersecting Forms of Oppression	Terms: personal and social (interaction) Space: sociality
Avoiding Hierarchies of Oppression	Terms: past, present, and future (continuity) Space: temporality
Experiencing At Least One Form of Intersectionality	Terms: place (situation) Space: place
Centering Voice(s) of Multiply Burdened	Terms: personal and social (interaction) Space:
Using Counter-Storytelling for Alternative Realities	Terms: past, present, and future (continuity); place (situation) Space: temporality

TABLE 8.3 Narrative (Process) and Intersectionality

Multiple Inequalities/Intersecting Forms of Oppression	Process: Attending, Telling, Transcribing, Analyzing, Reading
Avoiding Hierarchies of Oppression	Process: Telling, Analyzing, Reading
Experiencing At Least One Form of Intersectionality	Process: Attending, Telling, Analyzing
Centering Voice(s) of Multiply Burdened	Process: Attending, Telling, Transcribing
Using Counter-Storytelling for Alternative Realities	Process: Telling, Analyzing, Reading

Narrative research for intersectionality (1) focuses on multiple inequalities embedded in identities and intersecting forms of oppression, (2) avoids hierarchies of oppression, (3) articulates experiences of at least one of the three forms of intersectionality, (4) centers the voice(s) of the multiply burdened, and (5) uses counter-storytelling to provide alternative realities to debunk the master narrative(s). In doing so, authenticity of the participants' voice must be present in the work. In the representation of experience, intersectionality repositions talking to listening, valuing the centrality of the voice of the participants. Representation of text should strive to be reflective of the multi-dimensionality of voice; researchers should not limit themselves to word text but engage in the use of audio and/or photo text.

When engaging in narrative research for interaction and interpretation centering intersectionality, three things must be considered when investigating what we want to know: multiple and intersecting identities of the researcher; the multiple and intersecting identities of the individual(s) whose stories of experiences are told; the ways in which the identities of the researcher intersect with the identities of the storied individual(s). Centering intersectionality recognizes and acknowledges identities subjugated to any and all forms of oppression.

What We Know Now: Discussion and Conclusion

Centering intersectionality in narrative research provided three important lessons: (1) intersectionality within narrative research must be both phenomenon and inquiry; (2) intersectionality within narrative research must involve an inquiry of multiplicative praxis; and (3) intersectionality within narrative research must address the presence of multiple consciousness.

As stated earlier, narrative research is both phenomenon and inquiry. But, to understand the phenomenon, we must engage in inquiry. What we want to know is, in part, predicated on what we already know, our experiences. In order to systematically seek after the responses to our inquiry, we must follow a process that honors and centers voice. Intersectionality honors CRT's notion of uniqueness of voice of color. In fact, it centers the presence of this tenet by the very nature and naming of this tenet. This tenet clearly positions race and ____ as equally and significantly important. Narrative research with intersectionality positions the phenomenon (race and ____) and the inquiry (unique voice of color) as equally and significantly important. For us, it means that the way in which we engage with narrative research includes both our identities and the questions we pose within the context of our identities.

As such, intersectionality within narrative research is an inquiry of multiplicative praxis. Wing's (1990) notion of a multiplicative praxis informs us of the importance of our whole selves informing how we think about our work (reflection) as well as how we engage in our work (action) in the context of our intersecting identities. A multiplicative praxis connects the knowledge we gain from all of our experiences (based on our identities) to the spaces and places, the context of these experiences. It is these connections that inform our understandings of the lived experience as story and/or counterstory.

Intersectionality within narrative research involves recognizing and acknowledging the presence of multiple consciousness. Multiple consciousness is present in those whose lived experiences exist at the intersections, particularly race and ____; for the authors, this is specifically, true for race and gender. As such the stories of our lived experience, researching through narrative as both phenomenon and inquiry, centers the unique voice of color, and values intersectionality.

References

Austin, R. (1992). Black women, sisterhood, and the difference/deviance divide. *New England Law Review, 26*(3), 877.

Berry, T. R. (2018). *States of grace: Counterstories of a Black woman in the academy.* New York: Peter Lang.

Berry, T. R. & Stovall, D. O. (2013). Trayvon Martin and the curriculum of tragedy: Critical race lessons for education. *Race Ethnicity and Education, 16*(4), 587–602.

Bonilla-Silva, E. (2010). *Racism without racists: Color-blind racism and the persistence of racial inequality in the United States* (3rd ed.). Lanham: Rowman & Littlefield Publishers.

Chang, R. S (1993). Toward an Asian American legal scholarship: Critical race theory, post-structuralism, and narrative space. *California Law Review,* 81 (5), 1241–1323.

Chase, S. E. (2005). Narrative inquiry: Multiple lenses, approaches, voices. In N. K. Denzin & Y. S. Lincoln (Eds.), *The Sage Handbook of Qualitative Research* (3rd ed.). Thousand Oaks, CA: Sage.

Clandinin, D. J. & Connelly, F. M. (2000). *Narrative inquiry: Experience and story in qualitative research.* San Francisco, CA: Jossey-Bass.

Connelly, F. M. & Clandinin, D. J. (1990). Stories of experience and narrative inquiry. *Educational Researcher, 19*(5), 2–14.

Cook, E. B. (2017). *Black face – Brown space: Narratives of Black graduate women attending Hispanic-serving institutions.* Proquest Dissertation Publishing.

Crenshaw, K. W. (1989). Demarginalizing the intersection of race and sex: A Black feminist critique of antidiscrimination doctrine, feminist theory and antiracist politics. *The University of Chicago Legal Forum, 1*(8), 139–167.

Crenshaw, K. W. (1991). Mapping the margins: Intersectionality, identity politics, and violence against women of color. *Stanford Law Review, 43*(6), 1241–1299.

Creswell, J. W. (2013). *Qualitative inquiry and research design: Choosing among the five approaches.* Los Angeles: Sage.

Czarniawska, B. (2004). *Narratives in social science research.* London: Sage.

DeCuir, J. T. & Dixson, A. D. (2004). So when it comes out, they aren't surprised that it is there: Using critical race theory as a tool of analysis of race and racism in education. *Educational Researcher, 33*(5), 26–31.

Delgado, R. & Stefancic, J. (2012) *Critical race theory: An introduction* (2nd ed.). New York: New York University Press.

Delgado, R. & Stefancic, J. (Eds.) (2000). *Critical race theory: The cutting edge.* Chicago, IL: Temple University Press.

Duncan, G. A. (2005). Critical race ethnography in education: Narrative, inequality, and the problem of epistemology. *Race Ethnicity and Education, 8*(1), 93–114.

Evans-Winters, V. E. & Esposito, J. (2010). Other people's daughters: Critical race feminism and Black girls' education. *Journal of Education Foundations, 24*(1/2), 11–24.

Foster, M. (1998). *Black teachers on teaching.* New York: The New Press.

Harris, A. P. (2001). Forward. In R. Delgado & J. Stefancic, *Critical race theory: An introduction* (pp. xvii-xxi). New York: New York University Press.

Ladson-Billings, G. (2009). "Who you callin' nappy-headed?" A critical race theory look at the construction of Black women. *Race Ethnicity and Education, 12*(1), 87–99.

Ladson-Billings, G. & Tate, W. F. IV (1995). Toward a critical race theory of education. *Teachers College Record, 97*(1), 47–68.

Lynn, M., Jennings, M. E., & Hughes, S. (2013). Critical race pedagogy 2.0: Lessons from Derrick Bell. *Race Ethnicity and Education,* 16(4), 603–628.

MacKinnon, C. A. (2013). Intersectionality as method: A note. *Signs, 38*(4), 1019–1030.

Matsuda, M. (1995). Critical race theory and critical legal studies: Contestation and coalition. In K. W. Crenshaw, N. Gotanda, G. Peller, & K. Thomas (Eds.), *Critical race theory: The key writings that formed the movement* (pp. 63–79). New York: The New Press.

McCall, L. (2005). The complexities of intersectionality. *Signs, 30*(3), 1772–1799.

Parker, L. (1998). Race is, race ain't: An exploration of the utility of critical race theory in qualitative research. *International Journal of Qualitative Studies in Education, 11*(1), 43–55.

Parker. L., & Lynn, M. (2002). What's race got to do with it? Critical race theory's conflicts with and connections to qualitative research methodology and epistemology. *Qualitative Inquiry, 8*(1), 7–22.

Polkinghorne, D. E. (1995). Narrative configuration in qualitative analysis. *International Journal of Qualitative Studies in Education, 8*(1), 5–23.

Riessman, C. (1993). *Narrative analysis,* 1st ed. Series: Qualitative research methods, 30. Newbury Park, CA: Sage.

Romeo, M. & Stewart, A. J. (Eds.) (1999). *Women's untold stories: Breaking silence, talking back, voicing complexity.* New York: Routledge.

Schubert, W. H. & Ayers, W. C. (1999 [1992]). *Teacher Lore: Learning from our own experience.* Educators International Press.

Solórzano, D. G. (1998). Critical race theory, race and gender microaggressions, and the experience of Chicana and Chicano scholars. *International Journal of Qualitative Studies in Education, 11*(1), 121–136.

Solórzano, D. G. & Yosso, T. J. (2002). Critical race methodology: Counter-storytelling as an analytical framework for education research. *Qualitative Inquiry, 8*(1), 23–44.

Solórzano, D. G. & Yosso, T. J. (2001). Critical race and LatCrit theory and method: Counter-storytelling. *International Journal of Qualitative Studies in Education, 14*(4), 471–495.

Stovall, D. (2006). Forging community in race and class: Critical race theory and the quest for social justice in education. *Race Ethnicity and Education, 9*(3), 243–259.

Tate, W.F. (1994). From inner city to ivory tower: Does my voice matter in the academy? *Urban Education, 29*(3), 244–469.

Williams, P. (1987). Spirit-murdering the messenger: The discourse of finger pointing as the law's response to racism. *Miami Law Review, 42*(1), 127–157.

Wing, A. K. (2003). *Critical race feminism: A reader* (2nd ed.) Foreword, Richard Delgado (1st ed. Foreword, Derrick Bell). New York: New York University Press.

Wing, A. K. (1990). Brief reflections on a multiplicative theory and praxis of being. *Berkeley Journal of Gender, Law, and Justice, 6*(1), 181–201.

9

NOT ONE, BUT MANY

A CRT Research Team Approach to Investigate Student Experiences in Racially Diverse Settings

Thandeka K. Chapman, Nicholas D. Hartlep, May Vang, Talonda Lipsey-Brown, and Tatiana Joseph

Critical Race Theory (CRT) is not an overlay of traditional paradigms of research by researchers of color in which one simply "bends the rules" by questioning established understandings of epistemology, such as the roles of objectivity and "truth." Critical Race Theory offers researchers of color the opportunity to challenge the origin of the "rules" of scientific research and seek new forms of research that speak to the experiences, relationships, and perspectives of oppressed communities (Solórzano & Yosso, 2002). As researchers of color engage in CRT methodologies, the conversations concerning representation, relationships, and scholarly recognition become more intense and complicated (DeCuir & Dixson, 2004). Unfortunately, higher education provides minimal intellectual space to fully examine what it means for researchers of color to document the lives of their brothers and sisters who are often living truly painful realities (Delgado Bernal & Villalpando, 2002). To provide greater avenues for muted voices to be amplified, the intellectual space must be expanded so that the power and complexities of a CRT methodology, as a tool to prevent static, deficit representations of cultures, communities, and people, will be cultivated in education research (Fernández, 2002; Solórzano & Yosso, 2002).

Using critical race theory, we conceptualize what it means for researchers of color to conduct research with a racially diverse body of students in learning spaces where these students are academically and socially marginalized. This chapter contributes to the CRT in education literature by describing how researchers serve as methodological instruments in their work in the field and how researchers from different racial and educational backgrounds work as a team to excavate the complexities of race and racism in racially diverse learning spaces. The merits of conducting race-based research as a multi-racial team of scholars, who validate and challenge each other's assumptions and perceptions, should be embraced and not ignored by the research community; because when we fail to explore the ways we are able to more fully contextualize issues of race and racism we become guilty of "epistemological racism," in which our understandings ". . . logically reflect and reinforce that social history and that racial group (while excluding the epistemologies of other races/cultures)" (Scheurich & Young, 1997, p. 8).

Critical Race Research

An often forgotten or purposefully omitted tenet of critical race theory is the call for researchers of color to research their own racially marginalized communities. Race-based methodologies that are employed by researchers of color hold special importance for Critical Race Theory in the Academy as an instrument to break through traditional tropes of research and research methodologies (Chapman, 2007; DeCuir & Dixson, 2004; Delgado Bernal & Villalpando, 2002). Pillow states,

> Race-based methodology thus shifts the locus of power in the research process by situating subjects as knowers. Race-based methodology work describes and provides a way for the "raced" academic to think about our unique roles as researchers and theorists.
>
> *(2003, p. 187)*

Critical race scholars believe that their unique position(s) as racialized subjects gives them distinctive ways to view events, participants' perceptions, and group conversations. Moreover, as researchers who share common sets of racialized experiences, community ties, and concerns for the future of children of color with the research participants, we are indelibly linked to our work (Parker & Lynn, 2002). Ladson-Billings states,

> CRT asks the critical qualitative research to operate in a self-revelatory mode, to acknowledge the double (or multiple) consciousness in which he or she is operating. My decision to deploy a critical race theoretical framework in my scholarship is intimately linked to my understanding of the political and personal stake I have in the education of Black children.
>
> *(2000, p. 273)*

In CRT, these epistemological connections to one's community affiliations are valued and cultivated, not hidden or demonized. Yet, we also acknowledge the problematic nature of having a single researcher of color, whose intimate knowledge of race and racism is positioned around their primary racial identity, conducting research in a racially diverse setting. Thus, a racially diverse team approach becomes one avenue for capturing the multiple "truths" shared by the participants.

Details of the Study

The study was commissioned by a community organization, which consists of parents from suburban districts, university faculty from multiple universities that serve the surrounding metropolitan area, and high-ranking school district officials. This organization was created to address the achievement gap between students of color and White students in suburban districts. The goal of the study was to better understand the schooling experiences of students of color in predominately White high schools with hopes of changing various aspects of the school curriculum to increase students' engagement and academic achievement.

The study took place in five high schools in four suburban districts that share borders with a Midwest metropolitan area. In order to substantiate the findings through the voices of students of color, the data collection consisted of twenty-two focus group interviews of four and five students, with ninety students of color (Delgado, 2000; Delgado Bernal, 2002; Fernández, 2002). Students from racially and ethnically underrepresented groups were solicited for interviews that took place during the regular school day. The racial breakdown of the students included sixty-six African American, six Latino, six Asian American, six White/ Black bi-racial, one bi-racial Asian American/ Black, one Asian American/ White bi-racial, one Indian American, one Black/ Native American bi-racial, and one multi-racial student. In part, the disproportionate number of African American students reflects the racial percentages within the larger metropolitan district and the schools that participate in the open enrollment and inter-district desegregation busing programs. Although the research team did not have representation from all racial groups identified among the participants, nor could we match the intersectional and intergenerational differences between the team and the participants, having a racially, culturally, and linguistically diverse research team remained a significant strength during the research process.

The Research Team

The research team consisted of two African American women, one Latina, one Korean man, and one Hmong woman. Four of the five research team members are bilingual: two speak Spanish and English, one speaks Hmong and English, and one member purposefully code-switches between academic English and African American Vernacular English. Additionally, all of the researchers have past lives as teachers in K-12 schools and, at the time of the study, lived in the same neighborhoods as the student participants who participated in the inter-district enrollment programs. Each of the researchers shared similar K-12 education experiences as former students with our youth participants. The similarity of experiences shows the intransient nature of racism in institutions of higher learning. Through the following vignettes, the researchers discuss how their ontological and epistemological perspectives shaped their experiences in the field.

Thandeka, African American Female. Conducting this research was bitter-sweet because I was excited to raise the voices of the young people matriculating through these difficult spaces, but I dreaded the memories these interviews brought back from my own childhood. I was raised in an all-White community where my family and four other Black families integrated the school system. Now I hear the same pain, for the same reasons, in the voices of a new generation. My heart breaks for the children who continue to struggle under this meta-narrative of racially oppressive school contexts.

While conducting the interviews, I shared my story and the scholarship from researchers who have documented the experiences of students of color in pre-dominantly White schools to help the student participants situate their experiences as lingering forms of racism that resulted from *Brown v. Board I and II.* Students responded to the personal experiences and professional knowledge I inserted during the interviews with both anger and resolution: anger as to why the same injustices continued over time and resolve to "get through it" so they could have the lives they wanted for themselves and the lives the parents dreamed for them.

May, Hmong American Female. Although we lived in the heart of an urban metropolitan area, my parents understood the educational benefits of sending me to the wealthy suburban White schools through the inter-district busing program. As a result of my White-washed education, I struggled to become as "American," as possible. I became skilled at deciphering the nuances which would "give me away" as anything but "American," (i.e., language, appearance, food, and family). Yet, the constant awareness that my race meant that I could never be considered a "true" American served as a catalyst to push against the boundaries American schooling had set for me. Because K-12 learning spaces encouraged me to negate my Hmong identity and pursue an unobtainable American identity, I became an education researcher to challenge the racist institutional paradigms that continue to push Hmong youth and Hmong communities to disaffirm our culture, our beauty, and our strength. During the interviews I used my home language to help a few of the Hmong participants explain their experiences or feelings with English words or re-state their thoughts in Hmong when they struggled with English. During the analysis, I situated their voices within a cultural context to capture the gravity of their experiences as members of a refugee community with a particular relationship to the United States.

Nicholas, Korean American Male. As a Korean American kid, adopted by White parents, and raised in the Midwest, I never truly felt connected to the schools that I attended, nor the communities in which they were located. In addition to being a victim of racial bullying, it was challenging to attend public schools because I had no teachers that looked like me. This should not be surprising: Teranishi indicates that only "1.5% of America's K-12 teachers" are Asian American (2010, p. 131). I became an elementary teacher, and later an education researcher, as part of my passion to change the deficit positioning of Asian Americans and challenge

the model-minority stereotype. As an AsianCRT researcher, linking my education experiences and scholarship with the participants' experiences helped all the
students to share their painful experiences with racism, and provided the Asian
American students with a way to connect their "I'm no one's model minority,"
counter-stories to something larger and more systemic than themselves as individuals who would not comply with stereotypes of docile, dispassionate Asian
American youth.

Talonda, African American Female. My personal experiences as an African
American female who matriculated through under-resourced urban schools,
and my professional experiences as a teacher in schools with the same racial
and demographic profiles as the schools I attended, became guide posts for me
throughout the data collection and analysis processes. As a former student and
teacher in a larger urban district, I've witnessed the lack of resources, large class
sizes, high rates of teacher attrition, limited school funding, poor teacher quality, and low teacher expectations. I understand how the problems that plague
urban districts create a seemingly "forced choice" for parents of color to choose
predominantly White learning spaces for their children, even when they know
the emotional, cultural, and psychological injuries these schools pose for their
children. During the research process, I had several focus groups of just Black
girls. Staying focused was challenging, because the girls wanted to know more
about me, my background, and how I became a researcher. These interviews
often spilled beyond the forty-five minutes and into their lunch hours so that
the girls and I could both ask our questions. These interviews, filled with tears,
anger, and laughter for all of us, were the most rewarding and the most difficult. Through the interviews with the Black girls and the other mixed-race
and gender focus group interviews, it was apparent that parental perceptions of
academic rigor and greater access to educational opportunities were accurate;
however, the significant damage done to the students' self-esteem and identities was also crystal clear. Throughout analysis, I interrogated how to weigh the
negative consequences of majority-White suburban schools against strong academic outcomes and future financial gains; and I asked, "A better education—at
what cost?"

Tatiana, Latina. Born in San Jose, Costa Rica, I migrated to the United States
at the age of ten. For high school my parents moved me from an educational
environment that felt safe and protected to an elite White parochial school
with classmates who showed distain for my heritage and language. By changing my clothes and losing my accent, I tried to assimilate into a White, middle/
upper class environment for survival. Assimilation came at a price—the negation
of my racial and cultural identities and language (Lau, Yeh, Wood, McCabe,
Garland & Hough, 2005). Similar to the student participants, I lived through
the pain of attempted assimilation and the backlash of rejecting the dominant
culture as the sole mechanism for success. As a LatCrit researcher focused on
issues of institutional ethnic, cultural, and linguistic marginalization (Delgado

Bernal & Villalpando, 2002), I conveyed to all the students that they should demand more from their schools than college-bound curricula and activities constructed around whiteness and White privilege. I stood as an example of a Latina who embraces and does not view culture and language as barriers to success for Latinx students.

Research as a Multi-Racial Team

This study is distinctive because the researchers utilized their experiential positioning and incorporated theoretical constructs from CRT, LatCrit, and Asian-Crit to formulate a cohesive, racially diverse research team. In a cohesive research team, the members work on all aspects of the research together and the analysis does not rest on the sole understandings of one researcher. Researchers are able to challenge one another's behaviors and understandings of the work they are conducting together, and push team members to engage in deeper self-reflection around their roles in the research process (Russell & Kelly, 2002). As a multi-racial team, "we believe that by consciously locating our individual contexts, egos, biases, and agendas in the study, we enhanced the quality and integrity of the research project" (Stanley & Slattery, 2003, p. 724).

The professional capabilities of the researchers and what each team member offered to the process as individuals with different cultural backgrounds, schooling experiences, and epistemologies brought significant strengths to the data analysis. Concerns for trustworthiness were addressed through the use of a team process in which all five members of the research used identical instruments for data collection, conducted identical steps to analyze the data, and met as a group to engage in a collective analysis process. In the data analysis stage, all the researchers independently arrived at similar thematic units, which suggested clear uniformity among the emerging themes. The initial thematic uniformity, coupled with our constant conversations regarding the ways our epistemologies and ontologies functioned within our individual and collective understandings of the data, strengthened the research findings by incorporating a more nuanced understanding of the students' perceptions of and reactions to racism on their campuses. During the data analysis we had to make decisions about what data would receive a robust analysis and what data would be left for exploration at a future time period. Our analysis revealed strong themes that were supported by significant data from across the five schools in the study. We also noted the data from compelling issues we could not explore because of the limited number of students who engaged in particular conversations. For example, during one focus group with five African American girls, the young ladies complained about being exoticized and desired, but not considered for committed relationships by young men across racial groups. While this particular conversation resonated with a few other mentions of the privileged status of White girls in integrated spaces in interviews at other schools, we did not have enough substantive data, nor did we have previous research literature focused on the intersections of race and gender in adolescent romantic relationships, to explore this as a significant theme. Yet, we believe it is an under-theorized, under-researched, and important aspect of African American women's experiences in integrated high schools that deserves attention in education research. To resolve our conflicts over data representation, we presented the larger themes of institutional, structural, and social barriers to teachers, community members, and district officials because these themes had concrete resolutions directly related to student connectedness and academic achievement; meanwhile we continue to explore clusters of smaller, yet meaningful data in academic venues and professional papers.

Discussion

As researchers of color, we demarcate our ability to conduct research about students of color as a privileged position. We recognize that distinctive interactions occur, and particular types of information are disclosed when researchers document their own lived racial spaces (Delgado Bernal & Villalpando, 2002; Villenas, 1996). "There can be no complete or definitive solution to the problem of speaking for others, but there is a possibility that its dangers can be decreased" (Alcoff, 1995, p. 111). Given our privileged positions as university researchers, we also acknowledge and remain vigilant about the ways in which privilege and positionality work within and among groups to maintain hierarchies of power and instantiate the status quo. Although Alcoff (1995) is not a critical race theorist, her chapter, "The Problem with Speaking for Others," offers four practices that we as critical race researchers applied while conducting the research. These practices are useful for critical race researchers who conduct research that enmeshes their epistemological and ontological perspectives within the research process. In this section of the chapter we share incidents from the research process in which the researchers employed and inhibited their ontological and epistemological selves to facilitate the research process.

Alcoff reminds us that "anyone who speaks for others should only do so out of a concrete analysis of the particular power relations and discursive effects involved" (1995, p. 111). As university researchers, we guided the participants through the protocols, made meaning of their words, and held significant power over the presentation of their voices. While we did not lead students to give particular answers or alter the students' words, we used their words to support our analysis, which excluded or minimized information that various audiences may deem significant. As critical race theorists we understand that the story other researchers may view as an important 'truth' is often not the story we seek to examine (Solórzano & Yosso, 2002); thus, when the student voice data is compelling and triangulated with other forms of data, we use their words to highlight counter-stories that explicate how power relations and social and academic discourses affect educational outcomes for students of color.

Critical race theorists understand that issues of power and privilege are present at all times during the research process. During the data collection process, the power and control over participant voice means that, as Alcoff states, the "impetus to speak" must be controlled. As educated adults, in fact teachers, we resisted our desire to always be the speaker and provide the "teachable moment." Our resistance to "mastery and domination" through researcher over-participation is apparent throughout the interviews. As researchers with particular sets of similar schooling experiences, formal education, and adult life experiences, we stayed vigilant about the moments in which we inserted ourselves into the interviews with our adolescent participants. The closeness of the topic compelled us to want to engage in the discussion in various ways. During the interviews, Thandeka extended her wait-time to allow the students to reach their own conclusions about their experiences with race and racism, while Talonda tempered her desire to speak at length about her own experiences as a student. Tatiana and May found themselves masking their disappointment and holding their tongues when Latinx and Hmong students' responses demonstrated a lack of critical solidarity with other racial groups; similarly, Nicholas resisted dominating moments of critical conversation among the few Korean American student participants.

Secondly, we must understand the *"bearing of our location and context* on what we are saying" (Alcoff, 1995, p. 111). Alcoff suggests that researchers often state their positionality as a means to solicit forgiveness for mis-handling and misappropriating the words of their participants. Rather than stating our positionalities to present our weaknesses, we shared our personal experiences with the participants to help them understand the historical and structural nature of their experiences as students of color in a racist system. For example, because May was a former inter-district busing student, the students were eager to compare their current experiences with her previous experiences. However, the symbiotic relationship between May and the students meant that the students used more nicknames and acronyms to describe the school resources and practices; thus May took on the task of defining and positioning these terms during the analysis. Additionally, during the interviews we constantly solicited clarity from the students by asking follow-up questions, pushing for the students to give examples of what their statements meant, and re-stating their words back to them in Hmong, Spanish, African American Vernacular English, and/or academic prose. We wanted to fully understand the meanings of their words in order to properly represent their experiences and perceptions.

Thirdly, as critical race theorists, our ultimate "accountability and responsibility" is to the schools and students where we conducted our research. Our understandings of race and racism have developed and shifted as we have grown older—we are no longer teenagers, and we do not think like the teenagers in the study. Moreover, race and racism are not static constructions; because of the generational gaps between the researchers and those being researched, the racialized experiences of these young people were similar, yet different from our experiences in schools. Critical race theory recognizes the fluidity of social constructions and denies acontextual accounts of racism (DeCuir & Dixson, 2004; Chapman, 2007; Solórzano & Yosso, 2002). Therefore, we were responsible for representing participants' truths, as they see them, not as we believe them to be represented.

Our attempts to let the students' truths be heard were demonstrated by each of the researchers' concerns for capturing the words of the participants without judgment, even when we could not document a more critical understanding of race and racism from some of the student participants. For example, in the interviews there were instances where a minority number of participants rejected the presence of race or racism in their schools and articulated classist, meritocratic language about working hard, getting good grades, and not "acting ghetto" as a mode of behavior to avoid negative stereotypes and cultivate positive relationships with school adults. When asked about issues of racial bias, two young ladies who did not believe there was overt racism in their schools explained,

> That doesn't happen to me very much because I do kind of mingle. There is nothing I don't really like about the school. Sometimes you can tell people get nervous around you, but you kind of let it go.
>
> Not really. In elementary school there were some experiences. We used to talk about how you as an individual can use your personality and character to kind of over-compensate.

Rather than diminish the perceptions of these few students, given our disagreement with the way they rationalized the treatment of students of color from lower track classes and students who were viewed as discipline problems, we juxtaposed these instances of meritocratic language with other students' explicit articulations of race and racism concerning the treatment they received from teachers, school adults, and White students in their schools. For example, a young lady who acknowledged racism in her school explained:

> It kind of seems like they [teachers] assume I am wrong right away. And they will have to double check [my work] or even if they get it wrong they will act like I must have gotten lucky. I really have to watch what I say, what I do, how I act.

The two different perspectives demonstrated the diversity of experiences and perceptions within racial groups. Yet, the two groups of students were actually relating similar experiences, with the smaller group providing justifications for inequitable treatment and the larger number of students perceiving their experiences as examples of racist practices. The decision to incorporate both sets of perceptions, rather than solely articulating the dominant majority voice generated a more complex analysis of the data.

Additionally, the team closely examined the racial, gender, and economic demographics represented in the thematic categories, and the significance of the themes within and across the five school sites. To strengthen the trustworthiness of the research we consistently returned to the research literature to identify and interrogate the parallels and discontinuities between previous scholarship and the analysis of the data; additionally, we triangulated the interview data with material documents from the five schools, district documents, and informal observations of the physical school sites.

Lastly, as critical race theorists who align ourselves with the mission of racial justice, we needed to "analyze the probable or actual effects of the words on the discourse and material context" (Alcoff, 1995, p. 113). Because of the political nature of the project, we were extremely careful about protecting their anonymity so that the students would not feel "backlash" for truth-telling. Many of the students were "token" African American students in their AP (Advanced Placement) and honors courses; therefore, we could only represent parts of the data in aggregated form and infrequently school by school.

Even though we only shared details of the sample in particular ways, we were able to work with the schools and districts to create better learning environments for children of color. Tyson states that research operating within a transformative framework would require that the process of gathering data "would become a conscious political, economic, and personal conduit for empowerment" (2003, p. 24). To uphold the goal of racial justice and empowerment, we presented our findings in each of the five districts and to a meeting of superintendents and stakeholders. Several schools invited the team to design programs to build stronger relationships between teachers and students or create proposals advocating for resources targeting different racial groups in the schools.

Conclusion

Scholars have called for a deeper interrogation of race-based research to gain a better understanding of how intersections of race, class, gender and other positionalities impact the research process (Duncan, 2005; Villenas, 1996). Critical race theory privileges the stories of people of color in order to counter deficit discourses and partial story-tellings of their experiences (Delgado Bernal & Villalpando, 2002). After conducting this research, we are ever more keenly aware of the risks of privileging the epistemologies of people of color in the research process when issues of researcher power, position, and situation have gone underexamined (Villenas, 1996; Ramji, 2009). Heeding this warning, we express solidarity with Dillard's assertion that her African-centered self, "necessitates a different relationship between me, as the researcher, and the researched, between my knowing and the production of knowledge" (2000, p. 663). By individually employing our epistemologies and ontologies and collectively challenging our assumptions and biases as a multi-racial research team during the research process, we gleaned important information and constructed new knowledge concerning the lived experiences of students of color in predominantly White schools.

Critical race theorists are committed to disrupting "the allochronic discourses that give enduring forms of oppression and inequality their appearance of normalcy and naturalness" (Duncan 2005, p. 101). As we pursue our goals to challenge stock stories of young people of color, we are ever mindful of how our positions as researchers, community members, and individuals shape our research. Through our reflections as a multi-racial research team, we hope to further complicate and contextualize race-based team research and facilitate inroads for racial justice in education.

References

Alcoff, L. (1995). The problem of speaking for others. In J. Roof & R. Wiegman (Eds.), *Who can speak? Authority and critical identity* (pp. 97–119). Urbana: University of Illinois.

Chapman, T. K. (2007). Interrogating classroom relationships and events: Using portraiture and critical race theory in education research. *Educational Researcher, 36*(3), 156–162.

DeCuir, J. T., & Dixson, A. D. (2004). "So when it comes out, they aren't that surprised that it is there": Using critical race theory as a tool of analysis of race and racism in education. *Educational Researcher, 33*(5), 26–31.

Delgado, R. (2000). Storytelling for oppositionists and others: A plea for narrative. In R. Delgado & J. Stefancic (Eds.), *Critical race theory: The cutting edge* (2nd ed.) (pp. 60–70). Philadelphia, PA: Temple University Press.

Delgado Bernal, D. (2002). Critical race theory, Latino critical theory, and critical raced-gendered epistemologies: Recognizing students of color as holders and creators of knowledge. *Qualitative Inquiry, 8*(1), 105–126.

Delgado Bernal, D., & Villalpando, O. (2002). An apartheid of knowledge in academia: The struggle over the "legitimate" knowledge of faculty of color. *Equity & Excellence in Education, 35*(2), 169–180.

Dillard, C. B. (2000). The substance of things hoped for, the evidence of things not seen: Examining an endarkened feminist epistemology in educational research and leadership. *International Journal of Qualitative Studies in Education (QSE), 13*(6), 661–681.

Dixson, A. D., & Rousseau, C. K. (2005). And we are still not saved: Critical race theory in education ten years later. *Race Ethnicity and Education, 8*(1), 7–27.

Duncan, G. A. (2005). Critical race ethnography in education: Narrative, inequality and the problem of epistemology. *Race Ethnicity and Education, 8*(1), 93–114.

Fernández, L. (2002). Telling stories about school: Using critical race and Latino critical theories to document Latina/Latino education and resistance. *Qualitative Inquiry, 8*(1), 45–65.

Ladson-Billings, G. (2000). Racialized discourses and ethnic epistemologies. In N. K. Denzin & Y. S. Lincolns (Eds.), *The Sage handbook of qualitative research*, 2nd ed. (pp. 257–278). Thousand Oaks, CA: Sage Publications.

Lau, A. S., McCabe, K. M., Yeh, M., Garland, A. F., Wood, P. A., & Hough, R. L. (2005). The acculturation gap-distress hypothesis among high-risk Mexican American families. *Journal of Family Psychology, 19*(3), 367.

Lynn, M., & Parker, L. (2006). Critical race studies in education: Examining a decade of research on US schools. *The Urban Review, 38*(4), 257–290.

Parker, L., & Lynn, M. (2002). What's race got to do with it? Critical race theory's conflicts with and connections to qualitative research methodology and epistemology. *Qualitative Inquiry, 8*(1), 7–22.

Pillow, W. (2003). Race-based methodologies: Multicultural methods or epistemological shifts? In L. Parker and G. Lopez (Eds.), *Interrogating racism in qualitative research* (pp. 181–202). Peter Lang: New York.

Ramji, H. (2009). *Researching race: Theory, methods, and analysis.* New York: Open University Press.

Russell, G. M., & Kelly, N. H. (2002, September). Research as interacting dialogic processes: Implications for reflexivity. In *Forum Qualitative Sozialforschung/Forum: Qualitative Social Research, 3*(3), 1–18.

Scheurich, J., & Young, M. D. (1997). Coloring epistemologies: Are our epistemologies racially based? *Educational Researcher, 26*(4), 4–16.

Solórzano, D. G. (1998). Critical race theory, race and gender microaggressions, and the experience of Chicana and Chicana scholars. *Qualitative Studies in Education, 11*(1), 121–136.

Solórzano, D. G., & Yosso, T. J. (2002). Critical race methodology: Counter-storytelling as an analytical framework for education research. *Qualitative Inquiry, 8*(1), 23–44.

Stanley, C. A., & Slattery, P. (2003). Who reveals what to whom? Critical reflections on conducting qualitative inquiry as an interdisciplinary, biracial, male/female research team. *Qualitative Inquiry, 9*(5), 705–728.

Teranishi, R. T. (2010). *Asians in the ivory tower: Dilemmas of racial inequality in American higher education.* New York: Teachers College Press.

Tyson, C. (2003). Research, race, and an epistemology of emancipation. In G. Lopez & L. Parker (Eds.), *Interrogating racism in qualitative research methodology* (pp. 19–28). Peter Lang: New York.

Villenas, S. (1996). The colonizer/colonized Chicana ethnographer: Identity marginalization, and co-optation in the field. *Harvard Educational Review, 66*(4), 711–731.

Young, A. A. Jr. (2004) Experiences in ethnographic interviewing about race: The inside and outside of it. In M. Bulmir & J. Solomos (Eds.), *Researching Race and Racism* (pp. 187–202). London: Routledge.

10

BRIDGING THEORIES TO NAME AND CLAIM A CRITICAL RACE FEMINISTA METHODOLOGY

Dolores Delgado Bernal, Lindsay Pérez Huber, and María C. Malagón

In the preface to *This Bridge We Call Home*, Gloria Anzaldúa and AnaLouise Keating speak to building bridges between theoretical perspectives, extending ideas, and germinating new theories, particularly those that speak to marginalized peoples. They explain,

> I used to cross a trestle bridge near the Boardwalk until a winter storm demolished it. Recently, I watched the workers rebuild this historic land-mark, leaving intact some of the original foundation but supporting it with heavy buttresses and integrating it with other new materials . . . Like the trestle bridge, and other things that have reached their zenith, it [our bridge] will decline unless we attach it to new growth or append new growth to it, *this bridge we call home* is our attempt to continue the dialogue, rethink the old ideas, and germinate new theories.
>
> *(Anzaldúa & Keating, 2002, p. 2)*

Similarly, we are engaging in the ongoing methodological dialogues among critical race theory scholars and Chicana feminist scholars. In doing so, we bridge these dialogues and the theories that have informed the approaches we have each taken in our research. Separately, critical race theories (CRTs) and Chicana feminist theories (CFTs)[1] offer important critiques of dominant research paradigms, as well as analytical tools and methods to transform colonizing ways of doing research. CRTs have allowed us to study how intersecting oppressions operate at the institutional level via educational policies, practices, and discourses. They have also allowed us to understand our participants and ourselves as researchers in relation to issues such as our bodies, spirituality, relationships, healing, and critical consciousness. We argue that, when we append these perspectives to each other, they germinate a critical race feminista perspective that allows us to take approaches to our research (i.e., the questions we ask, the data collection and analysis, engagement with participants, reflections of subjectivity) in ways that neither approach does separately.

Our purpose in this chapter is twofold. First, we integrate analytical concepts and methodological approaches from CRTs and CFTs to name, claim, and build upon what has been called a critical race feminista methodology (Delgado Bernal & Alemán, 2017). To do this, we offer a brief overview of how CRTs have informed our research and point to some of the congruencies between CRTs and CFTs. We then provide a lengthier discussion of CFTs, introducing key concepts and approaches. Our second purpose is to provide not just a theoretical discussion of a critical race feminista methodology, but also a practical description of what it might look like in the field. To do this, we follow our theoretical discussion with snapshots from three different research projects highlighting how CFTs have extended the way we do critical race work.

Critical Race Theories

CRTs draw from multiple disciplines to challenge dominant ideologies embedded in educational theory and practice, build from the knowledge of communities of color to reveal how forms of oppression mediate educational trajectories, and are committed to empowering communities of color to work toward social and racial justice (Solórzano & Delgado Bernal, 2001). Several key concepts have been theorized from CRTs that have proved useful in our own work. We very briefly summarize three of these concepts.

Racial realism. Critical race legal scholar Derrick Bell names the acceptance of the centrality and pervasiveness of racism in society as racial realism, the notion that racism is a permanent aspect of our society, embedded in the everyday lives of all persons in the United States, and destructive to all of society's institutions and structures (Bell, 1995). We use the idea of racial realism to better understand how racism is embedded structurally into societies' institutions, especially educational institutions.

Racist nativism. Racist nativism is a conceptual tool used to examine the specific intersections of race and immigration status as it emerges in the experiences of Latinas/os[2] (Pérez Huber, Benavides Lopez, Malagón, Vélez, & Solórzano, 2008). This concept helps explain how race and immigration status are intricately tied processes of racialization and colonialism. It provides a lens to examine how perceived racial differences construct Latinas/os as "non-native" to the U.S. and not belonging to an "American" identity, historically tied to social constructions of whiteness.

Resistance. CRT scholars have drawn from sociological theories of resistance to provide a more complex understanding of how people of color resist substandard schooling practices (Solórzano & Delgado Bernal, 2001). CRT's analysis on resistance adds a more complex understanding of how the multiple subjectivities of participants/collaborators further inform marginalization within schooling structures and how they respond to these oppressive conditions (Solórzano & Delgado Bernal, 2001).

Chicana Feminist Theories

Chicana feminist theories are grounded in the life experiences of Chicanas and acknowledge that Chicanas/os inherit a legacy of two colonial projects: the Spanish Conquest that occurred during the 16th century, and the U.S. territorial imperial expansion that resulted with the U.S.-Mexican War (Anzaldúa, 1999; Pérez, 1999). The inscription of both conquests carries forward an ideological apparatus that racializes and exploits the brown body. CFTs interrogate the Western/European philosophical tenets that fragment the mind from the body, splintering racialized/gendered/sexed identities, reducing brown bodies to manageable objects designed for colonial/capitalist desire (Aldama, 1998; Cruz, 2001). A Chicana feminist epistemology is in a deliberate search of mending a colonized body complete (Cruz, 2001). The brown body serves as a discursive site that can interrogate constructions of normality, rooted in white supremacy and how Chicanas/os are regulated and governed in societal institutions, particularly schools. Chicana feminist perspectives offer many theoretical tools. We provide brief conceptualizations of five tools that have allowed us to bridge CRTs and CFTs.

Bodymindspirit. Chicana feminist scholarship disrupts Western colonial assumptions that research needs to be neutral or unbiased and that our bodymindspirit (Lara, 2002) must be separate entities. Suturing of the mind, body, and spirit provides a way to forefront "the sacred and the profane in our work, the spiritual and the political in our lives, and our mind with our body" (Lara, 2002, p. 436). This position affirms how through Western constructions of normality, bodies of color become "othered," regulated, and governed in schools and society (Cruz, 2001).

Conocimiento. Anzaldúa's (2002) path of *conocimiento* (knowledge) outlines seven interconnected spaces of coming to critical consciousness and gaining new knowledge. The process invokes ancestral wisdom, lived experiences, cultural knowledge, and a resiliency that allows people to heal from the effects of race-based trauma and other forms of oppression as we strategically navigate within and outside of hostile educational environments. One space of the path of *conocimiento* is the idea of spiritual activism, a "spirituality for social change, spirituality that recognizes the many differences among people yet insists on our commonalities and uses these commonalities as catalysts for transformation" (Keating, 2006, p. 11). *Conocimiento* in research comes from opening all physical, emotional, and spiritual senses. It is often a painful process that requires connecting "inner acts" and "public acts," and allows for researcher vulnerability.

Convivencia. Trinidad Galván (2015) describes *convivencia* as social relationships and practices that shed light on the ways Chicanas/Latinas draw from their cultural knowledge and experiences to live, learn, and teach together. Engaging *convivencia* in research means the deconstruction of power dynamics employed by the traditional researcher-subject dichotomy, and to acknowledge the "mutual humanity" of research participants (Trinidad Galván) 2011, p. 555). Working within a space of convivencia means working together with communities in a collective struggle for liberation. Further, the praxis of *convivencia* allows us to build bridges between school, home, community, and university spaces, creating the opportunity for a shared mutual humanity and collective liberation.

Methodological Nepantla. Anzaldúa (2005) reclaims the Nahuatl concept of *nepantla* as an in-between space of tension and possible formation. Methodological *nepantla* refers to the awkward, uncomfortable, and frustrating methodological tensions, as well as possibilities that are present in research (Alemán, Delgado Bernal, & Mendoza, 2013). Methodological *nepantla* is particularly useful to explore and embrace the tensions, contradictions, and mistakes of reflexive praxis. Anzaldúa (2002) argues that it is in *nepantla* where we often spend most of our time and that it might be advantageous to call *nepantla* "home." Methodological *nepantla* embraces that space where practice and theory meet and often grate against each other.

Sitios y lenguas. Pérez (1998) theorizes the process of *sitios y lenguas* as those spaces (*sitios*) where decolonized discourse (*lenguas*) can unfold. *Lengua* is a methodological tool that affords the opportunity to uncover the counter-discourses that challenge normative ways of thinking about race, class, gender, and sexuality. It also refers to the use of the multiple languages and dialects that marginalized people employ as resistant strategies. Sitio involves claiming a historical, geographical, or philosophical space that nurtures resistance. Pérez (1998) states, "for me, marginalized groups must have separate spaces to inaugurate their own discourses, *nuestra lengua en nuestro sitio* [our language in our space]" (p. 92).

Conceptualizing a Critical Race Feminista Methodology

We understand a critical race feminista methodology as the knowledge production by Chicana feminist scholars who are guided by the awareness of permanent, indestructible racism. We recognize the various ways that structural racism emerges in institutions, particularly educational institutions, and seek to bring nuanced forms of understanding oppression, resistance, and transformation. This praxis is guided by embracing a desire for memory prior to the ruptures incurred by colonial violence and a nostalgia for wholeness as an epistemology wrought with complications, liminality, and theorizing from a constant state of in-betweenness (Anzaldúa, 2002). It is also guided by an awareness that brown bodies have been "othered" and regulated, while reminding us to affirm the wisdom and experiences of our corporeality. A critical race feminista methodology ruptures oppressive structures in our scholarship, while pushing us toward spiritual activism, and building paradigms to replace those that are not suitable or do not seem adequate. The goal of such critical analysis is to interpret and dismantle conditions that oppress marginalized people's roles in society. Critical race feministas do this by creating theory and methodologies that consider how we form relationships in our research and build praxis that focuses on an analytical process of reflexivity and healing for the purpose of transformative social justice advocacy. Finally, we acknowledge that a critical race feminista methodology assumes many forms within creative and academic endeavors, legal efforts, personal and professional expression, and collective activism.

Using a Critical Race Feminista Methodology in Educational Research

A critical race feminista methodology is the result of bridging ideas and approaches of CRTs and CFTs. It is a methodology that requires researchers to be *nepantleras/os*, the bridge builders or "threshold people" (Keating, 2006, p. 9) who can work with racist/sexist institutions, advocate for social transformation, have a tolerance for contradictions, and bring their bodymindspirit (Lara, 2002) to the research process. How CRTs and CFTs are drawn upon to shape critical race feminista methodology depends on the research at hand. The three of us have engaged in separate research projects where we have bridged CRTs and CFTs. Our projects have looked differently and been guided by distinct questions. Collectively, our work has involved Chicana/o/Latina/o elementary school, high school, and college students as well as their families. Our work has also shared an intentionality to disrupt intersecting forms of oppression. In what follows, we provide three snapshots of what a critical race feminista methodology can look like in the field. These snapshots take up separate methodological concerns. Dolores addresses the importance of theorizing relationships in community-engaged research, pointing to the contradictions inherent in advocacy scholarship. Lindsay theorizes the healing of Chicana/Latina undocumented college students via her use of *testimonios* and the idea of *conocimiento*. María follows by describing how *sitios y lenguas* allow her to theorize the ideological, physical, discursive spaces where Chicano masculinities are located and articulated.

Convivencia and Methodological *Nepantla* (Dolores)

My collaborative research for over a decade, was grounded in Adelante, a university-school-community partnership that developed into a K-16 educational pathway (Delgado Bernal & Alemán, 2017).[3] The primary focus was to build college readiness and raise expectations of higher education attendance and success for elementary students. To do this, we collaborated with numerous elementary and university stakeholders, including students and parents. For my colleague,

Dr. Enrique Alemán, the graduate research assistants, and me, Adelante was not just a site for conducting "research," it was personal. I had children attending the school, was invited to family celebrations, and marched with immigrant parents. It was a space where I nurtured my spirit, shared meaningful *convivencias* with community members, and engaged in advocacy for a community of which I was a part.

Convivencia as methodology has to do with living together, forging relationships, creating union, and being aware of our mutual humanity (Trinidad Galván, 2015); something that too often is ignored in methodological discussions. Our *convivencias* in the Partnership allowed the Adelante team members to bring their bodymindspirit to the advocacy research and develop genuine reciprocal relationships with students, parents/guardians, and college student mentors. Our *convivencias* also allowed for numerous, sometimes alternative, forms of data collection including written *testimonios* with mothers, individual and group *pláticas* (conversations) with students and parents, digital projects with students, and participant observations. These methods, based on genuine relationships, worked best because they often took place alongside everyday interactions. They were able to reveal, in ways that other data collection methods may not, the leadership, resiliency, insights, triumphs, and immense pain that are present in communities of color.

Many feminista scholars point to the benefits and real necessity of bringing one's bodymindspirit to academia (Anzaldúa, 2005; Trinidad Galván, 2015). However, doing so can also contribute to a methodological *nepantla*—a research space of discomfort, contradictions, and possibility. For example, when we heard parents' pain about an unjust discipline policy or teachers they felt were racists, we felt the discomfort in trying to negotiate how to react as a parent/friend with privileges to leverage and/or a critical scholar building a sustainable university-community partnership with individuals about whom parents had concerns (Delgado Bernal & Alemán, 2017). Indeed, early in the Partnership's development, a principal attempted to discontinue Adelante because she viewed us as "activists" who asked her to hear parents' concerns about anti-immigrant sentiments. At other times, we had to realign our work as activist scholars to stay focused on what was most important to the parents. When the dual immersion program was under attack, parents demanded we collectively respond to a greater concern around the surveillance of their sons' brown bodies via an unjust discipline policy. And when parents who we shared *convivencias* needed "un favor" (Delgado Bernal & Alemán, 2017) it meant prioritizing their personal needs that contradicted the ever-present demands of a research-intensive university.

While we prioritized *convivencia*, the idea of a methodological *nepantla* helped us make sense of the uneasiness we felt in the asymmetrical relations of reciprocity and the contradictions of working from within/with racist institutions. Although we were able to leverage our privilege to impact school culture, curriculum, and academic opportunities for students and their families, the idea of racial realism points to how the material realities of most of the students and their families remained the same. Therefore, I remain uncomfortably cognizant of the fact that research, even when guided by a critical race feminista methodology, often benefits activist scholars in qualitatively and quantitatively different ways than it benefits students and communities of color.

Critical race theories shed light on the institutional structures that maintain oppression and place a high value on experiential knowledge of communities of color, but they did not give me a way to theorize the importance of relationships and the contradictions of my activist research. Bridging CRTs with CFTs, *convivencia* offers a more holistic means to bring one's bodymindspirit to the research process and forge reciprocal relationships to create spaces of transformation. The idea of a methodological *nepantla* makes room for the tensions and contradictions that result from our limited capacity to alter the material realities of communities of color and to reform educational systems that were not meant to serve students of color.

A Critical Race Feminista Approach to Healing (Lindsay)

A critical race feminista methodology has afforded me an opportunity to explore the possibilities for a holistic research process that considers healing, while working through the contradictions of dominant research modes. I was initially trained in CRTs which provided me with a powerful theoretical lens to examine how structural conditions mediate the intersectional experiences of Latinas/os. However, it was Chicana feminist scholars who provided me with a way to utilize my cultural intuition (Delgado Bernal, 1998) to theorize these intersectional experiences in relation to healing. Here, I discuss how a critical race feminista methodology has helped me theorize healing through *testimonios* and *conocimiento*.

I situate my work within a Chicana feminist epistemology under the premise that my personal, professional, and academic experiences are tied together and woven with those of my participants through a collective narrative of struggle, resistance, and resiliency. I incorporated this premise in the methodological approach of *testimonio*, a feminista research method that repositions Chicanas/Latinas as central to the analysis and reassigns agency to the *testimonialista*, the woman giving her *testimonio* (Latina Feminist Group, 2001). *Testimonio* allows Chicanas/Latinas to inscribe a social witness account of collective experiences, political injustices, and human struggles that are often erased by dominant discourses and offer a pathway toward healing (Delgado Bernal et. al., 2012).

Testimonio as methodology allows Chicana/Latina researchers and participants to enter ourselves—our knowledge, positionalities, and experiences—into the process of theorizing and healing. One way I have enacted this approach is through a three-phase data analysis process that includes participant collaboration (Delgado Bernal, 1998; Pérez Huber, 2009). Following preliminary analysis,

I enter a second phase with participants in a group setting where we discuss how data is analyzed, interpreted, and categorized, and to reflect on the process of *testimonio* itself. During one of these meetings, Beatriz, a fourth-year sociology major and undocumented student expressed:

> Just to have a space where I could start from the beginning. A lot of my close friends know a lot about me and my own history . . . my hopes and my faith and they know the struggle, but I think having this type of step, where you let enough space for us to say our stories, I feel like I was not rushed so it gave me freedom to say much more. I think in a way it also scratched *heridas que*, that I guess I have to say . . . because sometimes I was not able to say everything with such detail so it hurt at the end. It was healing as well, because . . . just to be able to say everything with detail and not holding back, it's just like having someone having enough time [to listen].

Beatriz explained that the process "scratched *heridas*" (wounds) that allowed her to speak freely, and with detail about difficult experiences that she does not often get to share with others. Not being able to fully explain these painful experiences leaves her feeling hurt, as if a wound had been scratched, because she can only begin to share these experiences and is not able to feel the relief of fully expressing herself. Beatriz described sharing her story in this way as "healing."

In later work, my co-author and I further explored how Chicana/Latina women engaged in a process of healing from racist nativism using the concepts of theory in the flesh and *conocimiento* (Pérez Huber & Cueva, 2012). We found the women embodied racist nativism through negative physiological effects they experienced over their lifetimes. For example, we found some participants internalized the low-expectations educators and peers held for them that resulted in lower academic performance. To engage in the process of healing from such effects, we also found that these women created opportunities for themselves to heal from the trauma caused by racist nativism. One example shared was creating counterspaces that provided a sense of community and empowerment. *Conocimiento* provided a way to bridge participants lived experiences with structural racism and healing, to explore how they engaged in transformative practices that supported their well-being and academic persistence.

Critical race theories in my work have proven useful to understand how racial realism and nativist perceptions of Latinas/os shape educational policies and practices, yet they have methodological limitations when considering how oppression becomes embodied or how people of color engage in healing processes. I have used Chicana feminist epistemological and theoretical frameworks to explore the possibilities of transformation through healing, both within the methodological approaches I utilize and in how I approach a holistic analysis of Chicana/Latina. A critical race feminista methodology has allowed me to explore the intimate relationship between structure and agency where possibilities of healing and transformation take place, and to bring together the bodymindspirit.

The *Sitios y Lenguas* in Data Analysis (María)

In my research on Chicano male youth in continuation high schools, CRTs and CFTs allow for a theorizing of the ideological, physical, and discursive spaces where Chicano masculinities are located within the U.S. imaginary. A significant finding in this work includes how a criminal/worker dichotomy operates to reproduce stringent constructions of Chicano masculinity that translate into schooling discourses and practices. Here, I discuss how my collaborators and I came to understand the ways this dichotomy contributes to a binary of over-surveillance/neglect within schooling structures (Malagón, 2011) and how a process of *sitios y lenguas* simultaneously disrupted and left some colonial discourses in place.

After preliminary data analysis of oral history interviews, I incorporated my collaborators into a focus group where we engaged in a collaborative process of "decoding" their stories within the context of perpetual educational inequities. This process included creating a physical and sociopolitical *sitio* where the youth and I discussed the colonizing discourses of Chicano racialized masculinities. In claiming our *lengua,* we challenged the colonized normative language that does not allow for decolonial constructions of Chicano masculinity. Our counter-discourse allowed for a language that revealed student resistance in response to multiple forms of oppression. *Lenguas* also furthered our theorizing by drawing from multiple languages that these youths employed as resistant strategies including the use of Spanish, local colloquialisms, and/or artistic forms of communication.

To come to an understanding of how a binary of neglect and over-surveillance occurs in schools, I created a series of activities that included bringing in themes from the data collection phase.[4] As the youth reflected on these texts and their own life experiences, they came to see a relationship between deficit schooling practices (zero tolerance, disengaging curriculum and teachers) and larger societal conditions (policing, low-wage work opportunities, racist nativism). Saul, a 17-year-old collaborator described this through what we referred to as a gangster/gardener dichotomy, "We're gangsters or gardeners and that's it. And like what we talked about, this has been true in history, we were savages then, we are aliens now . . ." This dichotomy translated into the binary of over-surveillance and neglect within schools and by extension, in their communities. In our *sitio*, we interrogated how the racialized male body navigates various social contexts embedded within systems of asymmetrical power relations. They articulated in their *lengua* the significance of their physical raced/gendered/ classed bodies as they crossed multiple imaginary and real borders in and out of schools. As we collectively came to this understanding, the youth connected their experiences in schools as sites of marginalization and often irrelevant to their occupational futures.

While these young men grappled with the implications of the over-surveillance/ neglect binary, *choques* (collisions/disagreements) occurred when I pushed them to interrogate the limited ways in which they challenged Chicano masculinity. For example, when talking about the emasculation of men of color in society they held onto colonial heteronormative assumptions.

> Omar: It's like to be a man, we make sure we're not acting gay but to them it's like different, they don't even let us move past their ideas of like being a troublemaker or that we don't care about school.
>
> María: But if we want the dominant community to see past the binary we've developed together earlier, being gay is part of the movement we want to build in schools that allow us to define ourselves?
>
> Kevin: . . . being gay has nothing to do with the racist shit we go through. Being gay is a personal problem.

These *choques* moved me into a methodological *nepantla* where I needed to embrace the tensions and contradictions in the data. For some of these youth, their *conocimiento* of how racism and gender intersect was limited by their inability to challenge heteronormative and sometimes heterosexist ideas. The uneasiness and disagreements with the youth pushed me to strategize about the difficulties and importance of theorizing a liberatory praxis that can challenge the limited, deficit, and oppressive constructions of Chicano masculinities.

A critical race feminista methodology includes theorizing the contradictions and messiness that come from the uncovering hidden voices that are simultaneously liberatory and colonial in a way that CRTs alone do not. It is a methodology that allows me to negotiate opposing positions and uncover the hidden voices of color that have been subverted by colonial constructions. It allows for the theorization of the physical, social, and discursive spaces of contradictions and possibilities that can uncover how culture, family and communities support one on their educational journey while at the same time it is the space that exposes patriarchy, sexism, heterosexism, and racism.

Conclusion

We concur with Anzaldúa and Keating (2002) that we must continue to push the theoretical boundaries of CRTs and build bridges with other theoretical perspectives to ensure its longevity as a robust framework in anti-racist research. We have offered our thinking around bridging critical race and Chicana feminist concepts to create a methodological space for sustaining meaningful relationships with our communities, for considering healing in our research process and findings, and for theorizing the ideological, discursive, and physical contradictions within the research processes we undertake. We name and claim a critical race feminista methodology, not just as a methodology that merely borrows concepts and ideas from CRTs and CFTs. Rather, a critical race feminista methodology is one that seeks to disrupt traditional research paradigms that (re)produce systemic oppression through an intentional praxis to build and create theoretical and methodological strategies that sustain our humanity and honor those with whom we engage in the research process. To engage this praxis, we continue to build and (re)construct the theoretical and methodological bridges that have been laid before us. We have shown how, in our own work, engaging a critical race feminista methodology has opened a discursive space within our research processes to focus on intentionally humanizing strategies for the purpose of transformative social justice advocacy. We look forward to seeing how future scholars will continue to (re)construct critical race feminista methodologies, building new approaches that seek to honor the communities with and for whom we research.

Notes

1 In this chapter, we use the term critical race theories (CRTs) and Chicana feminist theories (CFTs) to collectively refer to two bodies of theoretical thought. Critical race theories refer to critical race theory that developed in legal studies and the many branches that share its basic tenets such as LatCrit, FemCrit, AsianCrit, TribalCrit, DisabilityCrit, etc. While Chicana feminist theories are inclusive of the work of many Chicana scholars, this chapter will focus specifically on theories developed by Gloria Anzaldúa, Trinidad Galván, Emma Pérez, and Irene Lara.
2 We use Latinas/os as an umbrella term to refer to Mexican, Cuban, Puerto Rican, Central American, and South American peoples living in the US regardless of place of birth. We acknowledge the limited gendered dichotomy that the Spanish language creates, but choose to use the term Latinas/os to be inclusive of all genders across a spectrum of varied identities.
3 The Partnership was founded as one way of challenging racial realism and destabilizing the ubiquitous coloniality and unequal educational opportunities for Chicanas/os/ Latinas/os students.
4 These activities included viewing films on Chicano education and discussing relevant school attainment data, as well as discussing media and societal representations of Chicano males throughout history.

References

Aldama, A. J. (1998). Millennial anxieties: Borders, violence and the struggle for Chicana/o subjectivity. *Arizona Journal of Hispanic Cultural Studies*, 2(1), 41–62.
Alemán, E., Jr., Delgado Bernal, D., & Mendoza, S. (2013). Critical race methodological tensions: Nepantla in our community-based praxis. In M. Lynn & A. Dixson (Eds.), *Handbook of critical race theory in education* (pp. 325–338). New York, NY: Routledge.

Anzaldúa, G. (1987). *Borderlands/la* frontera: *The new mestiza* (2nd ed.). San Francisco, CA: Aunt Lute Books.

Anzaldúa, G. (2002). "Now let us shift . . . The path of conocimiento . . . Inner work, public acts." In G. Anzaldúa & A. Keating, (Eds.), *This bridge we call home: Radical visions for transformation* (pp. 540–578). New York, NY: Routledge.

Anzaldúa, G. (2005). Let us be the healing of the wound: The Coyolxauhqui imperative— La sombra y el sueno. In C. Joysmith & C. Lomas (Eds.), *One wound for another/Una herida por otra: Testimonios de Latin@s in the US through cyberspace* (pp. 92–103). Mexico City, Mexico: Universidad Nacional Autonoma de Mexico.

Anzaldúa, G., & Keating, A. (2002) (Eds.), *This bridge we call home: Radical visions for transformation*. New York, NY: Routledge.

Bell, D. A. (1995). Racial realism. In K. Crenshaw, N. Gotanda, G. Peller, & K. Thomas (Eds.), *Critical race theory: The key writings that formed the movement* (pp. 302–312). New York, NY: The New Press.

Cruz, C. (2001). Toward an epistemology of a brown body. *International Journal of Qualitative Studies in Education, 14*(5), 657–669.

Delgado Bernal, D. (1998). Using a Chicana feminist epistemology in educational research. *Harvard Educational Review, 68*(4), 555–579.

Delgado Bernal, D., & Alemán, E., Jr. (2017). *Transforming educational pathways for Chicana/o students: A critical race feminista praxis*. New York, NY: Teachers College Press.

Delgado Bernal, D., Burciaga, R., & Flores Carmona, J. (2012). Chicana/Latina testimonio: mapping the methodological, pedagogical, and political. *Equity & Excellence in Education, 45*(3), 363–372.

Keating, A. (2006). From borderlands and new mestizas to nepantlas and nepantleras: Anzaldúan theories for social change. *Human Architecture: Journal of the Sociology of Self Knowledge, 4*(3), 5–16.

Ladson-Billings, G. (2000). Racialized discourses and ethnic epistemologies. *Handbook of Qualitative research, 2*, 257–277.

Lara, I. (2002). Healing sueños for academia. In G. Anzaldúa & A. Keating (Eds.), *This bridge we call home: Radical visions for transformation* (pp. 433–438). New York, NY: Routledge.

Latina Feminist Group. (2001). *Telling to live: Latina feminist testimonios*. Durham, NC: Duke University Press.

Malagón M. C. (2011). *Trenches under the pipeline: The educational trajectories of Chicano continuation high school students in California* (Doctoral dissertation). Available from ProQuest Digital Dissertations. (UMI No. 3515055)

Moraga, C., & Anzaldúa, G. (Eds.). (2002). *This bridge called my back: Writing by radical women of color* (3rd ed.). Berkeley, CA: Third Woman Press.

Pérez, E. (1998). Irigaray's female symbolic in the making of Chicana lesbian sitios y lenguas (sites and discourses). In C. Trujillo (Ed.), *Living Chicana theory* (pp. 87–101). Berkeley: Third Woman Press.

Pérez, E. (1999) *The decolonial imaginary: Writing Chicanas into history*. Bloomington, IN: Indiana University Press.

Pérez Huber, L. (2009). Disrupting apartheid of knowledge: *Testimonio* as methodology in Latina/o critical race research in education. *International Journal of Qualitative Studies in Education, 22*(6), 639–654.

Pérez Huber, L., & Cueva, B. M. (2012). Chicana/Latina testimonios on effects and responses to microaggressions. *Equity & Excellence in Education, 45*(3), 392–410.

Pérez Huber, L., Benavides Lopez, C., Malagón, M. C., Vélez, V., & Solórzano, D. G. (2008). Getting beyond the "symptom," acknowledging the "disease": Theorizing racist nativism. *Contemporary Justice Review, 11*(1), 39–51.

Solórzano, D. G., & Delgado Bernal, D. (2001). Examining transformational resistance through a critical race and LatCrit theory framework: Chicana and Chicano students in an urban context. *Urban Education, 36*(3), 308–342.

Trinidad Galván, R. (2011). Chicana transborder vivencias and autoherteorías: Reflections from the field. *Qualitative Inquiry, 17*(6), 552–557.

Trinidad Galván, R. (2015). *Women who stay behind: Pedagogies of survival in rural transmigrant Mexico.* Tucson, AZ: University of Arizona Press.

PART IV

Critical Race Quantitative and Mixed Methodologies

11

QUANTS AND CRITS

Using Numbers for Social Justice (Or, How *Not* to be Lied to with Statistics)[1]

*Claire E. Crawford, Sean Demack,
David Gillborn, and Paul Warmington*

A day after a Black activist was kicked and punched by voters at a Donald Trump rally in Alabama, Trump tweeted an image packed with racially loaded and incorrect murder statistics . . . None of the numbers are supported by official sources. The figures . . . are wildly inaccurate. And, as several news organizations quickly noted, the 'Crime Statistics Bureau' [the claimed source for the statistics] doesn't exist (*PolitiFact*, 2015).

Numbers have a fascination for many people. Numbers are especially appealing to those in power when they appear to lend authoritative 'scientific' backing to a favored stereotype. Sometimes the numbers can be easily discredited, as was the case with the entirely fictitious crime stats retweeted by a soon-to-be President of the USA. In that case the media used its resources to prove that the numbers were invented. Unfortunately, education statistics rarely face this level of wider scrutiny. Indeed, many 'experts' (policy-makers and academics) create and/or publicize figures that do not stand up to critical race-conscious scrutiny.

A key problem is that many feel intimidated by numbers. When we encounter a news story, or a piece of research, that uses qualitative data (such as striking interview quotations) we know enough to question how the material was generated (e.g., what questions were interviewees asked? have the quotations been edited or taken out of context?). These basic critical inquiries come naturally because, in everyday life, people are used to judging the trustworthiness of qualitative data – the kinds of thing heard at work, on the street, and in the news. But such questions do not come so easily when faced with numbers. Statistics are widely viewed as an authoritative, 'factual' source of information. Even when people have a gut-feeling that the numbers (or their interpretation) are not correct, many lack the skills to seriously explore and critique quantitative data.

In this chapter, we explore and apply a series of principles (first outlined in Gillborn, Warmington, & Demack, 2018) to help guide a critical race-conscious use of statistics. We take inspiration from Darrell Huff's slim volume *How to Lie with Statistics* (first published in 1954). Described, in the journal *Statistical Science,* as 'the most widely read statistics book in the history of the world' (Steele, 2005), Huff's enduring appeal is the ability to demystify statistics by looking at how the everyday use of numbers (especially in news media) can give a false impression of reality. In a similar spirit, guided by the defining characteristics of Critical Race Theory (CRT) (Delgado & Stefancic, 2017; Ladson-Billings & Tate, 1995; Matsuda, Lawrence, Delgado, & Crenshaw, 1993; Taylor, Gillborn & Ladson-Billings, 2016), we offer a brief commentary on some common problems that are encountered when statistics are used in relation to race equity, social justice and education.

Quantitative Critical Race Theory (QuantCrit): A Working Guide

We are by no means the first to set out ways in which critical scholars should think more carefully about how quantitative data might be used to frustrate and/ or support the struggle for equity and social justice in education. We have sought to build upon previous work and develop the beginnings of a coherent CRT-inspired approach we call, for sake of simplicity, *QuantCrit:* both the name and the process were directly inspired by the ground-breaking work of scholars at the interface of CRT and Dis/ability Studies as they began to formulate the outline for Dis/ability Critical Race Theory (DisCrit) (cf. Annamma, Connor, & Ferri, 2013; Connor, Ferri, & Annamma, 2016). We view QuantCrit as a framework to help take forward a critical race methodology that takes seriously the potential of numbers to work in the service of equity and dismantle their frequent deployment in defense of White supremacy and oppression. QuantCrit uses the core principles of CRT to provide a set of sensitizing ideas that can be applied to any situation where quantitative data is being (or could be) used in relation to a race-conscious analysis, project, or argument. The five QuantCrit principles can be briefly summarized as:

I.   The centrality of racism: Racism is a complex, fluid and changing characteristic of society that is neither automatically nor obviously amenable to statistical inquiry. In the absence of a critical race-conscious perspective, quantitative analyses tend to remake and legitimate existing race inequities.

II. Numbers are not neutral: QuantCrit exposes how quantitative data is often gathered and analyzed in ways that reflect the interests, assumptions, and perceptions of White elites. One of the main tasks of QuantCrit, therefore, is to challenge the past and current ways in which quantitative research has served White supremacy: for example, by lending support to deficit theories without acknowledging alternative critical and radical interpretations; by removing racism from discussion by using tools, models, and techniques that fail to take account of racism as a central factor in daily life; and by lending supposedly 'objective' support to Eurocentric and White supremacist ideas.

III. Categories are not natural: for *race* read *racism*: QuantCrit interrogates the nature and consequences of the categories that are used within quantitative research. In particular, we must always remain sensitive to possibilities of 'categorical alignment' (Artiles, 2011; Epstein, 2007) where complex, historically situated and contested terms (like race and dis/ability) are normalized and mobilized as labeling, organizing, and controlling devices in research and measurement. Where 'race' is associated with an unequal outcome it is likely to indicate the operation of racism, but mainstream interpretations may erroneously impute 'race' as a cause in its own right, as if the minoritized group is inherently deficient somehow.

IV. Voice and Insight: Data cannot 'speak for itself' – QuantCrit recognizes that data is open to numerous (and conflicting) interpretations and, therefore, assigns particular importance to the experiential knowledge of people of color and other 'outsider' groups (including those marginalized by assumptions around class, gender, sexuality, and dis/ability). QuantCrit seeks to foreground their insights, knowledge, and understandings to inform research, analyses, and critique.

V. Social justice/equity orientation: A principled ambivalence to numbers – QuantCrit rejects false and self-serving notions of statistical research as value-free and politically neutral. CRT scholarship is oriented to support social justice goals and work to achieve equity, by critiquing official analyses that trade on deficit assumptions, and working with minoritized communities and activist groups to provide more insightful, sensitive, and useful research that adds a quantitative dimension to anti-oppressive praxis.

Conscious of the limitations of space, in the rest of this chapter we consider three of the five QuantCrit principles in detail and illustrate them with a series of examples drawn from real-world projects and problems. The examples are not exhaustive and several are relevant to more than one principle.

The Centrality of Racism

CRT views 'race' as 'more than just a variable' (Dixson & Lynn, 2013, 3). This is not only a methodological statement, it is also a political understanding that is integral to CRT's view of the World. Social relationships are hugely complex and fluid; they do not easily translate into simple categories and effects that are easily quantified.

Placing race at the center is less easy than one might expect, for one must do this with due recognition of its complexity. Race is not a stable category . . . "'It" is not a thing, a reified object that can be measured as if it were a simple biological entity. Race is a *construction*, a set of fully social *relationships*' (Apple, 2001, 204, original emphasis).

It follows that every attempt to 'measure' the social (especially in relation to 'race') can only offer a crude approximation of reality. We noted earlier that quantitative data are frequently assumed to be more trustworthy and robust than qualitative evidence; but this is turned on its head if we take seriously the *social* character of 'race'. Even the most basic numbers in relation to racial justice are open to multiple and profound threats to their meaning and use. In view of these problems (and the societal dominance of perspectives that are shaped by the interests, perceptions, and assumptions of White people) *the most sensible starting point in any quantitative analysis is to interrogate the collection, analysis, and representation of statistical material for likely bias in favor of White supremacy and the racial status quo.*

Don't accept numbers on trust. *Ever.*

Our first advice on dealing with statistics may seem glaringly obvious but experience suggests that numbers are rarely subjected to serious scrutiny; sometimes even the most cursory checks are not carried out by readers. For decades, the debate about race and educational achievement has been one of the most controversial areas of research on both sides of the Atlantic (Gillborn, Demack, Rollock, & Warmington, 2017). In the UK, a landmark study was published in the early 1980s which included the first ever cross-tabulation for achievement in relation to both race *and* social class simultaneously (Craft & Craft, 1983). The research showed that Black students had lower average attainment than their White counterparts regardless of class background. The research was cited frequently and a key table, setting out the findings, was reproduced *in full* in numerous publications, including an official government inquiry into the educational attainment of minoritized students (Swann, 1985, 60). And yet, the various columns in the table do not add up. In one of the columns, summarizing the results, there is a discrepancy between the constituent values and the 'total' given at the end[2] (Gillborn, 1990, 125). The discrepancy is relatively small but its constant repetition without query is significant: although the table had been reprinted numerous times, it seems no-one had bothered to check even that the table was internally consistent (let alone that the decisions about how to measure achievement and social class made sense).

Numbers are Not Color-Blind

Statistics do not simply lie around waiting for interested citizens to pick them up and use them. *Numbers are no more obvious, neutral and factual than any other form of data.* Statistics are socially constructed in exactly the same way as interview data and survey returns. Through a design process that includes, for example, decisions about which issues should (and should not) be researched, what kinds of question should be asked, how information is to be analyzed, and which findings should be shared publicly. Even given the very best intentions (and there is no guarantee that everyone involved *is* well-intentioned) at every stage there is the possibility for decisions to be taken that obscure or misrepresent issues that could be vital to those concerned with social justice. This point is well illustrated by two examples separated by an ocean and almost 30 years:

England: 1988

St. George's Hospital Medical School has been found guilty by the Commission for Racial Equality of practicing racial and sexual discrimination in its admissions policy . . . a computer program used in the initial screening of applicants for places at the school unfairly discriminated against women and people with non-European sounding names . . . By 1988 all initial selection was being done by computer . . . Women and those from racial minorities had a reduced chance of being interviewed independent of academic considerations.

(*Lowry & Macpherson, 1988*)

United States: 2016

. . . judges, police forces and parole officers across the US are now using a computer program to decide whether a criminal defendant is likely to reoffend or not. The basic idea is that an algorithm is likely to be more 'objective' and consistent than the more subjective judgment of human officials . . . But guess what? The algorithm is not color-blind. Black defendants who did not reoffend over a two-year period were nearly twice as likely to be misclassified as higher risk compared with their White counterparts; White defendants who reoffended within the next two years had been mistakenly labelled low risk almost twice as often as Black reoffenders.

(*Naughton, 2016*)

These quotations describe how calculations made by computers, assumed by definition to be objective and free from human bias, not only reflected existing racist stereotypes but then acted upon those stereotypes to create yet further racial injustice. The news coverage generated by the events is strikingly similar. In both cases there was a sense of amazement that computer calculations could make such gross and racially patterned errors. In the US example, the reporters who found the problem note that 'even when controlling for prior crimes, future recidivism, age, and gender, black defendants were 77 percent more likely to be assigned higher risk scores than white defendants' (Larson, Mattu, Kirchner, & Angwin, 2016). A UK news story was entitled '***Even algorithms*** are biased against black men' (Naughton,

2016, emphasis added). The surprise that accompanies such findings reflects a central problem that critical scholars encounter when they use, or are confronted by, quantitative data and processes. We argue that, far from being surprised that quantitative calculations can re-produce human bias and racist stereotypes, such patterns are entirely predictable and should lead us to treat quantitative analyses with at least as much caution as when considering qualitative research and its findings. Computer programs, the 'models' that they run, and the calculations that they perform are all the product of human labor. Simply because the mechanics of an analysis are performed by a machine does not mean that any biases are automatically stripped from the calculations. On the contrary, not only can computer-generated quantitative analyses embody human biases, such as racism, they also represent the added danger that their assumed objectivity can give the biases enhanced respectability and persuasiveness. Contrary to popular belief, and the assertions of many quantitative researchers, numbers are neither objective nor color-blind.

Voice and Insight: Data Cannot 'Speak for Itself'

As we have already noted, numbers are social constructs and, therefore, likely to embody the dominant (racist) assumptions that shape contemporary society. At every stage in the production of statistics there is the opportunity for racialized assumptions of the researchers to come into play. Consequently, in many cases, numbers speak for White racial interests; their presentation as objective and factual merely adds to the danger of racist stereotyping where uncritical taken-for-granted understandings lie at the heart of analyses. Some of the most important ways in which White interests and assumptions play out in quantitative research is through the questions that are asked and the analyses that produce the answers.

Asking the 'Right' Questions

'It is a scandal that ethnic minority kids are more likely to go to university than poor white ones' – so read the headline in *The Telegraph*, one of the UK's leading daily newspapers (Kirkup, 2015). The story reported official data showing that young people categorized as White British were less likely to attend university than their peers in most minoritized ethnic groups. The story echoes, and adds to, a familiar trope in British popular news reports which, for more than a decade, have systematically encouraged a myth of White racial victimization (see Gillborn, 2010a). The report focused on the overall percentage of young people in each ethnic group that were attending university. The focus on access to higher education as a whole helps to sustain an image of White disadvantage which disappears if we focus on access to elite institutions (that carry most weight in the field and the job market) and when minoritized groups are disaggregated in the analysis. For example, compared with their White counterparts, Black young people in Britain are more likely to attend university overall, but they

TABLE 11.1 Degree Attainment by Ethnic Origin (UK, 2014)

UK-domiciled first degree undergraduate qualifiers by degree class and ethnic group

	First		2:1		2:2		Third/pass		Total	
	No.	%	No.	%	No.	%	No.	%	No.	%
White	**58,385**	**22.4**	**138,990**	**53.3**	**53,805**	**20.6**	**9,755**	**3.7**	**260,935**	**100.0**
BME (black and minority ethnic) total	8,690	13.7	29,620	46.7	20,035	31.6	5,105	8.0	63,450	100.0
Black	**1,645**	**8.7**	**7,670**	**40.8**	**7,300**	**38.8**	**2,190**	**11.7**	**18,805**	**100.0**
Black or Black British: Caribbean	*440*	*9.5*	*1,990*	*43.2*	*1,670*	*36.2*	*510*	*11.0*	*4,610*	*100.0*
Black or Black British: African	*1,135*	*8.5*	*5,340*	*40.1*	*5,305*	*39.8*	*1,550*	*11.6*	*13,330*	*100.0*
Other black background	*70*	*8.3*	*335*	*39.0*	*320*	*37.3*	*130*	*15.3*	*865*	*100.0*
Asian	**4,035**	**14.7**	**13,265**	**48.2**	**8,320**	**30.2**	**1,925**	**7.0**	**27,550**	**100.0**
Asian or Asian British: Indian	*1,900*	*16.8*	*5,770*	*51.1*	*2,960*	*26.2*	*655*	*5.8*	*11,285*	*100.0*
Asian or Asian British: Pakistani	*1,020*	*12.6*	*3,705*	*45.9*	*2,720*	*33.7*	*630*	*7.8*	*8,075*	*100.0*
Asian or Asian British: Bangladeshi	*410*	*13.4*	*1,450*	*47.7*	*960*	*31.5*	*225*	*7.4*	*3,045*	*100.0*
Other Asian background	*710*	*13.8*	*2,340*	*45.5*	*1,685*	*32.7*	*415*	*8.1*	*5,145*	*100.0*
Chinese	**545**	**18.6**	**1,380**	**47.3**	**780**	**26.7**	**215**	**7.3**	**2,915**	**100.0**
Mixed	**1,985**	**18.1**	**5,785**	**52.7**	**2,685**	**24.4**	**530**	**4.8**	**10,990**	**100.0**
Other	**480**	**15.0**	**1,515**	**47.5**	**950**	**29.8**	**245**	**7.7**	**3,190**	**100.0**
Arab	*30*	*11.5*	*145*	*52.9*	*80*	*28.1*	*20*	*7.6*	*280*	*100.0*
Other	*445*	*15.3*	*1,370*	*47.0*	*875*	*30.0*	*225*	*7.7*	*2,915*	*100.0*
Total	67,075	20.7	168,610	52.0	73,840	22.8	14,860	4.6	324,385	100.0

"All counts of students have been rounded to the nearest five in accordance with HESA [Higher Education Statistics Agency] policy in order to protect the confidentiality of individuals. As totals have also been rounded based on unrounded values, some may be greater or less than the individual count numbers presented in the report. Percentages are based on those students for whom the data in question are known."

Source: Table 3.13 and preamble in Equality Challenge Unit, 2015

are significantly less likely to attend a research-intensive high-status institution (Gillborn et al., 2018). In addition to querying the question that is being asked, therefore, critical scholars should also think about which questions are *not* being asked. For example, education research frequently focuses on achievement, and yet none of the press coverage about access to higher education asked about possible differences in *outcome* at the end of university. In answer to this question we offer Table 11.1 showing the proportion of each main ethnic group attaining the different classes of degree available at the end of undergraduate study; ranging from the very best result (a first class degree) through to a 'third' or 'pass' degree classification. *White students are more likely to gain a 'First' than any other group* (22.4%); Black students are the least likely to be awarded first class degrees (8.7% of Black students overall). This means that the odds of White undergraduates achieving the highest degree classification are around three times higher than their Black peers.[3] This is a significant race inequity but, perhaps because the beneficiaries are White, it went entirely unremarked in the press furor about the 'scandalous' overall access statistics.

When 'Models' Replace Reality: The Hidden Danger of Regression Analyses

Quantitative analyses that claim to control for the separate influence of different factors are especially prone to misunderstanding and misrepresentation. Such 'regression' analyses rely on statistical models that are complex and often only partially explained in published accounts. Nevertheless, the results are generally reported as if they describe the real world rather than being a product of statistical manipulations. Regression analyses can turn reality on its head. For example, Gillborn (2010b: 261–263) describes a prominent research study (Strand, 2007) in which several minoritized groups were found to be less likely to gain access to a higher level of teaching and assessment. However, the researcher performed a regression analysis that claimed to control for the separate influence of numerous factors (such as maternal education, eligibility for free school meals and prior attainment): see Table 11.2.

The table shows the likelihood of students being placed in the higher 'tier' for mathematics exams – this is important because the highest pass grades are only available to these students. The data is presented as odds ratios that compare the minoritized students' chances of access to those of their White peers: odds that are higher than 1 show minoritized students as *more* likely to gain access, but a value *less* than 1 signals that they are less likely. The table lists values for several ethnic groups according to three calculations, presented in three columns. The original researcher labeled the first column the 'base model' but we prefer the term 'reality', since these values are generated by the distribution of the students in the real world. The distribution of students in the top tier signaled a significant under-representation for those who classified their ethnic identity as

TABLE 11.2 How Models Change Findings: Cumulative Odds Ratios from Ordinal Logistic Regression for Mathematics Tier of Entry by Ethnic Group

Ethnic group	Reality (Base Model)	Adjustment 1 (Prior attainment)	Adjustment 2 (Family background)
Indian	(1.34)	(1.63)	(1.86)
Pakistani	[0.55]	1.19	(1.55)
Bangladeshi	[0.65]	1.08	(1.72)
Black Caribbean	[0.44]	[0.68]	[0.72]
Black African	[0.62]	(1.56)	(1.75)

Notes

Base	Ethnic group.
PA	Ethnic group, Key Stage 2 maths test marks.
FB	Ethnic group, Key Stage 2 maths test marks, gender, social class, maternal education, FSM, home ownership, single parent households.

(oval value) significantly **more** likely than White British to be entered for higher tiers.

[boxed value] significantly **less** likely than White British to be entered for higher tiers.

Source: Adapted from Strand, 2007, 87, Table 42: Gillborn, 2010b, 262.

Black Caribbean (0.44), Pakistani (0.55), Black African (0.62) and Bangladeshi (0.65) heritage. In the table, we have boxed these values to help them stand out. In the second and third columns, the researcher performed regression analyses that try to build in ('model') the results that would have been predicted based on the performance of students with certain other identities (including their prior attainment earlier in their school careers, whether they receive free meals, their mothers' education etc.). Each calculation adjusts the results and creates more cases of apparent *over*-representation (which we have signaled by an oval around the relevant value). The effect is dramatic; a situation that showed an under-representation of four out of five minoritized groups has now become a pattern claiming to reveal an over-representation of four of the five groups. By applying a statistical model (which assumes that poverty, income, maternal education and other 'family' characteristics are entirely unrelated to race/racism) the statistician has turned under-representation (minority disadvantage) into over-representation (White disadvantage).

A Social Justice/Equity Orientation: Principled Ambivalence to Numbers

There are no inherent reasons why critical race theorists should dispense with quantitative approaches entirely but they should adopt a position of *principled ambivalence*, neither rejecting numbers out of hand nor falling into the trap of imagining that numeric data have any kind of enhanced status or value. This is a stance that anti-racist scholars and activists have long practiced, for example, when they contest supposedly scientific claims about the biological nature of race – sometimes by invoking what science tells us about the unscientific status of race (Warmington, 2009, 2014). Critical race theorists work simultaneously *with* and *against* race, (i.e., we know that race only exists as a social construct, but we recognize the, sometimes murderous, power of the fiction and seek to engage, resist and ultimately destroy race/racism). Similarly, QuantCrit should work *with* and *against* numbers by engaging with statistics as a fully social aspect of how race/racism is constantly made and legitimated in society.

Comparing 'Like With Like'

A social justice orientation requires researchers to be sensitive to ways in which racism might operate through the everyday assumptions and processes of education. This is especially challenging in relation to quantitative research because most quantitative analyses are not informed by a critical understanding of social relations, let alone a CRT perspective on racism's complex and fluid character. Racism does not operate separately to factors such as prior attainment, income, and parental education: racism operates *through* and *between* many of these factors simultaneously. Quantitative research sometimes claims to disentangle these elements (e.g., by using regression analyses) and assumes that numerous factors (such as prior attainment, socio-economic status and parental education) are entirely independent of racist influences. Worse still, they treat inequalities in those indicators as if they are a sign of internal **deficit** on the part of the minoritized group rather than a socially constituted **injustice**. The use of 'prior attainment' scores is a particularly important example of this. Quantitative researchers frequently use students' test results at an earlier stage of their education as a way to group people of similar 'ability' (a maneuver that they claim compares 'like with like') but this erases racism and blames the students:

> the racism that the kids experience on a daily basis [in ranked teaching groups, with restricted curricula and less-experienced teachers] translates into lower scores . . . But those scores are then used to gauge 'ability' and 'prior attainment' . . . the differences in prior attainment are treated as if they were deficits in the students themselves and nothing to do with their schools.
>
> *(Gillborn, 2010b, 266)*

Conclusion

> Bill O'Reilly: 'You tweeted out that whites killed by blacks, these were statistics you picked up from somewhere, at a rate of 81 percent. And that's totally wrong. Whites killed by blacks is 15 percent, yet you tweeted it was 81 percent.'

Donald Trump: 'Bill, I didn't tweet, I retweeted somebody that was supposedly an expert . . . Bill, am I gonna check every statistic? I get millions and millions of people, @RealDonaldTrump, by the way . . . this was a retweet. Bill, I'm sure you're looking out for me, everybody is. This was a retweet. And it comes from sources that are very credible, what can I tell you.'

(Farley, 2015)

Donald Trump's 2015 retweet of entirely false and racist 'crime statistics' is instructive. Trump was not the only person to gleefully share the graphic, which appears to have originated on a Nazi sympathizer's account (Johnson, 2015). We tend to subject numbers to relatively little scrutiny, especially when they align with our beliefs. Of course, one might expect politicians, policy-makers and academics to be more circumspect in their behavior but, as we have shown in multiple examples above, this is often far from the case. We do not imagine that QuantCrit will spell the end of racist and misleading quantitative material in educational research. As critical race theorists we know that such changes are a matter of interest convergence and public protest, not a question of technical accuracy and reason. Nevertheless, we hope that the QuantCrit principles, and the examples we have set out above, will go some way to supporting greater critical scrutiny of quantitative data and the potential to harness its status in the cause of social justice.

Notes

1 This chapter explores and develops ideas that were first set out in the journal *Race Ethnicity and Education* (Gillborn, Warmington, & Demack, 2018). The original paper was shaped through a process of debate, challenge and support with colleagues in the Critical Race Studies in Education Association (CRSEA) and, in particular, in dialogue with the editors of the special issue on CRT and quantitative approaches, Nichole M. Garcia, Nancy López, and Verónica N. Vélez.
2 The original table gives the total number of 'middle class' respondents as 761 but this is six more than the figure that is produced by adding together the constituent values for middle class students elsewhere in the table.
3 This is based on the 'odds ratio' (also known as 'cross-product ratio') calculated by comparing the odds of success for White students compared with the odds of success for Black students (see Connolly, 2007, 107–108).

References

Annamma, S. A., Connor, D. J., & Ferri, B. A. (2013). Dis/ability critical race studies (DisCrit): theorizing at the intersections of race and dis/ability. *Race Ethnicity and Education, 16*(1), 1–31.

Apple, M. W. (2001). *Educating the 'right' way: Markets, standards, God, and inequality.* New York: RoutledgeFalmer.

Artiles, A. J. (2011). Toward an interdisciplinary understanding of educational equity and difference: The case of the racialization of ability. *Educational Researcher,* 40(9), 431–445.

Connolly, P. (2007). *Quantitative data analysis in education.* London: Routledge.

Connor, D. J., Ferri, B. A., & Annamma, S. A. (Eds.), (2016). *DisCrit: Disability studies and critical race theory in education.* New York: Teachers College Press.

Craft, M. & Craft, A. (1983). The participation of ethnic minority pupils in further and higher education. *Educational Research,* 25(1), 10–19.

Delgado, R. & Stefancic, J. (2017). *Critical race theory: An introduction,* 3rd ed. New York: New York University Press.

Dixson, A. D. & Lynn, M. (2013). Introduction. In M. Lynn & A. D. Dixson (Eds.), *Handbook of critical race theory in education* (pp. 1–6). New York: Routledge.

Epstein, S. (2007). *Inclusion: The politics of difference in medical research.* Chicago, IL: University of Chicago Press.

Equality Challenge Unit (2014). *Equality in higher education: Statistical report 2014.* London: Equality Challenge Unit. Retrieved from http://www.ecu.ac.uk/wp-content/uploads/2014/11/Equality-in-HE-student-data-2014.xlsx and http://www.ecu.ac.uk/wp-content/uploads/2018/01/2015-equality-in-higher-education-student-tables.xlsx.

Farley, R. (2015). Trump retweets bogus crime graphic. *FactCheck.org.* Retrieved from http://www.factcheck.org/2015/11/trump-retweets-bogus-crime-graphic.

Gillborn, D. (1990). *'Race', ethnicity & education: Teaching and learning in multi-ethnic schools.* London: Routledge.

Gillborn, D. (2010a). The White working class, racism and respectability: Victims, degenerates and interest-convergence. *British Journal of Educational Studies,* 58(1), 2–25.

Gillborn, D. (2010b). The colour of numbers: Surveys, statistics and deficit-thinking about race and class. *Journal of Education Policy,* 25(2), 253–276.

Gillborn, D., Demack, S., Rollock, N., & Warmington, P. (2017). Moving the goalposts: Education policy and 25 years of the Black/White achievement gap. *British Educational Research Journal,* 43(5), 848–874.

Gillborn, D., Warmington, P., & Demack, S. (2018). QuantCrit: Education policy, 'Big Data' and principles for a critical race theory of statistics. Special issue, Quantitative methods and critical race theory of *Race Ethnicity and Education,* 21(2), 158–179.

Huff, D. (1993 [1954]). *How to lie with statistics.* London: W.W. Norton & Company.

Johnson, C. (2015, November 22). We found where Donald Trump's 'Black crimes' graphic came from, *Little Green Footballs.* Retrieved from http://littlegreenfootballs.com/article/45291_We_Found_Where_Donald_Trumps_Black_Crimes_Graphic_Came_From.

Kirkup, J. (2015, November 10). It is a scandal that ethnic minority kids are more likely to go to university than poor white ones. *The Telegraph.* Retrieved from https://www.telegraph.co.uk/education/universityeducation/11986204/It-is-a-scandal-that-ethnic-minority-kids-are-more-likely-to-goto-university-than-white-ones.html.

Ladson-Billings, G. & Tate, W. F. (1995). Toward a critical race theory of education. *Teachers College Record,* 97(1), 47–68.

Larson, J., Mattu, S., Kirchner, L., & Angwin, J. (2016, May 23). How we analyzed the COMPAS recidivism algorithm, *ProPublica: Journalism in the Public Interest.* Retrieved from https://www.propublica.org/article/how-we-analyzed-the-compas-recidivism-algorithm.

Lowry, S. & Macpherson, G. (1988). A blot on the profession. *British Medical Journal*, 296(6623), 657–658.

Matsuda, M. J., Lawrence, C. R., Delgado, R. & Crenshaw, K. W. (Eds.), (1993). *Words that wound: Critical race theory, assaultive speech, and the First Amendment.* Boulder CO: Westview Press.

Naughton, J. (2016, June 26). Even algorithms are biased against Black men, *The Guardian*. Retrieved from https://www.theguardian.com/commentisfree/2016/jun/26/algorithms-racial-bias-offenders-florida.

PolitiFact (2015, November 23). Trump's pants on fire tweet that blacks killed 81% of white homicide victims, *PolitiFact*. Retrieved from http://www.politifact.com/truth-o-meter/statements/2015/nov/23/donald-trump/trump-tweet-blacks-white-homicide-victims

Steele, M. J. (2005). Darrell Huff and fifty years of *How to lie with statistics*, *Statistical Science*, 20(3), 205–209.

Strand, S. (2007). *Minority ethnic pupils in the Longitudinal Study of Young People in England* (LSYPE). Research Report DCSF-RR002. London: Department for Children, Schools and Families.

Swann, Lord (1985). *Education for all: Final report of the Committee of Inquiry into the education of children from ethnic minority groups*. Cmnd 9453. London: HMSO.

Taylor, E., Gillborn, D., & Ladson-Billings, G. (Eds.), (2016). *Foundations of critical race theory in education*, 2nd ed. New York: Routledge.

Warmington, P. (2009). Taking race out of scare quotes: Race-conscious social analysis in an ostensibly post-racial world, *Race Ethnicity and Education*, 12(3), 281–296.

Warmington, P. (2014). *Black British intellectuals and education: Multiculturalism's hidden history*. London: Routledge.

12

EXPANDING EDUCATIONAL PIPELINES

Critical Race Quantitative Intersectionality as a Transactional Methodology

Alejandro Covarrubias, Pedro E. Nava, Argelia Lara, Rebeca Burciaga, and Daniel G. Solórzano

The Critical Race Intersectional Think Tank (CRITT) is a praxis-based collective of Latina/o scholars trained in critical race theory (CRT), Latino critical theory (LatCrit), and critical feminist theories (CFT). Together, we are working to innovate research methodologies to produce structural, institutional, cultural, and personal transformative ruptures in and outside of academia. Delgado Bernal and Alemán (2017) describe these ruptures as *chóques*, or "incidents, interactions, experiences and moments that ***expose*** and ***interrupt*** pervasive coloniality and structural inequities" (p. 5, emphasis added). These *chóques*, or fundamental ideological collisions, create conditions that can position critical scholars in liminal theoretical and methodological practices and spaces also known as *nepantla*, a liminal space of knowledge creation (Anzaldúa, 1987). The *chóque* that catalyzed this project is the limitation of the educational pipeline model. In this chapter, we describe methodological approaches that reframe our analysis of educational pipeline models by conjoining theory, action, and reflection grounded in critical race and feminist community-building practices. While this is not always easy in the academy, we see community building as a necessary precursor to critical research and publication. Furthermore, this grounding provides the foundation for the Critical Race Intersectional Think Tank and the Critical Race Quantitative Intersectionality (CRQI) framework that informs our praxis.

Producing collaborative research that strives to create transformative ruptures in thought and practice means we must analyze our own methodological training, theoretical perspectives, and the limitations of our previous work. Our work on educational pipeline research (Burciaga, Pérez Huber, & Solórzano, 2010; Covarrubias, 2011; Pérez Huber, Huidor, Malagón, Sánchez, and Solórzano, 2006; Pérez Huber, Malagón, Ramirez, Gonzalez, Jimenez, and Vélez, 2015; Watford, Rivas, Burciaga, & Solórzano, 2006) serves as a foundation for these analyses. In doing so, we explore the limitations of the educational pipeline model that draws from our own work (Covarrubias, Nava, Lara, Burciaga, Vélez, & Solórzano, 2018) but also work from ethnographers, *testimoniadoras* [*testimonio* practice and research] (Delgado Bernal, Burciaga, & Flores Carmona, 2012), cartographers (Solórzano & Vélez, 2015), and policy makers. These methodological (re)considerations sharpen our ability to reveal structural inequities about educational attainment across different ethno-racial groups. They have also inspired a new rupture in our research, as we innovate methodological approaches, skills, and tools for educational research.

Although historically used to categorize, objectify, and dehumanize Communities of Color, quantitative approaches can serve as a critical starting point for revealing patterns of racial disparity. Analyzing enumerated data can verify important patterns that help researchers make meaning of social phenomena. Yet, the complexity of lived experiences in relationship to power can only be captured by methodological strategies that seek to understand and theorize from the flesh. Gloria E. Anzaldúa (1990), for example, states,

> Theory, then, is a set of knowledges. Some of these knowledges have been kept from us—entry into some professions and academia denied us. Because we are not allowed to enter discourse, because we are often disqualified and excluded from it, because what passes for theory these days is forbidden territory for us, it is *vital* that we occupy theorizing space, that we not allow white men and women solely to occupy it. By bringing in our own approaches and methodologies, we transform that theorizing space.
>
> *(p. xxv, emphasis original)*

We heed Anzaldúa's call to occupy theorizing space in building decolonizing methodologies (L. T. Smith 1999) to conduct research. Developed and deepened by CRITT, CRQI is our approach to juxtapose our academic training alongside our lived experiences and memories in exploring new openings into methodological insights. Often our theories, methodologies, and perspectives clash – *chocan*. It is in working through these clashes – intellectually and personally – that we transcend the siloed boundaries of academic fields. We call these *trans-sectional* methodologies – methodologies that bridge academic fields, communities, and our cultural intuitions that hold collective memories.

We position CRQI as a historically situated, transdisciplinary methodology grounded in the resistance of Feminists of Color, Indigenous Communities, and People of Color (Anzaldúa, 1987; hooks, 1994; B. Smith, 1978; L. T. Smith, 1999). Native scholars have long highlighted the necessity to center Indigenous intellectual project(s) in the process of anticolonial work (Wolfe, 2006; Tuck & Yang, 2012). Feminists of Color formalized researchers' understanding of intersectionality, and specifically the relationships of power between people, ideologies, and institutions (Crenshaw, 1989; Hill Collins, 1998).

Critical Race Quantitative Intersectionality: Exploring "Numbers" as Anti-Racist Praxis

Although there remain important critiques and considerations when working with "numbers" (Bonilla-Silva & Zuberi, 2008; Zuberi, 2001), anti-racist contributions are possible using quantitative inquiry (Covarrubias et al., 2018). Reflective of its roots in Critical Race Theory, CRQI (Covarrubias & Vélez, 2013) insists that the intersectional construction of difference frames how we develop, contest, and examine policies, practices, and procedures that institutionalize oppressive ideologies in educational systems. CRQI is defined as "an explanatory framework and methodological approach that utilizes quantitative methods to account for the material impact of race and racism at its intersections with other forms of subordination" (Covarrubias & Vélez, 2013, p. 275). While not an instructional manual for specific quantitative approaches or the use of selective statistical software packages, CRQI makes an explicit commitment to foregrounding intersectionality and centering the lives of People of Color at each stage of the quantitative research process – from deriving questions to disseminating findings. Earlier iterations of CRQI focus on establishing the necessity, explaining the rationale, delineating restrictions, and expanding the utility of quantitative research from a critical race perspective (Covarrubias, 2011; Covarrubias & Lara, 2014, Covarrubias & Liou, 2014; Covarrubias & Vélez, 2013; Covarrubias et al., 2018). In this chapter, we revisit the original tenets of CRQI, describe research projects as examples that use and shape CRQI, and reflect on the framework's limitations and potential for critical race scholarship in education.

CRQI Working Tenets

1) Numbers Do Not Speak for Themselves

Convention teaches that statistical significance of difference is warranted when a "p" value is less than 0.05. This gold standard of improbability is a construct that relies on problematic underlying assumptions (Bonilla-Silva & Zuberi, 2008; Zuberi, 2001). While statistical significance indicates whether results fit into our abstract, hypothesized models, it gives validity to the data that is framed within parameters of accepted norms. This narrow framing limits opportunities for new insights and is rooted in the sociopolitical and cultural position of its authors, telling us more about the context than what was ostensibly measured. Indeed, "significance, reduced to its narrow and statistical meaning only, has little to do with a defensible notion of scientific inference, error analysis, or rational decision making" (Ziliak & McCloskey, 2008, p. 2).

The U.S.' fascination with the "achievement gap" rests primarily on ahistorical quantitative analyses of high-stakes test scores (Ladson-Billings, 2006).

These seemingly neutral, decontextualized statistics serve to normalize deficit-based ideas that blame Students of Color for their inability to "achieve" in school; when instead, opportunities are tied to the preservation of White supremacy, capitalism, and patriarchy (hooks, 2000). CRQI asserts that numbers cannot speak for themselves. It exposes the ideological investments in White supremacy that inform how quantitative analyses, and their corresponding portraits, such as the "achievement gap," can be used to misrepresent Communities of Color. CRQI commits to exposing how power undergirds all relationships, institutions, ideologies, and systems that numbers are used to represent, measure, and rationalize.

2) *Quantifying Intersectionally*

Educational pipelines capture snapshots of educational attainment along the PreK-PhD educational trajectory (see Figure 12.1). CRQI was first conceptualized to explore how educational pipelines could highlight varying educational attainment patterns for Communities of Color. While educational pipelines provide an overview of who attains educational degrees (e.g. high school diploma, Bachelor's degree, etc.), U.S. Census data used to construct them obscure root causes of inequities (Rodríguez, 2000). Educational opportunities are mediated by how we experience racialization *intersectionally*, namely in relationship to gender, social class, citizenship, and other social constructions. As such, the development of educational pipelines involves more than just analyzing data intersectionally; we must commit to centering intersectionality throughout the entire research process (Covarrubias, 2011).

Intersectional quantitative data have been used to reveal and contest oppressive educational conditions and contextualize the lived experiences of People of Color. For example, Covarrubias and Lara (2014) innovate a unique method for calculating an intersectional pipeline for people of Mexican origin that helps better approximate their demographic dispersal across different categories of immigration status. Grounded in cultural intuition (Delgado Bernal, 1998), this method relies on the authors' experiential and intellectual knowledge of immigration policies, personal memories of migration, and a conceptual understanding of census data limitations. As a result, racial analyses are layered in relation to other social markers, such as gender, citizenship status, and class; categories that are not static variables, but historically situated realities of how positions of power mediate opportunity (e.g. White people in relationship to People of Color). These layered tabulations using the large-scale census data are the foundations for portraits of education (in)opportunity for Communities of Color at nested levels of geography (i.e. census tract, cities, counties, states, etc.). Intersectional calculations help us visualize and pinpoint potential ruptures for further analysis. Yet, even data collected and analyzed intersectionally does not speak for itself. CRQI requires analyses that are contextualized and challenge claims of neutrality, as part of a broader project to expose "hidden assumptions" and "ideological inscriptions" (Stage, 2007, p. 9).

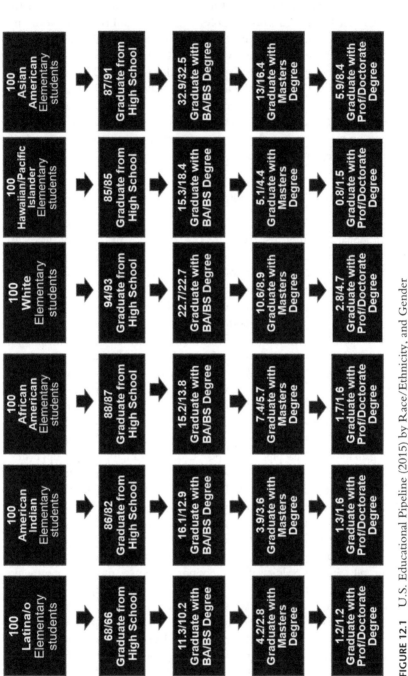

FIGURE 12.1 U.S. Educational Pipeline (2015) by Race/Ethnicity, and Gender

Current Population Survey, March Supplement of the US Census Bureau Annual Social and Economic Supplement, 2015

3) Experientially Grounding Data

Critical Race Quantitative Intersectionality insists that CRT scholars start from the lived experiences of Communities of Color, or those "at the bottom of the well" (Bell, 1992). More specifically, we call for intersectional interrogations of quantitative research that includes localized knowledges and collective memories. Experientially grounding quantitative data is an iterative process – one that bridges "neutral" numbers with intersectional factors that produce outcomes. It is within this *nepantla* (liminal space) of critical mixed-methodological analyses that *chóques*, or transformative ruptures, expose and unpack majoritarian stories.

Although we create intersectional pipelines to study the impact of inequitable educational conditions, we fall short of our intended goal when we produce work that inadequately demonstrates the lived complexities of societal stratification. For example, without experientially grounding data, the pipeline remains vulnerable to deficit interpretations that attribute educational leakages to individual traits instead of structural conditions.

Critical Race Quantitative Intersectionality argues that *significance*, as measured by potential statistical variance, is not the only measure of import that can be utilized to provide meaning to difference when represented and measured by numbers. Dominant analyses of quantitative data can lose sight of the fact that numbers are simply symbols representing reality. These abstractions, and their subsequent manipulation, can be restrictive for other types of contextualization and meaning-making of those numbers. Alternatively, the importance of quantitative findings can be given substantive meaning (significance) using *experiential significance* – the magnitude of the measurement is captured and assessed through the production of various qualitative methods that speak to the impact on the lived experiences of people represented by otherwise impersonal numbers. This not only shifts the center of knowledge production but allows for reliance on cultural intuition and community memory (Delgado Bernal, 1998), fourth-person accounts/narratives (Vizenor 2008), and other epistemological and ontological groundings. The concept of experiential significance draws directly from the strengths of rebellious standpoints—outsider within, feminista standpoints—to make meaning of numerically measured differences and situated knowledge. We make meaning of the numbers by remembering, living, and acting.

4) Commitment to Structural Transformation of Intersectional Subordination

Dill and Kohlman (2012) argue that intersectionality is a spectrum with weak and strong applications, depending on the theoretical and methodological approaches to understand the interdependence of cause and effect. Intersectionality cannot be disconnected from discussions of structural transformation and decoloniality, nor can we view the concept as encompassing mere identity or differences. CRQI was developed to *expose* and *transform* persistent structural inequities grounded in critical applications of intersectionality.

Critical Race Quantitative Intersectionality is used best in the service of producing applicable research that evolves our understanding of opportunity structures. CRQI is grounded in quantitative criticalism, described by Stage (2007) as an approach that "seeks to forge challenges, illuminate conflict, and develop critique through quantitative methods in an effort to move theory, knowledge, and policy to a higher plane" (p. 8). In the academy, CRQI begins with re-imagining possibilities through centering an intersectional critique of dynamic systems of power in research and practice. Outside of the academy, this work continues through our work with and continuous learning from community-based efforts. In the spirit of la paperson's (2017) work, we acknowledge our positionalities as *scyborgs* who are "subversively part of the machinery" but *not of* the machine (p. xiii).

Intersectionalizing Quantitative Data

To construct the educational pipeline, we mined data from the American Community Survey (ACS),[1] collected by the U.S. Census Bureau monthly and aggregated in 1-year, 3-year, and 5-year datasets. Using DataFerret,[2] we collected and analyzed 5-year ACS data files with a focus on a range of variables, including race, ethnicity, citizenship, class, sex, geography, and educational attainment.

In addition to disaggregating what is arguably homogenizing US Census data, our work involves reconceptualizing how data captures power relationships and experiences within specific material conditions. This approach embraces the assumption that educational systems have underlying ideologies that drive policies, practices, and procedures. Thus, systems either fail to create conditions for students to successfully navigate the actual educational pipeline, or they intentionally produce conditions that lead to disparate outcomes among People of Color. Although the educational pipeline clearly depicts disparate outcomes for diverse groups, the use of the pipeline can reinforce dominant achievement ideologies. In contrast, CRQI (re)imagines possibilities for producing intersectional pipelines that lend themselves to reveal material structural inequities. In the process, we consult our educational journeys, shared experiences, collective memories, and experiential knowledge to make sense of how opportunity is mediated by multiple and intersecting social locations and relationships.

For example, the California San Joaquin Valley has an extended history of educational disinvestment throughout many of its small, rural, agricultural communities. Over the past 40 years and as a response to the agricultural labor demands, migration from Mexico and Central America has resulted in the remaking of its demographic landscape of the Valley with a majority Latinx population. Yet, an educational pipeline of the region reveals that over half of the Latinx population has less than a full high school education. A CRQI analysis for the San Joaquin

Valley would focus on the social context leading to disparate educational out-comes along with other structural factors including citizenship status and context of migration, language, housing and food insecurity, and need for educators to teach from culturally responsive approaches.

Critical Examination of Research Assumptions

Institutions have been created with problematic ideologies that maintain patriar-chy, White supremacy, and meritocracy. These ideologies shape the conditions, opportunities, and outcomes produced by schools. Outcomes data (e.g. levels of educational attainment) has often been used to frame the success/failure of People of Color. Yet in order to critically examine outcomes, we must also reconsider why data is collected, how data is collected, and how data is interpreted.

Producing Testimonios as a Collective: Experientially Grounding Data

The CRITT collective weaves qualitative methods into CRQI and situates quantitative data alongside *testimonios* of People of Color (see Covarrubias, et al., 2018). A CRQI with *Testimonio* (CRQI+T) framework allows more nuanced analyses to emerge from quantitative findings. Rooted in the oral history tra-ditions and scholarship of human rights' struggles across the Americas, *testimo-nio* is purposeful storytelling, grounded in praxis, utilized to **expose** and **disrupt** histories that are otherwise subsumed (Cruz, 2012). *Testimonios* are a collective endeavor because they place individual experiences in conversation with socio-historical factors and memories that help demonstrate context. A *testimonio* can be prepared individually or a collectively, but its analysis must include context and intent to further illuminate silenced experiences within majoritarian stories. CRQI+T challenges us to critically examine our own intersectional positionali-ties and experiences in relationship to our work. It became necessary for us to reflect on the ways that our exceptional educational experiences highlight institu-tional inequities through scrutinizing the privileges we were granted in our vari-ous sociopolitical locations. These experiences illuminate patterns of institutional neglect, microaggressions, whitestreaming of educational spaces, and generally under-resourced conditions that uniquely explain the variety of ways people are schooled within distinct regions across the state of California.

The creation of individual and collective *testimonios* involves a complex pro-cess with shared vulnerability. We begin with educational pipelines, using our *testimonios* to flesh out our own experiences alongside attainment data within regions, across local cities, and in our neighborhoods. Our stories, as well as the stories of our families and the narratives from our communities, give substance to the range of outcomes we see in education and give meaning to the magnitude of the material impact those numbers represent. We partner our CRQI framework with the long-standing *feminista* and Latinx traditions of *testimonio* to affirm an *experiential significance* that substantiates the numerically measured findings.

Intentional Community Building Within Academia

Creating a research collective that can work "in community" is in direct opposition to our academic training to publish as individuals. Within professional communities, we grow apart from natural allies because of policies and procedures that reward ongoing competition for limited resources, publications, jobs, grants, and even mentorship opportunities. While we belong to many academic communities, some of which resist such an atmosphere and others that relish in it, CRQI prepares us as CRITT scholars to transform destructive relationships and conditions while working "in community" towards the creation of purposeful scholarship. Not only is our research grounded in CRT, our relationships and working processes strive for a CRT community-building model, which we find are instrumental to the methodological ruptures experienced through this process.

Discussion and Conclusion

Critical Race Quantitative Intersectionality is focused on rethinking why we measure, who we measure, and how we can reimagine ways that quantitative tools can support justice praxis. More importantly, this trans-sectional approach is about building bridges by deliberately inserting our own lived experiences into the quantitative narratives. Without these lenses, quantitative narratives are left to dominant interpretations, often reproducing cultural deficit ideas that are devoid of historic and political context. CRQI is a methodological resistance that subverts normative and normalizing research processes, relationships, and analyses. It rejects hierarchical research relationships, disconnected involvement in analytical processes, and privileging of dominant ideological constructs related to quantitative research.

Throughout our efforts to build and work in community through the production of scholarship, as CRITT scholars, we continue to confront our own methodological limitations. It is in working through these clashes – intellectually and personally – that we transcend the siloed boundaries of academic fields. We insist on trans-sectional approaches to this work. Sharing our *testimonios*, for example, was an important methodological process that pushed our thinking around CRQI. In fact, new revelations and improved analyses of our data most developed when we produced and shared individual critical *testimonios* that exposed our intersectional experiences of privilege and punishment. This process helps us understand how experiential significance grounded in *testimonio* provides equally, if not more, substantive, meaning to quantitative data than does statistical significance. These trans-sectional methodologies bridge academic fields, communities, and call upon cultural intuition that holds collective memories. These approaches require individual and collective risk-taking and courage-making, as well as community building, offers new ways to expose and address patterns of inequities across and within regions as relational, personal, intentional, and historic.

Notes

1 "The American Community Survey (ACS) is an ongoing survey by the U.S. Census Bureau. It regularly gathers information previously contained only in the long form of the decennial census, such as ancestry, educational attainment, income, language proficiency, migration, disability, employment, and housing characteristics. Sent to approximately 295,000 addresses monthly (or 3.5 million per year), it is the largest household survey that the Census Bureau administers." (US Census Bureau. ACS Information Guide. www.census.gov., p. 8)
2 See https://dataferrett.census.gov. According to the U.S. Census, "DataFerrett is a data analysis and extraction tool to customize federal, state, and local data to suit your requirements. Using DataFerrett, an unlimited array of customized spreadsheets can be developed that are as versatile and complex as usage demands. The spreadsheets can then be turned into graphs and maps without any additional software."

References

Anzaldúa, G. (1987). *Borderlands: La frontera* (Vol. 3). San Francisco, CA: Aunt Lute.

Anzaldúa, G. (1990). *Haciendo caras/making face, making soul: Creative and critical perspectives by women of Color*. San Francisco, CA: Aunt Lute.

Bell, D. (1992). *Faces at the bottom of the well: The permanence of racism*. New York: Basic Books.

Bonilla-Silva, E., & Zuberi, T. (2008). Toward a definition of White logic and White methods. In T. Zuberi, & E. Bonilla-Silva, *White logic, White methods: Racism and methodology* (pp. 3–27). Lanham, MD: Rowman & Littlefield.

Burciaga, R., Pérez Huber, L., & Solórzano, D. G. (2010). Going back to the headwaters: Examining Latina/o educational attainment and achievement through a framework of hope. In E. G. Murillo, S. A. Villenas, R. Trinidad Galván, J. S. Muñoz, C. Martínez, & M. Machado-Casas (Eds.), *Handbook of Latinos and education: Theory, research, and practice* (pp. 422–437). London: Routledge.

Covarrubias, A. (2011). Quantitative intersectionality: A critical race analysis of the Chicana/o educational pipeline. *Journal of Latinos and Education, 10*(2), 86–105.

Covarrubias, A., & Lara, A. (2014). The undocumented (im)migrant educational pipeline: The influence of citizenship status on educational attainment for people of Mexican origin. *Urban Education, 49*(1), 75–110.

Covarrubias, A., & Liou, D. D. (2014). Asian American education and income attainment in the era of post-racial America. *Teachers College Record, 116*(6).

Covarrubias, A., & Vélez, V. (2013). Critical race quantitative intersectionality: An anti-racist research paradigm that refuses to "let the numbers speak for themselves." In M. Lynn & A. Dixson (Eds.), *Handbook of critical race theory in education* (pp. 270–285). New York: Routledge.

Covarrubias, A., Nava, P. E., Lara, A., Burciaga, R., Vélez, V. N., & Solórzano, D. G. (2018). Critical race quantitative intersections: A *testimonio* analysis. *Race, Ethnicity and Education, 21*(2), 253–273.

Crenshaw, K. (1989). Demarginalizing the intersection of race and sex: A Black feminist critique of antidiscrimination doctrine, feminist theory and antiracist politics. *University of Chicago Legal Forum*, 139–166.

Cruz, C. (2012). Making curriculum from scratch: *Testimonio* in an urban classroom. *Equity & Excellence in Education*, *45*(3), 460–471.

Delgado Bernal, D. (1998). Using a Chicana feminist epistemology in educational research. *Harvard Educational Review*, *68*(4), 555–582.

Delgado Bernal, D., & Alemán, Jr., E. (2017). Transforming educational pathways for Chicana/o students. New York: Teachers College Press.

Delgado Bernal, D., Burciaga, R., & Flores Carmona, J. (2012). Chicana/Latina testimonios: Mapping the methodological, pedagogical, and political. *Equity & Excellence in Education*, *45*(3), 363–372.

Dill, B. T., & Kohlman, M. H. (2012). Intersectionality: A transformative paradigm in feminist theory and social justice. *Handbook of Feminist Research: Theory and Praxis*, *2*, 154–174.

Hill Collins, P. (1998). *Fighting words: Black women and the search for justice*. Minneapolis: University of Minnesota Press.

hooks, b. (1994). Teaching to transgress: Education as the practice of freedom. New York: Routledge.

hooks, b. (2000). All about love: New visions. New York: William Morrow.

Ladson-Billings, G. (2006). From the achievement gap to the education debt: Understanding achievement in US schools. *Educational Researcher*, *35*(7), 3–12.

Paperson, l. (2017). *A third university is possible*. University of Minnesota Press.

Pérez Huber, L., Huidor, O., Malagón, M. C., Sánchez, G., & Solórzano, D. G. (2006). *Falling through the cracks: Critical transitions in the Latina/o educational pipeline. 2006 Latina/o Education Summit Report*. CSRC Research Report, No. 7. Los Angeles, CA: UCLA Chicano Studies Research Center (NJ1).

Pérez Huber, L., Malagón, M. C., Ramirez, B. R., Gonzalez, L. C., Jimenez, A., & Vélez, V. N. (2015). Still falling through the cracks: Revisiting the Latina/o education pipeline. CSRC Research Report No. 19. Los Angeles, CA: UCLA Chicano Studies Research Center.

Rodríguez, C. E. (2000). *Changing race: Latinos, the census, and the history of ethnicity in the United States*. New York: NY University Press.

Smith, B. (1978). Toward a Black feminist criticism. *The Radical Teacher*, (7), 20–27.

Smith, L. T. (1999). *Decolonizing methodologies: Research and Indigenous peoples*. London: Zed Books.

Solórzano, D. G., & Vélez, V. N. (2015). Using critical race spatial analysis to examine the Du Boisian color-line along the Alameda Corridor in Southern California. *Whittier Law Review*, *37*, 423.

Stage, F. K. (2007). Answering critical questions using quantitative data. *New Directions for Institutional Research*, *2007*(133), 5–16.

Tuck, E., & Yang, K. W. (2012). Decolonization is not a metaphor. *Decolonization: Indigeneity, Education & Society*, *1*(1).

Vélez, V., & Solórzano, D. G. (2017). Critical race spatial analysis: Conceptualizing GIS as a tool for critical race research in education. In D. Morrison, S. Annamma, & D. Jackson (Eds.), *Critical race spatial analysis: Mapping to understand and address educational inequity* (pp. 8–31). Sterling, VA: Stylus.

Vizenor, G. (Ed.). (2008). *Survivance: Narratives of native presence.* Lincoln, NE: University of Nebraska Press.

Watford, T., Rivas, M. A., Burciaga, R., & Solórzano, D. G. (2006). Latinas and the doctorate: The "status" of attainment and experiences from the margin. In J, Castellanos, A. M. Gloria, & M. Kamimura (Eds.), *The Latina/o pathway to the Ph. D.: Abriendo caminos* (113–133). Sterling, VA: Stylus.

Wolfe, P. (2006). Settler colonialism and the elimination of the Native. *Journal of Genocide Research, 8*(4), 387–409.

Ziliak, S., & McCloskey, D. N. (2008). *The cult of statistical significance: How the standard error costs us jobs, justice, and lives.* Ann Arbor, MI: University of Michigan Press.

Zuberi, T. (2001). *Thicker than blood: How racial statistics lie.* Minneapolis, MN: University of Minnesota Press.

13

CRITICAL RACE CARTOGRAPHIES

Exploring Map-Making as Anti-Racist Praxis

Verónica N. Vélez and Daniel G. Solórzano

Over the course of several years, we have been intrigued about the possibility of *the map* to provide an innovative portrait on the intersection of race and space (Solórzano & Vélez, 2007). We originally created digital maps, using geographic information systems (GIS), to help us understand the geohistorical and geopolitical markers of race and racism in South Los Angeles, specifically along the Alameda Corridor,[1] and their impact on the educational experiences of Students of Color[2] (Solórzano & Vélez, 2016). Our intent was to create a counter-*cartographic* narrative (Knigge & Cope, 2006) that could illuminate the relationship between the social and the spatial and make evident how power intervenes at this intersection to mediate lived experience. The response from students, families, community organizers, and researchers with whom we have shared these maps, have become a driving force for the work highlighted in this chapter, which aims toward further theorizing in the field of education about the relationship between space and race, particularly the role of *the map*, and developing a methodological approach to the study of space and map-making that could rightfully be called an anti-racist practice.

As we pursued our interests, we looked for models that employed GIS map-making in educational research. A few examples emerged that introduced GIS as a visual display of spatially related demographic and statistical data concerning schools (Caughey, 1967; Hogrebe & Tate, 2012; Horng, Renee, Silver, & Goode, 2004; Riles, 1966; Tate, 2008). As an extension of this work, we were particularly interested in how cartographic tools, like GIS, could be utilized to challenge racism and other forms of subordination. We asked ourselves: *What types of education-related questions could GIS help us answer? What would it take to envision GIS as both a conceptual and methodological tool for critical race scholars and educators? Can GIS map-making, given its use in surveillance, be (re)imagined to challenge racism and other forms of subordination?*

Although the use of GIS technologies within education is increasing (Dache-Gerbino, 2017; Rodríguez, Amador, & Tarango, 2016; Tate, Jones, Thorne-Wallington, & Hogrebe, 2012), maps are often viewed as static visual representations of quantitative data, a shortcoming that many critical geographers warn could lead to reinstating the dominant power hierarchies that our work seeks to dismantle. We argue that the construction and use of maps in educational scholarship, particularly in critical *race* scholarship, must treat the technique of map-making as both an epistemological and methodological practice that requires attention to issues of positionality, power, knowledge construction, multiple subjectivities, and the politicized nature of representation. Only by doing so can maps be deployed as a discursive *tool* in the service of anti-racist aims.

This chapter ventures to align GIS map-making with the goals of, and critiques put forth by, critical race theorists in education. We begin with the work of W. E. B. Du Bois to articulate the relationship between space, race, and power. Using CRT as our guide, we journey into geographical developments on race and space and draw on the critiques of feminist geographers, critical cartographers, and indigenous scholars for (re)imaging *the map* in critical race research. By addressing the epistemological premises, critiques, and applications of GIS through the lens of CRT, we offer an approach that utilizes maps critically to spatially analyze the role of race and racism in the historical and contemporary context of schools. We define this approach as *critical race spatial analysis* (CRSA) and provide two case studies of our work to highlight CRSA's potential. Finally, we conclude with possibilities for developing critical race cartographies moving forward.

A Du Boisian Understanding of Space

In 1903, W. E. B. Du Bois reminded his readers that the single greatest problem of the twentieth century would be the problem of the color-line.[3] Perhaps inspired by the article, *The Color Line*, by Frederick Douglass in 1881, Du Bois reflected on the color-line in the opening article in *The Crisis* magazine, which was the voice of the recently formed NAACP (Du Bois, 1910). The scholar and activist observed the growing mountain of evidence surfacing within and beyond the United States, and constructed the following, now famous, question through which the Black experience had come to be defined: "*How does it feel to be a problem?*"

In his seminal work, *The Souls of Black Folk*, Du Bois furthered the notion of the *color-line* as a socio-spatial phenomena:

> Since then a new adjustment of relations in economic and political affairs has grown up . . . which leaves still that frightful chasm as the *color-line* across which men pass at their peril. Thus, then and now, there stand in the South two separate worlds; and separate not simply in the higher realms of social intercourse, but also in church and school, on railway and street-car,

in hotels and theatres, in streets and city sections, in books and newspapers, in asylums and jails, in hospitals and graveyards.

(Du Bois, 1903/1999, p. 66)

Although Du Bois first articulated the concept of the color-line more than 115 years ago, the relevance of his words still bears contemporary significance.[4] He underscored the intimate relationship between race and space in shaping our social landscapes. For Du Bois, the two cannot be disarticulated. In describing Southern communities in the United States during the period he was writing, for example, he describes the intricacies of form and shape the color-line assumes, while noting that its function still serves the same purpose; namely, that of separating, dividing, and shaping the experiences of individuals based on their social "location" to "the line." He writes,

I know some towns where a straight line drawn through the middle of the main street separates nine-tenths of the whites from nine-tenths of the blacks. In other towns the older settlement of whites has been encircled by a broad band of blacks; in still other cases little settlements or nuclei of blacks have sprung up amid surrounding whites.

(Du Bois, 1903/1999, pp. 106–107)

It isn't difficult to imagine how the notion of the color-line could be applied today. Continued segregation in schools and neighborhoods, educational tracking, and gentrification are just a few examples of where the color-line could be appropriately applied to examine our social world at present.

Drawing from Du Bois, we argue that the color-line is key in framing a critical race understanding of space. It exposes the central role of race and racism in the purposeful construction of the physical, perceived, and conceptualized notions of the places[5] that make up our social world. The lens of CRT makes visible the fingerprints of White supremacy in shaping every neighborhood, city center and suburb, school and prison, and their social construction as "safe" or "ghetto," "rich" or "poor." The color-line powerfully defines privilege and opportunity, as well as subordination and marginality, largely determining the distribution of opportunities, material or symbolic, across geographies.

Yet, the color-line cannot just be seen as an oppressive delineation within a CRT framework. It must also be viewed as a space of anti-racist transformation and possibility.[6] While we acknowledge color-lines as boundaries of exclusion, we also acknowledge how they are *resisted* through complex daily cultural practices. People of Color invest daily in efforts to (re)define and (re)claim space. One example is the Ovarian Psycos Bicycle Brigade in Los Angeles (O.V.A.S), a Womxn of Color-led bicycle group that travels across Los Angeles neighborhood to solidify local networks under a credo that believes in "feminist ideals with an *indígena* understanding and an urban/hood mentality."[7] Groups like the O.V.A.S.

remind us that Communities of Color interrupt the function of color-lines, making them porous over time. Thus, while undoubtedly the product of White supremacy, color-lines are also places of anti-racist interventions.

Transdisciplinary Connections in the Study of Space, Race, and Schools

According to Delaney (2002), interest in race, racism, and racialization has grown substantially in the field of geography over the past twenty years. Today, a growing body of scholarship exists that can be referenced about geographical inquiry on the topic (Bonnet, 1997, 2000; Delaney, 2002; Dwyer & Jones, 2000; Jackson, 1998; Kobayashi & Peake, 2000; Neely & Samura, 2011; Peake & Kobayashi, 2002; Price, 2010, 2015; Pulido, 2000; Rose, 1970; Silvern, 1995; Zavella, 2000). Much of this work has emerged from a critical line of transdisciplinary work on spatial theory that includes the well-known work of Lefebvre (1974), Harvey (1990), and Soja (1989, 1996, 2000, 2010). A few broad categories of research in this field include race-based segregation, labor market participation and segmentation of People of Color, and geopolitical inquiry on the spatial effects of the civil rights movement and affirmative action (Peake & Schein, 2000).

Many geographers interested in how ideologies of race, racism, and racial consciousness, or racial formation (Omi & Winant, 1994) constitute space, and vice versa, argue that space can be viewed as a form of "enabling technology" (Delaney, 2002), through which race is produced. This suggests that "race . . . is what it is and does what it does precisely because of how it is given spatial expression" (Delaney, 2002, p. 7). This perspective aligns with a fundamental premise of critical geographical theories that stress how the social and spatial mutually constitute each other, in that social dynamics, such as race, don't simply exist in space but are reinforced and constituted by it (Delaney, 2002).

Scholars in this area are also examining how racial formations are a product of historically specific geographies (Kobayashi & Peake, 2000). These geohistorical accounts illuminate how historical processes of colonialism and labor markets, for example, interact with race-based ideologies to produce the highly textured, power-laden aspects of space. In line with a critical race approach, this work explores how "Whiteness," in particular, is crucial to any study of the relationship between race and space because "to understand the normativity accorded to 'White' landscapes requires reopening a view of past landscapes where the terms of today's normalization were laid down" (Kobayashi & Peake, 2000, p. 400). Acknowledging "White" spaces as racialized spaces unmasks the normative and manipulative power Whiteness has "to mark 'White' as a location of social privileges" (Kobayashi & Peake, 2000, p. 393). The study of race across a range of spaces has led many critical geographers into the field of anthropology, gender studies, legal studies, sociology, labor history, and postcolonial studies (Peake & Schein, 2000).

The transdisciplinary connections that link several modes and fields of study in the quest to understand the socio-spatial dynamics of society offer important insights for investigating the connection between space, race, and *schools*. Schools are undeniably political, economic, cultural, and *racialized* spaces. Consequently, critical race scholars in education could benefit by incorporating the transdisciplinary inquiry laid out above, to study the role of race and racism in shaping spaces *within* schools as well as the spatial relationship *between* schools and their larger contexts. In the remainder of the chapter, we outline our approach—CRSA—that incorporates spatial analysis, specifically GIS map-making, within the broader framework of CRT in education. Before addressing the nuts and bolts of this approach, we first turn to a discussion of the purpose, limitations, and possibilities of *the map*.

GIS Map-Making: A Tool for Critical Race Scholars?

Map-making is one of the most important tools geographers use to study space. In recent history, the construction of maps has been greatly facilitated by the use of computerized technologies known as geographic information systems (GIS). GIS has made it easier to visualize data on a map and conduct certain analyses to reveal patterns and concentrations of spatial phenomena. It does this by constructing maps through layers of information, thereby helping to reveal spatial relationships among different sets of data. According to Elwood and Leitner (2003), "GIS is a computer technology that enables storage, analysis, and mapping of a wide range of geographic information, including demographic, socio-economic, housing, crime, environmental, and land-use data" (p. 140).

Despite its many uses, GIS has been heavily critiqued by feminist geographers, critical cartographers, and indigenous scholars. Summing feminist critiques, Kwan (2002a) states that GIS has been challenged "for its inadequate representation of space and subjectivity, its positivist epistemology, its instrumental rationality, its technique-driven and data-led methods, and its role as surveillance . . . technology deployed by the state" (p. 645). Knigge and Cope (2006) further add that social theorists are concerned with how GIS is "used in ways that rigidify power structures while simultaneously *masking*—through the legitimizing strength of 'science' and gee-whiz displays—the possibility of multiple versions of reality or 'truth,' socially constructed knowledges, and other sources of subjectivity that are inherent in all social research" (p. 2022). Most of these critiques are based in the often exclusive association between GIS and quantitative spatial analysis, and the politics of representation inherent in maps, a concern that stems from the use of early maps whose generalizations of the world drove imperialist and colonial efforts. L. T. Smith (2012), for example, argues that most maps reflect a Western conceptualization of space. She describes how maps were used to define territories, survey land, and mark the boundaries of colonial power in the nineteenth century. The center was typically the "mother country" that oriented the viewer to what was most significant. Outside of the center was typically empty space. Smith argues that the "outside" is important because "it positioned territory and people in an oppositional relation to the colonial centre" (Smith, 2012, p. 55). For indigenous peoples, an existence outside and apart from the colonial power, in empty space, meant non-existence. Over time, maps became artifacts, tools reflecting a particular worldview—only specific European nations were "civilized" enough to maintain control over vast areas of land and their natural resources. Maps, thus, functioned as one piece in a complex puzzle that encouraged and supported the conquest of indigenous land. This was further enforced in school lessons that taught us to use maps as if they are complete, true representations of the world.

This analysis forces us to view maps as inextricably tied to their makers, who become a necessary and critical component of understanding what a map represents and how it is supposed to function. In addition, it reveals that maps are not the static, one-dimensional objects we have been trained to see them as, but rather active artifacts, representing and constructing knowledge as individuals engage with them. According to Crampton and Krygier (2006), "maps are active . . . they exercise power . . . maps sweat, they strain, they apply themselves. The ends achieved with so much effort? The ceaseless reproduction of the culture that brings them into being" (p. 15). Thus, the inherent power of maps lies in their ability to not just represent society, but also in their ability to reproduce it.

Given these critiques, can GIS be employed in critical race educational research? Laying the groundwork for a theoretical and methodological approach that critically utilizes GIS technologies to investigate questions on schools and space, particularly the role of race and racism in shaping these spaces, we offer CRSA. While the implications of this approach extend beyond using GIS as a tool for educational inquiry on space, we focus our attention here on describing how GIS can be used to address spatial inquiries within a critical race framework.

Critical Race Spatial Analysis: Constructing Critical Race Cartographies

Although we have provided a conceptual argument for deepening our spatial consciousness as critical race scholars, we also consider the methodological implications for building critical race cartographies. The goal here is to make explicit the connection between critical race geography and CRT in education and offer an approach for constructing counter-cartographic narratives (Knigge & Cope, 2006).

Toward this end, we provide the following working definition for CRSA[8] in education (Vélez & Solórzano, 2017):

> Critical race spatial analysis (CRSA) is an explanatory framework and methodological approach that accounts for the role of race, racism, and white

supremacy in examining geographic and social spaces and that works toward identifying and challenging racism and white supremacy within these spaces as part of a larger goal of identifying and challenging all forms of subordination. CRSA goes beyond description to spatially examine how structural and institutional factors influence and shape racial dynamics and the power associated with those dynamics over time. Within educational research, CRSA is particularly interested in how structural and institutional factors divide, constrict, and construct space to impact the educational experiences and opportunities available to students based on race.

Drawing from the tenets of CRT in education, employing CRSA in educational research requires:

- foregrounding the color-line, underscoring the relationship between race, racism, memory, and space; its intersection with other forms of subordination; and its material and perceived impact on the daily lives of Students of Color, their families, and their communities;
- challenging race-neutral representations of space by exposing how racism operates to construct space in ways that limit educational opportunity for Students of Color, their families, and communities;
- focusing research, curriculum, practice, and activism on mapping the spatial expression of the lived experiences of Students of Color, their families, and their communities and constructing a socio-spatial narrative that portrays these experiences as sources of strength;
- centering a transformative solution by investing in and reimagining "spatial" research and teaching tools that work for racial justice, and expanding the reach and use of these tools to eliminate subordination in and beyond the academy;
- utilizing the transdisciplinary knowledge base of critical race studies in education (ethnic studies, women's studies, sociology, feminist geography, history, humanities, and the law) as well as visual sociology, critical geography, and radical/tactical cartography to inform praxis; and
- emphasizing maps and map-making as a point of departure for analyzing the socio-spatial relationship between race and space and refusing to allow maps to speak for themselves.

It is important to acknowledge that CRSA, and the GIS technologies it may use, is a *conceptual* and *methodological* approach and not simply an analytical technique. The epistemological and ontological implications of geographical research tools, especially GIS, as many critical geographers have pointed out, require a broader and more nuanced framing of CRSA. Based on this working definition, *how can critical race education scholars use CRSA in their work? How can it be utilized as a transformative, anti-racist practice?* We offer the following case studies as examples.

Case Study #1: The Alameda Corridor

Having grown up in Southern California, particularly near downtown Los Angeles, one of the authors was particularly interested in the Alameda Corridor and the role it played in shaping the experiences of Communities of Color who resided, worked, and went to school in its proximity (Solórzano & Vélez, 2016). We asked, *how has the color-line shaped and been shaped by the social, economic, and educational history along one of Los Angeles's most prominent color-lines—the Alameda Corridor?*

Grounded in this author's lived experience, we constructed a series of maps of Los Angeles County from 1960 to 2010. The goal was to visually show the demographic racial/ethnic population shifts that took place during a fifty-year period. Employing CRSA, we layered demographic information digitally on a map, and then analyzed the data to explore socio-spatial connections with an explicitly race-based lens. As a first step, GIS helped establish the robustness of the Alameda Corridor as a color-line. In 1960 (as today), Los Angeles was one of the most racially and ethnically segregated cities in the United States. Our map of 1960 Los Angeles showed that Black majorities were found in communities of Los Angeles County that ran along the Alameda Corridor, from just south of downtown Los Angeles to the community of Watts. Black communities resided just west of the Corridor, with little to no representation to the east of "the line."

We explored the significance of this demographic reality on schools along the Alameda Corridor during this time. Two of these Los Angeles Unified School District high schools (Jordan and South Gate) were part of a desegregation lawsuit filed in 1963 known as *Crawford v. Los Angeles Board of Education*. The judge in this case ruled that one of the remedies for both the *de jure* and *de facto* segregation was a mandatory busing program for all Los Angeles city schools, which was staunchly opposed by White parents and residents. Fast forward, by 2010, our maps showed that the region, and its schools, had become solidly Latinx/a/o.[9] The Black population continued to move out of South Central Los Angeles and into the communities to the west and south along the Alameda Corridor, such as Inglewood and Lynwood. In this fifty-year period, the vestiges of *de jure* and *de facto* racial segregation in communities east and west of the Alameda Corridor, events such as the 1965 Watts Rebellion, the legal remedy of educational busing to de-segregate Los Angeles schools, and the industrial and manufacturing plant closures from 1970 to 1980 all contributed to precipitate a "White flight" from these and other neighborhoods in Los Angeles (Solórzano & Vélez, 2016).

The evidence provided in the 1960–2010 maps along the Alameda Corridor, together with the demographic, social, political, and educational analyses, are clear examples of how race is both a socially and spatially constructed category used to differentiate and marginalize racial groups. These maps display how the superiority, dominance, and separation of one race over another (i.e. institutional racism and White supremacy) manifests in the form of racially and economically homogenous neighborhoods and becomes structurally facilitated through the creation and maintenance of geographic color-lines (Solórzano & Vélez, 2016).

Case Study #2: Redlining in Southern California

Our second case study was interested in exploring color-lines in Mexican American communities as evidenced through segregated housing patterns (Solórzano & Vélez, 2017). Specifically, we wanted to find out how Mexican American communities became and remained racially segregated and what impact this had for the institutions (i.e. schools, healthcare, and social services) that serve them. We started by examining racially restrictive covenants[10] and redlining.[11]

Our first step was to look for the actual grants deeds that prohibited Mexican Americans from purchasing or leasing property. A facsimile of a November 1949 property grant deed from Oxnard, California shows Mildred Nye's transfer of property to Hurshel Keeter in the city of Oxnard in Ventura County California. The second page of the grant deed states:

> This deed is made and accented subject to the restrictions and conditions as follows: No part of said premises shall ever be occupied (other than in capacity of servant to the occupant) by any person or persons other than of the White or Caucasian race and for the purpose of this paragraph no Japanese, Chinese, Mexican, Hindu, or any other person or persons of the Ethiopian, Indian, or Mongolian races shall be deemed to be Caucasian.

While these racially restrictive covenants were outlawed in the *Shelly v. Kramer* (334 U.S. 1, 1948) U.S. Supreme Court decision in 1948, the justices ruled that state courts could not constitutionally prevent the sale of real property to Blacks, even if that property was covered by a racially restrictive covenant. The Court held that racially restrictive covenants violated no rights. To this day one can go to local county offices where property transactions are recorded and find examples of grant deeds that continue to have the racially restrictive language similar to the language above. Although we had succeeded in finding the grant deeds that targeted Mexican Americans, we realized there were other tools used to keep People of Color and the poor out of more affluent White neighborhoods—redlining.

In 1933, as part of New Deal legislation, the Federal Government created the Home Owners Loan Corporation (HOLC) to assist the refinancing of small home mortgages in foreclosure during and after the Great Depression (see Lipsitz, 2006; Marciano, Goldberg, & Hou, 2011). One of the tools of the HOLC in the late 1930s was the creation of "appraisal maps" or "residential security maps" (Marciano et al., 2011). These color-coded maps in 239 cities across the United States, combined with the Federal Housing Administration's (FHA) strict lending standards, determined which kinds of properties it would approve for mortgages (see Avila, 2006; Lipsitz, 2006; Marciano et al., 2011; Weaver, 1948). In addition to physical quality standards of the properties, the FHA also based its lending decisions on these "residential security maps" which indicated the location, and the racial and ethnic composition of the neighborhood where the property existed (Avila, 2006; Lipsitz, 2006; Weaver, 1948). These color-coded maps used racial criteria to categorize lending and insurance risks and showed the level of security for real estate investments in these 239 U.S. cities. The color-coded designations on the maps were based on descriptive assumptions about the community and not on the ability of various households to satisfy lending criteria. For instance, using these appraisal maps, the HOLC, the FHA, and private lenders granted the vast majority of loans to the predominately White suburbs of Los Angeles and not in the neediest areas of inner-city Los Angeles (Nicolaides, 2002; Weaver, 1948).

To show how this worked, we applied CRSA to examine a 1939 HOLC *Los Angeles and Vicinity Residential Security Map*. This map shows the color-coded classifications that HOLC appraisers developed to differentiate neighborhoods so as to categorize lending and insurance risks. These classifications were determined based in part on the HOLC appraisers' descriptions of the occupation, income and ethnicity of the inhabitants, along with the physical conditions of the neighborhoods and dwellings. A closer look at the *Residential Security Map* shows that in addition to being color-coded, they have alpha-numeric designations attached to these communities. The following descriptions of the color-coded neighborhoods are hierarchical with **"A"** (Green) being the most desirable and **"D"** (Red) being the least desirable (see Crossney & Bartelt, 2005):

- **A (Green):** Best; new; homogenous
- **B (Blue):** Still desirable; area has reached peak
- **C (Yellow):** Definitely declining
- **D (Red):** Hazardous.

Using the *Residential Security Maps* as our guide, we journeyed to communities south and east of downtown Los Angeles. We looked at the neighborhoods that, in 1939, had sizeable and growing Mexican American and Black populations and the least desirable or "red" designation. These *Residential Security Maps* and *Area Descriptions*, which separated neighborhoods primarily by race, paved the way for segregation and discrimination in lending and other resources. We argue that the HOLC *Residential Security Maps* and *Area Descriptions* were blatant examples of institutional racism in U.S. housing and lending (Avila, 2006; Lipsitz, 2006; Marciano et al., 2011; Weaver, 1948). The narratives used by the HOLC appraisers in their *Area Descriptions* to describe Black and Mexican populations in Los Angeles and the San Gabriel Valley reflect framing language that is part of an ideology that creates and maintains the *color-line*. Some examples of that language include "slums," "subversive racial elements," and "peon Mexicans." In addition to segregating neighborhoods, we argue that the *Residential Security Maps* and the language used in the *Area Descriptions* were also used to justify poor conditions in schools and substandard social and commercial services (e.g. health care, supermarkets, and banking) in Communities of Color (Solórzano & Vélez, 2017).

Charting Future Cartographic Possibilities Toward Racial Justice

Citing the practices of critical, feminist, and postcolonial cartographers, Kwan (2002a) argues that GIS can be renegotiated as a discursive tactic to create "countermaps," or what Crampton and Krygier (2006) refer to as "subversive cartographies" that challenge dominant representations of the world. Kwan (2002a) refuses to accept the "technological determinism" of associating GIS with a particular positivist epistemology, asserting that the very subjectivities and agency of GIS users can help illuminate the meaningful aspects of everyday life. Kwan (2002a, 2002b) challenges GIS users to complement their quantitative data with other contextual information and using primary sources from individuals to complement secondary sources that can often overgeneralize communities, such as census data.

Similarly, Knigge and Cope (2006) suggest using *grounded visualization*, an approach that combines grounded theory and GIS visualization, as a way of representing multiple interpretations of the world. Their work honors the concept of "situated knowledges" by acknowledging the positionality of the GIS mapmaker and recognizing the political, social, and historical subjectivity embedded in map-making. Kwan (2002b) also suggests that GIS users need to practice reflexivity when using GIS methods by reflecting on what we want to "produce" through maps; the actual image of the map to examine the possible exclusions, silences, and marginalizing power of our representations; and our target audience as a way of thinking ahead about how our maps may be contested and negotiated. Inspired by these (re)imaginings and critiques of GIS, we are currently developing the concept of *groundtruthing* as a core component of CRSA (Vélez & Solórzano, 2017). Although traditionally used to describe the process whereby GIS technicians verify the satellite imagery of maps "on the ground," we argue that within CRSA, *groundtruthing* relies on the expertise of Communities of Color to determine the accuracy of geographic maps to portray socio-spatial relationships, particularly how race mediates access to a range of resources and opportunities across geographies.

Heeding these insights and innovations, we believe maps and map-making have the potential to illuminate how the spaces that define our lives are not arbitrary, but rather concrete manifestations of the complexity of social life. We believe, as critical race scholars, that GIS can transform how we imagine, understand, and disrupt spatial arrangements as core to our commitment toward racial justice. Beyond research endeavors, GIS can also serve as a pedagogical tool to illuminate how color-lines become erected and lead to residential segregation, limited access to educational and social services, and so forth.

Lastly, with the availability of GIS technologies to a larger audience, it holds great potential for use by non-academicians in constructing *their own* meaningful maps of their environments. The emerging field of public participation geographic information science (PPGIS) is hoping to make GIS more accessible and user friendly to nontraditional audiences (Ghose, 2001; Elwood, 2002a, 2002b). By equipping students, teachers, and local community members with this tool in the critical ways that we have described, we move from observation to active participation *with* local communities to achieve an anti-racist agenda.

Notes

1 The Alameda Corridor is a street that travels from downtown Los Angeles to the Los Angeles harbor. It has been a rail, industrial, and community corridor for well over 100 years.

2 "Students of Color" is intentionally capitalized to reject the standard grammatical norm. Capitalization here represents a grammatical move toward social and racial justice. This rule also applies to "People of Color," "Students of Color," and "Communities of Color" used throughout this chapter.

3 In 1897, W. E. B. Du Bois wrote an article in the *Atlantic Monthly* called "Strivings of the Negro People" in which he first introduced us to early elements that in *The Souls of Black Folk* would help us understand the concept of the color-line—the veil, second-sight, double-consciousness, and twoness (Du Bois 1897, 1995 [1903], p. 45). At the 1900 World's Fair in Paris, France, Du Bois curated a collection of photos and other artifacts in an exhibit called "The American Negro in Paris" (1900, p. 575). One of these artifacts, a social study, was called "The Georgia Negro." In this piece, Du Bois first uses the line, "The problem of the twentieth century is the problem of the color-line" (S. M. Smith, 2004, p. 22).

4 See Wells & Crain, 1997, p. 7; Cooperman, 2014; Vanhemert, 2013. In 1925 Du Bois reaffirmed his views of the color-line: "And thus again in 1925, as in 1899, I seem to see the problem of the Twentieth Century as the Problem of the Color-Line" (Du Bois, 1925, p. 444).

5 For our purposes here, we use "place" and "space" interchangeably but acknowledge their distinct, albeit related, meanings as several scholars have noted and theorized. For example, according to Friedland (1992), "place is the fusion of space and experience, a space filled with meaning, a source of identity" (p. 14). For Patel (2015), "the interactions [that] take place and are experienced by the beings in those places, that is space. Space is contoured, collapsed, made abrasive, and molded through lived experience in specific places . . . places become spaces through interactions, imbued with dynamics of power, and, more often than not, inequity." These definitions underscore the multifaceted dimensions of both "space" and "place." They also highlight very different understandings of the two concepts, which points to both their complexity and the range of interpretations.

6 See bell hooks (1990).

7 For more on O.V.A.S., see https://ovarianpsycos.com.

8 This working definition originally emerged from collaborative work that explores the role of race and racism in shaping the historic, evolving spatial relationship between South Los Angeles high schools near the Alameda Corridor, and their surrounding

communities. Our initial work in CRSA was presented at the 2007 American Education Research Association annual conference in Chicago, IL (Solórzano & Vélez, 2007).

9 We acknowledge that this chapter comes at a time when the label "Latina/o" is being challenged to better reflect intersectional identities, particularly gender fluid and gender non-conforming individuals. We have seen various iterations of the term, including (but not limited to) Latinx and Latinx/a/o. We recognize and applaud these efforts, often engaging in conversations about the meaning of rejecting grammatical norms as we seek social justice. These conversations have also revealed the concern that the evolution of labels can often be taken up uncritically, noting that symbols and rhetoric are often the first to be co-opted in struggles for inclusivity. In the midst of these debates, we recognize the need to re-imagine language to reflect intersectional experiences while making sure we do so in a way that centers those that will be most affected by the change in representative labels. Thus, we have decided to use Latinx/a/o for now as we continue to wrestle with how best to represent the complexity of experiences among Latinxs/as/os in our writing and teaching.

10 A racially restrictive covenant is a clause in a property deed or lease that restricts the sale or lease to particular racial or ethnic groups.

11 Redlining is the practice of denying or limiting financial services to certain neighborhoods based on racial or ethnic composition without regard to the residents' qualifications or creditworthiness. The term "redlining" refers to the practice of using a red line on a map to delineate the area where financial institutions would not lend or invest.

References

Avila, E. (2006). *Popular culture in the age of White flight: Fear and fantasy in suburban Los Angeles.* Berkeley, CA: University of California Press.

Bonnet, A. (1997). Geography, "race," and whiteness: Invisible traditions and current challenges. *Area, 29,* 193–199.

Bonnet, A. (2000). *Antiracism.* New York, NY: Routledge.

Caughey, J. (1967). *Segregation blights our schools.* Los Angeles, CA: Quail Books.

Cooperman, J. (2014). The story of segregation in St. Louis, *St. Louis Mag.* October 17. http://www.stlmag.com/news/the-color-line-race-in-st.-louis.

Crampton, J. W., & Krygier, J. (2006). An introduction to critical cartography. *An International E-Journal for Critical Geographies, 4*(1), 11–33.

Crossney, K. & Bartelt, D. (2005). Residential security, risk, and race: The Home Owners' Loan Corporation and mortgage access in two cities. *Urban Geography, 26,* 707–736.

Dache-Gerbino, A. (2017). Mapping the postcolonial across urban and suburban college access geographies. *Equity & Excellence in Education, 50*(4), 368–386.

Delaney, D. (2002). The space that race makes. *The Professional Geographer, 54*(1), 6–14.

Douglass, F. (1881, June). The color line. *The North American Review, 132*(295), 567–577.

DuBois, W.E.B. (1897). Strivings of the negro people, *Atlantic Monthly* (August). http://www.theatlantic.com/magazine/archive/1897/08/strivings-of-the-negro- people/305446.

Du Bois W. E. B. (1900). The American negro in Paris. *Monthly Review of Reviews, 22*(5), 575–76.

Du Bois, W. E. B. ([1903] 1995). *The souls of Black folk.* New York, NY: Signet.

Du Bois, W. E. B. ([1903] 1999). *The souls of Black folk.* New York, NY: W.W. Norton.

Du Bois, W. E. B. (1910, November). *The Crisis: Record of the Darker Races, 1*(1).

Du Bois, W. E. B. (1925). Worlds of color. *Foreign Affairs, 3*, 423–444.

Dwyer, O., & Jones, J. P. III (2000). White sociospational epistemology. *Social and Cultural Geography, 1*(2), 209–221.

Elwood, S. (2002a). GIS use in community planning: A multidimensional analysis of empowerment. *Environment and Planning A, 34*(5), 905–922.

Elwood, S. (2002b). GIS and collaborative urban governance: Understanding their implication for community action and power. *Urban Geography, 22*(8), 737–759.

Elwood, S., & Leitner, H. (2003). GIS and spatial knowledge production for neighborhood revitalization: Negotiating state priorities and neighborhood visions. *Journal of Urban Affairs, 25*(2), 139–157.

Friedland, R. (1992). Space, place, and modernity: The geographical moment *Contemporary Sociology, 21*(1), 11–15.

Ghose, R. (2001). Use of information technology for community empowerment: Transforming geographic information systems into community information systems. *Transactions in GIS, 5*(2), 141–163.

Harvey, D. (1990). Between space and time: Reflections on the geographical imagination. *Annals of the Association of American Geographers, 80*(3), 418–434.

Hogrebe, M., & Tate, W. F. (2012). Research and geospatial perspective: Toward a visual political project in education, health, and human services. Review of Research in Education, 36, 67–94.

hooks, b. (1990). Homeplace: A site of resistance. In *Yearning: Race, gender, and cultural politics* (pp. 41–49). Boston, MA: South End Press.

Horng, E., Renee, M., Silver, D., & Goode, J. (2004). *The education gap in Los Angeles County*. Los Angeles, CA: The Institute for Democracy, Education, and Access.

Jackson, P. (1998). Constructions of "whiteness" in the geographical imagination. *Area, 30*, 99–106.

Knigge, L., & Cope, M. (2006). Grounded visualization: Integrating the analysis of qualitative and quantitative data through grounded theory and visualization. *Environment and Planning, 38*, 2021–2037.

Kobayashi, A., & Peake, L. (2000). Racism out of place: Thoughts on whiteness and an antiracist geography in the new millennium. *Annals of the Association of American Geographers, 90*(2), 392–403.

Kwan, M. (2002a). Feminist visualization: Re-envisioning GIS as a method in feminist geographic research. *Annals of the Association of American Geographers, 92*(4), 645–661.

Kwan, M. (2002b). Is GIS for women? Reflection on the critical discourse in the 1990s. *Gender, Place and Culture, 9*(3), 271–279.

Lefebvre, H. (1974). The production of space. Oxford, UK: Blackwell.

Lipsitz, G. (2006). *The possessive investment in whiteness: How White people profit from identity politics*. Philadelphia, PA: Temple University Press.

Marciano, R., Goldberg, D., Hou, C.-Y., & McKeon, R. (2011). T-RACES: A testbed for the redlining archives of California's exclusionary spaces. Home Owners Loan Corporation City Survey Files, Area D-53, Los Angeles, 1939.

Neely, B., & Samura, M. (2011). Social geographies of race: Connecting race and space, *Ethnic and Racial Studies, 34*, 1933–1952.

Nicolaides, B. (2002). *My blue heaven: Life and politics in the working-class suburbs of Los Angeles, 1920–1965*. Chicago, IL: University of Chicago Press.

Omi, M., & Winant, H. (1994). *Racial formation in the United States: From the 1960s to the 1990s* (2nd ed.). New York, NY: Routledge.

Patel, L. (2015, July 17). Places become space: Structural oppression in situ. [Web log comment.] *Decolonizing Educational Research.* https://decolonizing.wordpress. com/2015/07/17/place-becomes-space-structural-oppression-in-situ.

Peake, L., & Kobayashi, A. (2002). Policies and practices for an antiracist geography at the millennium. *The Professional Geographer, 54*(1), 50–61.

Peake, L., & Schein, R. H. (2000). Racing geography into the new millennium: Studies of "race" and North American geographies. *Social and Cultural Geography, 1*(2), 133–142.

Price, P. L. (2010). At the crossroads: Critical race theory and critical geographies of race. *Progress in Human Geography, 34*(2), 147–174.

Price, P. L. (2015). Race and ethnicity III: Geographies of diversity. *Progress in Human Geography, 39*(4), 497–506.

Pulido, L. (2000). Rethinking environmental racism: White privilege and urban development in Southern California. *Annals of the Association of American Geographers, 90*, 12–40.

Riles, W. (1966). *Racial and ethnic survey of California public schools.* Sacramento, California. California Office of Compensatory Education, Bureau of Intergroup Relations, 5–14.

Rodríguez, C., Amador, A., Tarango, B. (2016). Mapping educational equity and reform policy in the borderlands: Latcrit spatial analysis of grade retention. *Equity & Excellence in Education, 49*(2), 228–240.

Rose, H. M. (1970). The development of an urban subsystem: The case of the Negro ghetto. *Annals of the Association of American Geographers, 60*(1), 1–17.

Silvern, S. (1995). Nature, territory, and identity in the Wisconsin treaty rights controversy. *Ecumene, 2*, 267–292.

Smith, L. T. (2012). *Decolonizing methodologies: Research and indigenous peoples.* London: Zed Books.

Smith, S. M. (2004). *Photography on the color line: W. E. B. Du Bois, race, and visual culture.* Durham, NC: Duke University Press.

Soja, E. W. (1989). *Postmodern geographies.* London, UK: Verso.

Soja, E. W. (1996). *Thirdspace: Journeys to Los Angeles and other real and imagined places.* Cambridge, MA: Blackwell.

Soja, E. W. (2000). *Postmetropolis: Critical studies of cities and regions.* Cambridge, MA: Blackwell.

Soja, E. W. (2010). *Seeking spatial justice.* Minneapolis, MN: University of Minnesota Press.

Solórzano, D., & Vélez, V. (2007). *Critical race spatial analysis along the Alameda Corridor in Los Angeles.* Presented to the American Education Research Association Conference, Chicago, IL.

Solórzano, D. & Vélez, V. (2016). Using critical race spatial analysis to examine the Du Boisian color-line along the Alameda Corridor in Southern California. *Whittier Law Review, 27*, 423–437.

Solórzano, D. & Vélez, V. (2017). Using critical race spatial analysis to examine Redlining in Southern California Communities of Color—*circa* 1939. In D. Morrison, S. Annamma, & D. Jackson (Eds.), *The spatial search to understand and address educational inequity to inform praxis* (pp. 91–108). Sterling, VA: Stylus.

Tate, W., Jones, B., Thorne-Wallington, E., Hogrebe, M. (2012). Science and the city: Thinking geospatially about opportunity to learn. *Urban Education, 47*(2), 399–433.

Tate, W. (2008). "Geography of opportunity": Poverty, place, and educational outcomes. *Educational Researcher, 37*(7), 397–411.

Vanhemert, K. (2013). The best map ever made of America's racial segregation, *Wired*, August 26. http://www.wired.com/2013/08/how-segregated-is-your-city-this-eye-opening-map-shows-you.

Vélez, V. & Solórzano, D. (2017). Critical race spatial analysis: Conceptualizing GIS as a tool for critical race research in education. In D. Morrison, S. Annamma, & D. Jackson, *The spatial search to understand and address educational inequity to inform praxis* (pp. 8–31). Sterling, VA: Stylus.

Wells, A. S., & Crain, R. L. (1997). *Stepping over the color line: African-American students in white suburban schools*. New Haven, CT: Yale University Press.

Weaver, R. (1948). *The Negro Ghetto*. New York, NY: Harcourt, Brace & Company.

Zavella, P. (2000). Latinos in the USA: Changing socioeconomic patterns. *Social and Cultural Geography, 1*(2), 155–167.

14

CRITICAL RACE MIXED METHODOLOGY

Designing a Research Study Combining Critical Race Theory and Mixed Methods Research

Jessica T. DeCuir-Gunby and Paul A. Schutz

The use of mixed methods research has seen considerable growth in education (DeCuir-Gunby & Schutz, 2017; Johnson & Onwuegbuzie, 2004). In addition, as racism-related issues continue to increase and are more recognized in schools and other contexts, Critical Race Theory (CRT) has become frequently utilized as a means of understanding issues of racial inequity (Dixson & Rousseau, 2005; Howard & Navarro, 2016; McCoy & Rodricks, 2015). Because both mixed methods and CRT have gained popularity in education research, their combination is ripe for development. As such, the purpose of this chapter is to discuss how to design a research study that combines CRT and mixed methods research. As an illustration, we propose a research study[1] on African American women college students' experiences with racial microaggressions, also known as subtle racial insults that can intentionally or unintentionally denigrate People of Color (Sue, Capodilupo, Torino, Bucceri, Holder, Nadal, & Esquilin, 2007). We use CRT to help frame the explanatory sequential mixed methods design (QUANT → qual), including the creation of an example that includes potential research questions, instrumentation, data collection, and data analysis. In the chapter, we explain Critical Race Mixed Methodology (CRMM), our approach to combining CRT and mixed methods research, as well as the steps to take in maintaining the fidelity of the mixed methods design/analysis process while adhering to a critical race theory framework.

Critical Race Mixed Methods Theoretical Framework: Towards a Critical Race Mixed Methodology

Mixed methods can be described as a research that combines both quantitative (e.g., survey data with statistical analysis) and qualitative approaches (e.g., interview data with narrative analysis). More specifically, we see mixed methods as involving "research in which the investigator collects and analyzes data, integrates the findings, and draws inferences using both qualitative and quantitative approaches or methods in a single study or program of inquiry" (Tashakkori & Creswell, 2007, p. 4). In addition, we look at mixed methods inquiry from a Pragmatic perspective and advocate the use a variety of approaches and research methods to solve problems (DeCuir-Gunby & Schutz, 2017; Schutz, Chambless, & DeCuir, 2004). In order to explicate our approach to CRMM, it is important begin with our inquiry world-views.

Inquiry World-View: Subjectivity

We use the term "inquiry world-view" to describe our current beliefs and assumptions about the nature and purpose of inquiry. Our approach to inquiry has emerged through examining both our ontological (i.e., what is the nature of reality?) and epistemological (i.e., what is the nature of knowledge and knowing?) assumptions about the world. We see this self-examination as essential in that one's inquiry world-view overtly or covertly informs every aspect of a research study (DeCuir-Gunby & Schutz, 2017; Schutz, Chambless, & DeCuir, 2004). Elsewhere we have elaborated more fully on our inquiry world-views (see DeCuir-Gunby & Schutz, 2017; Schutz, Chambless, & DeCuir, 2004): here we summarize those beliefs and provide a brief discussion of our subjectivities.

In terms of the nature of reality, we acknowledge external realities; however, the boundaries between, for example, our internal conceptions of ourselves as a student, and the external realities of interacting as a student within a particular university vary based on social constructions and reconstructions. Who we are is not independent of our communities and collective histories. Thus, for example, the identities of minoritized people may include identity self-statements with internal boundaries that include their family, gender, and/or their race.

Our views on the nature of the knower and knowledge currently include a Universalist perspective (Zusho & Clayton, 2011). As such, we tend to think that there are probably some basic "truths" that tend to be influenced by particular social-historical contexts. For example, we see humans as social animals and have a Need for Relatedness or to feel an attachment with meaningful others (e.g., believing that you belong to the university you are attending) (Deci & Ryan, 2000). Yet that need is influenced by personal and social-historical contextual factors which include the impact of race and gender.

As researchers, we believe it is important to acknowledge our multiple identities and the impact they can have on the research process. *Jessica* is an African American woman who has always lived and worked in the Southern US. She has personal experiences with both attending and working at predominate White institutions (PWIs). *Paul*, on the other hand, is an aging White heterosexual male who has lived and worked in various regions in the US, including the south and

Texas. Our respective experiences undoubtedly shape our approach to research design as well as any interpretations that would potentially be made from conducting such a study.

Inquiry World-View: Critical Race Theory

In embracing a Pragmatic inquiry world-view (DeCuir-Gunby & Schutz, 2014; Dewey, 1910; James, 1907) we focus on the use of research methods to solve problems. In order to address issues of race and racism we are also informed by four assumptions from CRT: (1) race is a social construction (Bell, 1992, 1993; DeCuir-Gunby & Schutz, 2014; Ladson-Billings, 2013; Omi & Winant, 1994, 2014); (2) racism is normal and ordinary (Delgado & Stefancic, 2012; Ladson-Billings, 2013; Pérez Huber & Solórzano, 2015; Solórzano, Ceja, & Yosso, 2000); (3) race intersects with other identities (Crenshaw, 1989); and (4) counterstorytelling can be used to challenge dominant discourses (Delgado, 1989; Ladson-Billings, 2013; Solórzano, Ceja, & Yosso, 2000).

In terms of *race as a social construction*, there is evidence from a variety of disciplines (e.g., biologists, geneticists, psychologists) that race is not biologically based but rather socially constructed (Bell, 1992, 1993; DeCuir-Gunby & Schutz, 2014; Ladson-Billings, 2013; Lehrman, 2003; Ossorio & Duster, 2005; Smedley & Smedley, 2005). However, once constructed, race as a social construct normalizes the sorting of people throughout US society. Because of this implicit/explicit hierarchy which privileges some and not others, racial microaggressions become *normal and ordinary* in higher educational contexts (DeCuir-Gunby & Schutz, 2017; Pérez Huber & Solórzano, 2015; Solórzano, Ceja, & Yosso, 2000). In addition, race *intersects with other identities* (Crenshaw, 1989). Identity is important in terms of understanding intersectionality, which tends to exacerbate the experiences of Women of Color with racial microaggressions in that racial experiences are gendered. Therefore, our intent is to use the CRMM to tell the *counterstories* of successful African American women college students' transactions with microaggressions. Counterstorytelling is a way of allowing marginalized groups to challenge dominant narratives through the telling of their experiences through stories (Delgado, 1989; Solórzano & Yosso, 2002). As such, the CRT theoretical framework shapes our approach to all components of the mixed methods research study (i.e., research purpose, research questions, data collection, and data analysis) and the use of mixed methods facilitates our central goal of understanding the manifestation of race and racism for African American women college students.

CRT and Mixed Methods

In our effort to integrate CRT with mixed methods, to form CRMM, we acknowledge that traditionally mixed methods research has been a quantitative-dominant approach (Giddings, 2006); however, more recently, mixed methods research has been growing to include more qualitative-dominant work (Hesse-Biber, 2010). In addition, some mixed methods researchers take a transformative stance to address social justice and challenge oppression (Mertens, 2007). Conversely, CRT research has been dominated by qualitative approaches and is beginning to expand to both quantitative and mixed methods approaches (Covarrubias, 2011; Covarrubias & Vélez, 2013; Teranishi, 2007). However, CRT research using quantitative and especially mixed methods approaches are limited (Covarrubias, Nava, Lara, Burciaga, Vélez, & Solórzano, 2018; DeCuir-Gunby & Walker-DeVose, 2013; Garcia & Mayorga, 2017; McCoy & Rodricks, 2015). Because we are combining mixed methods and critical race theory, two approaches that are rooted in somewhat different paradigms (quantitative and qualitative), we use a definition that incorporates key elements of both: "Mixed methods inquiry, influenced by one's theoretical perspective, involves the collecting and analyzing of both quantitative and qualitative data within one study and, when applicable, is used to address issues of power" (Schutz, DeCuir-Gunby, & Williams-Johnson, pp. 224). We suggest this approach to CRMM inquiry will be useful in the exploration of issues of race and racism.

Combining Critical Race Theory and Mixed Methods: A Critical Race Mixed Methodology Example

For our example study, we describe an explanatory sequential mixed methods design (quan→QUAL). This design involves first collecting quantitative data and then using the findings to inform the selection of participants and the collection of the qualitative data (See Figure 14.1). The process is recursive in that the findings from the qualitative data will then be compared to the findings from the quantitative data, a key component of mixed methods research (Creswell & Plano Clark, 2018). The explanatory sequential design can be either quantitative or qualitative dominant (Hesse-Biber, 2010). In this case, because the counterstories of African American women college students are the focus of the study, the qualitative component is the dominant component (DeCuir-Gunby & Walker-DeVose, 2013).[2]

Research Questions

Research questions are guided by one's inquiry world-view, the research literature, and one's experiences (DeCuir-Gunby & Schutz, 2017). Crafting good research questions is essential to any research study because research questions help to dictate a study's research methods. Research questions allow researchers to focus on specific issues and constructs. In a CRMM study, the research questions focus directly on aspects of race, racism, and/or power. For phase one of the explanatory mixed methods design, the quantitative phase, we propose

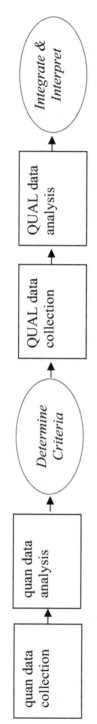

quan data collection

Procedures:
- Recruit participants (n = 225–250)
- Likert-format surveys (online)

Products:
- Racial Microaggressions Scale scores
- Need for relatedness scale scores
- Demographics

quan data analysis

Procedures:
- Descriptives
- Correlation Analysis
- Cluster Analysis Factor Analysis

Products:
- Cronbach's alpha
- Factor loadings
- Correlations

Determine Criteria

Procedures:
- Consider interesting findings
- Create profiles participant selection

Products:
- List of demographic criteria for participant selection
- Interview protocol

QUAL data collection

Procedures:
- Recruit Black women college students (n = 20–25)
- Conduct Interviews

Products:
- Transcripts

QUAL data analysis

Procedures:
- Critical Events Analysis
- Inter-rater reliability
- Member checking

Products:
- Coded transcripts
- Qualitative Data Base (Atlas.ti)
- Counterstories

Integrate & Interpret

Procedures:
- Compare Quan & Qual data (CRT)
- Integrate Quan & Qual data (CRT)

Products:
- Summary of Quan Data
- Summary of Qual Data
- Comparison of Quan & Qual Data

FIGURE 14.1 Explanatory Sequential Mixed Methods Diagram

the following research questions: *What are African American women college students' experiences with racial microaggressions at predominately White institutions?* In this question, we explicitly focus on African American women's racialized and gendered experiences. Specifically, we focus on their experiencing of racial microaggressions within the context of predominately White college institutions (i.e., race is a social construction and racism is normal and ordinary). Second, *Do African American women college students' at predominately White institutions report a sense of relatedness to their university?* The Need for Relatedness construct is important in that we are interested in African American women college students' level of felt connectedness or relatedness to their particular school. Developing a sense of belonging to ones' school is key to success and degree competition at the university one attends (Deci & Ryan, 2000; Glass & Westmont, 2014; Osterman, 2000; Won, Wolters, & Mueller, 2017)

The second phase of the study, the qualitative phase, focuses on the following research question: *How do African American women college students who score high on a scale of Need for Relatedness experience racial microaggressions at predominately White institutions?* Basically, we want to understand how some African American women college students feel a sense of belonging or relatedness to their school despite the racial microaggressions they experience. In this question, we examine how racial microaggressions impact the college experiences and sense of belonging of African American women in their college contexts (i.e., race is a social construction, racism is normal and ordinary, intersectionality, and counterstory-telling can be used to challenge dominant discourses).

Instrumentation

Researchers need to select instruments that most appropriately address their research questions. For a critical race mixed methods study, the instruments used should center around issues of race and racism. For the proposed study, selected instruments address African American women college students' experiences with race, racism, and Need for Relatedness to their particular university. As such, we will be including both race-focused constructs (e.g., Microaggressions) which centers around issues of race and are developed from racial categorizations and racial categorization theories (Helms, Jernigan, & Mascher, 2005), and race-reimaged constructs (e.g., Need for Relatedness) that are reconceptualized to include racially influenced, sociocultural perspectives (DeCuir-Gunby & Schutz, 2014).

As such, for the quantitative component (research question one and two), participants would answer a demographics questionnaire, the Racial and Ethnic Microaggressions Scale (Nadal, 2011), and the Need for Relatedness scale (Deci & Ryan, 2000). The demographics questionnaire would feature questions that focus on participants' personal characteristics including age, classification, major, as well as other important demographic issues. The Racial and Ethnic Microaggressions Scale (REMS) (Nadal, 2011) is a survey that attempts to capture People of Color's experiencing of racial microaggressions in a variety of contexts. The REMS has six subscales: (a) Assumptions of Inferiority, (b) Second-Class Citizen and Assumptions of Criminality, (c) Microinvalidations, (d) Exoticization/Assumptions of Similarity, (e) Environmental Microaggressions, and (f) Workplace and School Microaggressions. For this example, we would focus on three subscales: Assumptions of Inferiority (Sample item: Someone assumed that I would not be educated because of my race), microinvalidations (Sample item: Someone told me that they do not see race), and exoticization/assumptions of similarity (Sample item: Someone told me that all people in my racial group look alike).

In addition, we would also use the Basic Psychological Needs at College Scale (adapted from Deci, Ryan, Gagné, Leone, Usunov, & Kornazheva, 2001). This scale attempts to capture students' basic needs for Autonomy (i.e., being in control of ones' action), Competency (i.e., beliefs about being a successful student), and relatedness at College (i.e., feeling attached to meaningful others). In this example, we focus on the Need for Relatedness (Sample item: I feel that the people I care about at college also care about me.).

The qualitative component (research question three) would utilize a semi-structured interview schedule, featuring a series of open-ended questions (Merriam & Tisdell, 2015). The open-ended questions would allow participants to share their stories regarding their experiences with racial microaggressions on campus. Sample interview questions could include: "Tell me about a time where you where you thought that an instructor made assumptions about your race." We would focus on how those experiences ultimately impact participants' feelings of belonging on campus, helping to create their counterstories. Again, the counterstories are the central focus on the research design and considerable emphasis would be placed upon data collection and data reporting component.

Context

Since our proposed study focuses on African American women college students' experiences at PWIs, it is necessary for us to define PWIs. We consider PWIs as universities that historically practiced the exclusion of People of Color and are currently 50 percent or more White (Brown & Dancy, 2010). In our study, we propose focusing on both public and private, four-year PWIs throughout the US because African American women are underrepresented at PWIs.

Participants

It is important to recruit a wide range of participants to capture a variety of experiences with racial microaggressions. As such, African American women enrolled in undergraduate programs throughout the US would be recruited to complete an online survey. We would target 225–250 participants. This range is needed to engage in specific statistical analyses (Williams, Brown, & Onsman, 2010.). In recruiting our sample, we would take care to recruit students with a variety of experiences (e.g., age, major, school type, etc.). This would enable us to better understand the wide range of experiences with racial microaggressions. Once the quantitative data has been collected and analyzed, 20–25 women would be selected to participate in the qualitative portion. Participation in the qualitative portion of the study will be based upon responses on the quantitative portion and will allow us to tell their stories related to racial microaggressions. In other words, in this example, we would be looking for African American women college students who were aware of and have experienced microaggressions as well as scored high on a measure of Need for Relatedness to their particular PWI.

Procedures

The explanatory mixed methods design requires that the data be collected in two distinct phases. In the first phase, the quantitative phase, participants would be given an online survey (demographics questionnaire, the REMS, Need for Relatedness survey). The second phase of the study, the qualitative phase, could not begin until after analyzing the quantitative data. The findings of the quantitative data would indicate which participants should be chosen for the qualitative component. We would focus on 20–25 participants chosen from identity profiles created by participants' scores on the subscales of the REMS (assumptions of inferiority, microinvalidations, exoticization/assumptions of similarity) and Need for Relatedness. This would give us a range of experiences with racial microaggressions. In addition, this would allow us to better compare the findings from the quantitative and qualitative data in that the counterstories are detailed illustrations of the identity profiles. All interviews would be audio-recorded and conducted in-person or by using video conferencing software, featuring the semi-structured interview schedules. Follow-up interviews would be conducted if needed to more thoroughly explore issues and ideas discussed in the initial interviews.

Data Analysis

Data analysis for explanatory mixed methods designs generally occurs in two distinct stages. For the first stage, after the data has been cleaned and inspected for completeness, we would engage in a variety of statistical analyses including descriptive statistics (means, standard deviations, etc.) and confirmatory factor analysis. Using the REMS (assumptions of inferiority, microinvalidations, exoticization/assumptions of similarity) and the Need for Relatedness scale, we would engage in cluster analyses to create identity profiles of the women participants (e.g., low REMS/low relatedness; high REMS/high relatedness, etc.). Cluster analysis would be used because it allows for the systematic selection (creation) of groups of students who are similar on the basis of statistical variance on the various measures used in the study (see Aldenderfer & Blashfield, 1984; Milligan & Cooper, 1987). ANOVAs would then be used to examine differences between the identity profile groups. For example, via cluster analysis we may uncover a group of students, as discussed earlier, who feel a sense of belonging or relatedness to their school and are successful despite the racial microaggressions they experience (e.g., high REMS/high relatedness).

The second stage, the qualitative component, would focus on analyzing the interviews of the women from the various identity profiles. All interviews would be transcribed verbatim and coded using both a priori and emergent codes (Corbin & Strauss, 2015). We would use critical event/incident narrative analysis (Webster & Mertova, 2007) to help tell each participant's counterstory. This will allow us to focus on the significant critical racial events (microaggressions) that occurred on campus and impacted the participants' feelings of belonging. In exploring the common themes of all the counterstories, we will use the analysis of narratives approach (see Polkinghorne, 1995).

Data Integration

An essential component of mixed methods research is data integration, or the actual combining of both the quantitative and qualitative findings. In an explanatory sequential design, the quantitative and qualitative results are discussed separately with the qualitative data being used to expand, corroborate, or even contradict the quantitative data (Creswell, 2015; Fetters, Curry, & Creswell, 2013). For the example study, the counterstories are the focus of the study and would be used to elaborate the minimal findings provided by the quantitative data (e.g., using the counterstories to illustrate the initial identity profiles created by the quantitative profile data).

Role of the Inquiry World-Views

The inquiry world-view, including the theoretical framework, is essential to helping shape any study, and this is the case for a CRMM study. As previously stated, for a mixed methods study to be considered a CRMM study, CRT will need to be intertwined within all aspects of the study. In our example study, aspects of race are included in the development of the research questions (e.g., focusing on African American women college students' experiences with racial microaggressions and the Need for Relatedness) as well as the data collection for the quantitative data (e.g., using an instrument designed to examine experiences with various types of racial microaggressions) and the qualitative data (e.g., collecting interviews from African American women college students, focusing on their experiences with racial microaggressions and the impact on their feelings of belonging). CRT especially plays an important role in data analyses including using the quantitative data to create identity profiles based upon participants' experiences with racial microaggressions and then choosing participants according to identity profiles to collect counterstories that focus on their intersecting identities and experiences with race and racism. CRT would also play in important role when the data is written up by focusing on various tenets of CRT that are relevant to the experiences of African American women, particularly intersectionality. In addition, as researchers, our aforementioned personal experiences as well as beliefs are also integral in shaping all aspects of the research process, particularly the interpretation of the results and the providing of implications that support and/or challenge current research findings.

Validity and Reliability in Mixed Methods Research

In mixed method research, it is important to address issues of validity, reliability, trustworthiness and credibility. Validity addresses how well a construct is being measured/assessed while reliability addresses the consistency in which a construct is measured/assessed. For constructing validity, we would engage in exploratory/confirmatory factor analysis to explore the underlying structure of the various surveys used (Benson, 1998). To address reliability, we will calculate internal consistency (Cronbach's Alpha) using those same surveys. Trustworthiness, on the other hand, involves ensuring the theoretical framework generated is based on the data from the study while credibility is the extent to which one can believe in the research findings. To establish trustworthiness, we would engage in member checking, provide thick and rich descriptions, and utilize negative/deviant cases (Suri, 2011). To establish credibility for the qualitative data, we will develop a codebook, use peer reviewers, and calculate interrater agreement (Hruschka, Schwartz, St. John, Picone-Decaro, Jenkins, & Carey, 2004). We would also embrace Dellinger and Leech's (2007) unified validation framework model for mixed method research that suggests addressing a utilization/historical element that explores how well and accurately the research is implemented, focusing on issues of cultural congruence or aspects of multicultural validity (Kirkhart, 2010). We would also address Dellinger and Leech's (2007) consequential element by focusing on the potential impact that participating in our study could have on our participants, particularly their interactions within their respective PWIs and their future experiences with racial microaggressions.

Implications for Implementing Critical Race Mixed Methodology

As CRT research in education continues to increase, it is important to expand the methodologies that are used to engage in this research. Most CRT research uses qualitative approaches, yet the use of quantitative research approaches is on the rise. Likewise, mixed methods research approaches are increasing in education research. As such, CRMM has the potential to further both the fields of CRT and mixed methods research. This chapter is an attempt to provide a needed beginning framework for CRMM.

In this chapter, we describe a CRMM perspective and provide a discussion on how to design such research through illustrating a research example that uses an explanatory sequential mixed methods design (quan→QUAL). Our perspective on CRMM has developed out of merging a critical race view of the intersections of race, racism, and/or power with a pragmatic problem-solving view of research methods. In other words, there are many challenging problems related to issues of race, racism, and/or power. As such, it is important to utilize the most appropriate research methods and methodologies available to help understand how to solve challenging problems related to issues of race, racism, and/or power.

With that in mind, when implementing CRMM it is essential that researchers using this perspective adhere to the following three suggestions. First, Critical Race Theory should play integral roles in all phases of the study. This means that elements of race, racism, and/or power are explicitly necessary within research questions, instrumentation, data collection (e.g., context selection, participant selection, etc.), and data analysis (e.g., counterstorytelling and cluster analysis). This includes establishing validity/trustworthiness and reliability/credibility. Second, it is necessary to adhere to all the regulations/procedures pertaining to specific mixed methods research designs. Like qualitative and quantitative research methods, mixed methods researchers have developed specific guidelines that should be adhered to when possible (see Creswell & Plano Clark, 2018; DeCuir-Gunby, & Schutz, 2017). Third, in mixed methods research, the data integration portion (combining the quantitative and qualitative data) is one of the most important, if not the most important, elements of the study. Likewise, in CRMM, data integration is essential. However, it is important that data integration not only focuses on the study's general findings but serves to support the broader CRT framework.

Notes

1 The research study presented in this chapter is a derivation of the study presented in DeCuir-Gunby & Schutz (2017).
2 There are other mixed methods designs besides the explanatory sequential design; for more information on those designs see Creswell and Plano Clark, (2018), or DeCuir-Gunby and Schutz (2017).

References

Aldenderfer, M. S., & Blashfield, R. K. (1984). *Cluster analysis.* Thousand Oaks, CA: Sage.
Bell, D. (1993). *Faces at the bottom of the well: The permanence of racism.* NY: Basic Books.
Bell, D. (1992). Racial realism. *Connecticut Law Review, 24*(2), 363–379.

Benson, J. (1998). Developing a strong program of construct validation: A test anxiety example. *Educational Measurement: Issues and Practice, 17*(1), 10–17.

Brown II, M.C., & Dancy II, T. E. (2010). Predominantly White institutions. In K. Lomotey (Ed.), *Encyclopedia of African American education* (pp. 524–527). Thousand Oaks, CA: Sage. doi: http://dx.doi.org/10.4135/9781412971966.n193.

Corbin, J. M., & Strauss, A. L. (2015). *Basics of qualitative research: Techniques and procedures for developing grounded theory* (4th ed.). Thousand Oaks, CA: Sage.

Covarrubias, A. (2011). Quantitative intersectionality: A critical race analysis of the Chicana/o educational pipeline. *Journal of Latinos and Education, 10*(2), 86–105.

Covarrubias, A., & Vélez, V. (2013). Critical race quantitative intersectionality: An anti-racist research paradigm that refuses to "let the numbers speak for themselves." In M. Lynn & A. D. Dixson (Eds.), *Handbook of critical race theory in education* (pp. 270–285). NY: Routledge.

Covarrubias, A., Nava, P. E., Lara, A., Burciaga, R., Vélez, V. N., & Solórzano, D. G. (2018).

Critical race quantitative intersections: A testimonio analysis. *Race Ethnicity and Education, 21*(2), 253–273.

Crenshaw, K. (1989). Demarginalizing the intersection of race and sex: A Black feminist critique of antidiscrimination doctrine, feminist theory and antiracist politics. *University of Chicago Legal Forum, 1*(8), 139–167.

Creswell, J. W. (2015). A concise introduction to mixed methods research. Thousand Oaks, CA: Sage.

Creswell, J., & Plano Clark, V. (2018 [2011]). *Designing and conducting mixed methods research* (3rd ed.). Thousand Oaks, CA: Sage.

Deci, E. L., & Ryan, R. M. (2000). The "what" and "why" of goal pursuits: Human needs and the self-determination of behavior. *Psychological Inquiry, 11*(4), 227–268.

Deci, E. L., Ryan, R. M., Gagné, M., Leone, D. R., Usunov, J., & Kornazheva, B. P. (2001). Need satisfaction, motivation, and well-being in the work organizations of a former eastern bloc country: A cross-cultural study of self-determination. *Personality and Social Psychology Bulletin, 27*(8), 930–942.

DeCuir-Gunby, J. T. & Schutz, P. A. (2017). *Developing a mixed methods proposal: A practical guide for beginning researchers.* Thousand Oaks, CA: Sage.

DeCuir-Gunby, J. T. & Schutz, P. A. (2014). *Researching race within educational psychology contexts. Educational Psychologist, 49*(4), 244–260.

DeCuir-Gunby, J. T. & Walker-DeVose, D. C. (2013). Expanding the counterstory: The potential for Critical Race Mixed Methods studies in education. In M. Lynn & A.D. Dixson (Eds.), *Handbook of critical race theory in education* (pp. 248–259). New York: Routledge.

Delgado, R. (1989). Storytelling for oppositionists and others: A plea for narrative. *Michigan Law Review, 87*, 2411–2441.

Delgado, R. & Stefancic, J. (2012). *Critical race theory: An introduction* (2nd ed.). New York: New York University Press.

Dellinger, A. B., & Leech, N. L. (2007). Towards a unified validation framework in mixed methods research. *Journal of Mixed Methods Research, 1*(4), 309–332.

Dewey, J. (1910). *How we think.* Lexington, MA: D.C. Heath.

Dixson, A. D., & Rousseau, C. K. (2005). And we are still not saved: Critical race theory in education ten years later. *Race Ethnicity and Education, 8*(1), 7–27.

Fetters, M. D., Curry, L. A., & Creswell, J. W. (2013). Achieving integration in mixed methods designs: Principals and practices. *Health Services Research, 48*(6), 2134–2156.

Garcia, N. M., & Mayorga, O. J. (2018). The threat of unexamined secondary data: A critical race transformative convergent mixed methods. *Race Ethnicity and Education, 21*(2), 231–252.

Giddings, L. S. (2006). Mixed-methods research: Positivism dressed in drag? *Journal of Research in Nursing, 11*(3), 195–203.

Glass, C. R., & Westmont, C. M. (2014). Comparative effects of belongingness on the academic success and cross-cultural interactions of domestic and international students. *International Journal of Intercultural Relations, 38*, 106–119.

Helms, J. E., Jernigan, M., & Mascher, J. (2005). The meaning of race in psychology and how to change it: A methodological perspective. *American Psychologist, 60*(1), 27.

Hesse-Biber, S. (2010). Qualitative approaches to mixed methods practice. *Qualitative Inquiry, 16*(6), 455–468.

Howard, T. C., & Navarro, O. (2016). Critical race theory 20 years later: Where do we go from here? *Urban Education, 51*(3), 253–273.

Hruschka, D. J., Schwartz, D., St. John, D. C., Picone-Decaro, E., Jenkins, R. A., & Carey, J. W. (2004). Reliability in coding open-ended data: Lessons learned from coding HIV behavioral research. *Field Methods, 16*(3), 307–331.

Kirkhart, K. E. (2010). Eyes on the prize: Multicultural validity and evaluation theory. *American Journal of Evaluation, 31*(3), 400–413.

James, W. (1907). *Pragmatism: A new name for some old ways of thinking.* New York: Longmans, Green, and Company.

Johnson, R. B., & Onwuegbuzie, A. J. (2004). Mixed methods research: A research paradigm whose time has come. *Educational researcher, 33*(7), 14–26.

Ladson-Billings, G. (2013). Critical race theory: What it is not! In M. Lynn, & A. D. Dixson, (Eds.), *Handbook of critical race theory in education* (pp. 34–47). New York: Routledge.

Lehrman, S. (2003). The reality of race. *Scientific American*, (288), 32.

McCoy, D. L., & Rodricks, D. J. (2015). Critical race theory in higher education: 20 years of theoretical and research innovations. *ASHE Higher Education Report, 41*(3), 1–117.

Merriam, S. B., & Tisdell, E. J. (2015). *Qualitative research: A guide to design and implementation.* Hoboken, NJ: John Wiley & Sons.

Mertens, D. M. (2007). Transformative paradigm mixed methods and social justice. *Journal of Mixed Methods Research, 1*(3), 212–225.

Milligan, G. W., & Cooper, M. C. (1987). Methodology review: Clustering methods. *Applied Psychological Measurement, 11*(4), 329–354.

Nadal, K. (2011). The racial and ethnic microaggressions scale (REMS): Construction, reliability, and validity. *Journal of Counseling Psychology, 58*(4), 470–480.

Omi, M., & Winant, H. (2014). *Racial formation in the United States.* New York: Routledge.

Omi, M., & Winant, H. (1994). *Racial formation in the United States: From the 1960s to the 1990s* (2nd ed.). New York: Routledge.

Ossorio, P., & Duster, T. (2005). Race and genetics: Controversies in biomedical, behavioral, and forensic sciences. *American Psychologist, 60*(1), 115–128.

Osterman, K. F. (2000). Students' need for belonging in the school community. *Review of educational research, 70*(3), 323–367.

Pérez Huber, L., & Solórzano, D. G. (2015). Racial microaggressions as a tool for critical race research. *Race Ethnicity and Education, 18*(3), 297–320.

Polkinghorne, D. E. (1995). Narrative configuration in qualitative analysis. *Qualitative Studies in Education, 8*(1), 5–23.

Schutz, P. A., DeCuir-Gunby, J. T. & Williams-Johnson, M. R. (2016). Using multiple and mixed methods to investigate emotions in educational contexts. In M. Zembylas, and P. A. Schutz (eds.) *Methodological advances in research on emotion in education.* New York: Springer.

Schutz, P. A., Chambless, C. B., & DeCuir, J. T. (2004). Multimethods research. In K. B. deMarrais & S. D. Lapan (Eds.), *Research methods in the social sciences: Frameworks for knowing and doing* (pp. 267–281). Hillsdale, NJ: Erlbaum.

Smedley, A., & Smedley, B. D. (2005). Race as biology is fiction, racism as a social problem is real. *American Psychologist, 60*(1), 16–26.

Solórzano, D. G., & Yosso, T. J. (2002). Critical race methodology: Counter-storytelling as an analytical framework for education research. *Qualitative Inquiry, 8*(1), 23–44.

Solórzano, D., Ceja, M., & Yosso, T. (2000). Critical race theory, racial microaggressions, and campus racial climate: The experiences of African American college students. *Journal of Negro Education, 69*(1–2), 60–73.

Sue, D., Capodilupo, C., Torino, G., Bucceri, J., Holder, A., Nadal, K., & Esquilin, M. (2007). Racial microaggressions in everyday life: Implications for clinical practice. *American Psychologist, 62*(4), 271–286.

Suri, H. (2011). Purposeful sampling in qualitative research synthesis. *Qualitative Research Journal, 11*(2), 63–75.

Tashakkori, A., & Creswell, J. W. (2007). The new era of mixed methods. *Journal of Mixed Methods Research, 1*, 3–7.

Teranishi, R. T. (2007). Race, ethnicity, and higher education policy: The use of critical quantitative research. *New Directions for Institutional Research, 2007*(133), 37–49.

Webster, L., & Mertova, P. (2007). *Using narrative inquiry as a research method: An introduction to using critical event narrative analysis in research on learning and teaching.* New York: Routledge.

Williams, B., Brown, T., & Onsman, A. (2010). Exploratory factor analysis: A five-step guide for novices. *Australasian Journal of Paramedicine, 8*(3).

Won, S., Wolters, C. A., & Mueller, S. A. (2017). Sense of belonging and self-regulated learning: Testing achievement goals as mediators. *The Journal of Experimental Education,* 1–17.

Zusho, A., & Clayton, K. (2011). Culturalizing achievement goal theory and research. *Educational Psychologist, 46*(4), 239–260.

PART V

Future Directions in Critical Race Methods and Methodologies

15

"WHERE DO WE GO FROM HERE?"

A Future Agenda for Understanding Critical Race Research Methods and Methodologies

Thandeka K. Chapman and Jessica T. DeCuir-Gunby

In an explication of "What is CRT," and who are critical race theorists, Derrick Bell states, "We seek to empower and include traditionally excluded views and see all-inclusiveness as the ideal because of our belief in collective wisdom" (Bell, 1995, p. 901). We, the editors of this book, view this edited text as a form of collective wisdom focused on the multiple ways scholars who use critical race theory in education employ various research methods to document the lived experiences of people of color. Each chapter stands alone in the unique deployment of methods, yet the chapters hold together as a weapon against race and racism. Bringing together the diverse research methods used to forward racial justice in education allows the reader to grapple with the different approaches while seeing the collective binding of critical race theory.

Moreover, the book was developed in response to a distinct need for scholarly guidance when one says he/she is committed to using critical race theory. As the use of critical race theory continues to expand in education scholarship, all too often we see the theory distilled into an oversimplification of storytelling or statements about counter-stories when challenging deficit notions of students of color (Donnor & Ladson-Billings, 2017; Ladson-Billings, 2013). The stories told by germinal theorists such as Derrick Bell, Richard Delgado, Cheryl Harris, and Patricia Hill Collins are academic and intricate works of scholarship that weave history, law, contexts, and experiences into complex quilts of critique, voice, and empowerment. Scholarship that intellectually enlightens and deeply resonates with the lives of people of color is sincerely the goal for critical race theorists. However, in the field of critical race theory in education CRT, the element of storytelling appears to be misunderstood. Ladson-Billings explains,

Critical race theorists use storytelling as a way to illustrate and underscore broad legal principles regarding race and racial/social justice. The point of storytelling is not to vent or rant or be an exhibitionist regarding one's own racial struggle. Unfortunately, far too many would-be critical race theorists in education use the narrative or counter-story in just that way.

(2013, p. 42)

Ladson-Billings continues:

The work of the critical race scholar must be as rigorous as that of any other scholarship (or perhaps more so). We have an obligation to point out the endemic racism that is extant in our schools, colleges, and other public spaces. We must deconstruct laws, ordinances, and policies that work to re-inscribe racism and deny people their full rights.

(2013, p. 45)

Critical Race Theory, as both theory and methodology, must be held to a higher standard in order to expose the insidious applications of race and racism in education. To meet the high standard of scholarship, "Critical race scholars are engaged in a dynamic process seeking to explain the realities of race in an ever-changing society" (Tate, 1997, p. 235). The dynamic process includes: articulating how race and racism are deeply ingrained in society, crossing epistemological boundaries, reinterpreting the stimuli and outcomes of civil rights law, exposing "legal claims of neutrality, objectivity, color blindness, and meritocracy" in light of the self-interests of the powerful, challenging ahistoricism, contextualizing law and policy, and valuing the experiences of people of color (Tate, 1997). These ambitious goals necessitate the use of all the tools at our disposal. And, while we recognize that the tools of the master's house can never completely dismantle racism, critical race theory demands that scholars who use the theory use their privileged positions to at least expose and erode it (Bell, 1995; Lawrence, 2002; Valdes, Culp, & Harris, 2002).

William Tate poses several crucial questions when articulating the application of critical race theory to the field of education. He challenges education scholars when he states:

Thus, the question for the education scholar employing CRT is not so much whether or how racial discrimination can be eradicated while maintaining the vitality of other interests linked to the status quo such as federalism, traditional values, standards, established property interests, and choice. Rather, the new question would ask how these traditional interests and cultural artifacts serve as vehicles to limit and bind the educational opportunities of students of color.

By exploring different research methods to document the extensive and embedded nature of race and racism in education, the authors in this book respond to Tate's call to answer new questions about traditional interests and the culling of educational opportunities for students of color. Ladson-Billings and Donnor state:

> Thus, we argue that the work of critical scholars (from any variety of perspectives) is not merely to try to replicate the work of previous scholars in a cookie-cutter fashion but rather to break new epistemological, methodological, social activist, and moral ground.
>
> *(2005, p. 291)*

The new combinations of research methods and CRT are ways to more fully disclose how institutional and societal forces shape the education experiences of students of color. "Rather, CRT is a new analytic rubric for considering difference and inequity using multiple methodologies—story, voice, metaphor, analogy, critical social science, feminism, and postmodernism" (Ladson-Billings & Donnor, 2005, p. 290). In the book, each author answers this challenge in different, but equally important, ways to reveal the how people of color have responded to multifaceted, complex constructions of race and racism.

For the quantitative and mixed methods scholars in the book, the answers lie within dismantling and re-appropriating methods that are often revered for formulating generalities and supposed objective suppositions about the behaviors, perceptions, and experiences of people of color. For example, Crawford et al. directly challenge the well-worn trope that statistics do not hold bias. Additionally, the authors explicate the consequences of using the master's tools against the powerful majority voice. Here we see the close guarding of academic scholarship as the realm of White supremacy.

Similarly, Covarrubias et al. challenge the common-sense notion of the neutrality of numbers. They explain that "[d]ominant analyses of quantitative data can lose sight of the fact that numbers are simply symbols representing reality." These authors combined quantitative methods with Latina feminist theory to create a new way to use quantitative methods to expose patterns of inequality and oppression in education and name the realities of people of color.

Importantly, Vélez and Solórzano re-envision the roles of maps and mapping as empowering methodology. Maps remain one of the most colonizing forces in the history of civilization. From the distorted sizing of land masses, such as the United States and Europe, in K-12 globes, to the topographical explanations that reinforce the dominance of Western civilization and Christianity, maps have been used to as legal and psychological tools of oppression.[1] Yet, Vélez and Solórzano demonstrate how maps can be used to highlight the impact of social and political forces on communities of color. Each of these quantitative methodologies contests majoritarian stock stories of deficit behaviors and meritocracy to reveal the connections between the dismantling of communities of color and public policy.

Lastly, DeCuir-Gunby and Schutz combine quantitative driven mixed methods with critical race theory to unpack the racialized experiences of Black women on a college campus. Whereas mixed methods can be perceived from a post-positive theoretical framework, the authors locate their suggested model in counter-stories. Again, these authors demonstrate how quantitative methods can be employed to expose inequity in education contexts.

To best answer the call to explore new ways to interrogate racial and ethnic oppression, several of the qualitative scholars in the book have embraced the elements of CRT that invite them to cross epistemological boundaries. Just as CRT theoretically borrows from multiple traditions, the authors have borrowed methodologies from indigenous knowledges, feminist methodologies, and participatory action research. In the return of Henry Sampson, Brayboy and Chin (Chapter 5) reassert the power of critical race storytelling as a tool to examine the many roles of scholar activists and the capricious relationship between universities and indigenous communities they purport to serve. Relatedly, Berry and Cook explore their roles as Black women professors and the constraints of higher education through narrative inquiry. Dixson, James, and Frieson, and Stovall take a more involved and active approach to research by combining CRT with participatory action research in schools. Delgado Bernal et al. utilize both aspects of participatory action research and Latina feminist works to describe their research projects working with Latinx students and families.

Other authors in the text focus on the goal to "reinterpret civil rights law in light of its limitations, illustrating that laws to remedy racial inequality are often undermined before they [are] implemented" Tate, 1997, p. 235). Donnor's analysis of law and the consequences of law borrows from legal studies, and demonstrates how an analysis of law gives us insights into historic and current constructions of racial and ethnic marginalization in education. To capture historic implementations of law and policy, and how communities of color responded to those events, Morris and Parker access historical artifacts and re-construct the stories that were disregarded. These two chapters also challenge ahistoricism and provide a contextual examination of past events that allows the reader to better understand the current racial contexts of public schools.

Additionally, two chapters expose concealed "claims of neutrality, objectivity, color blindness, and meritocracy" (Tate, 1997, p. 235) that maintain barriers in education. Lanehart conducts a document analysis of the journal publication process to expose the racial discrepancies in authorship concerning African Americans and language. Chapman et al. use a team research approach with CRT to document the racially uneven experiences of students of color in mixed-raced schools. These two chapters critique how enactments of seemingly neutral policies such as the journal review process and school discipline policies are racialized through their implementations.

The Role of Scholar Activism in CRT

In the words of William F. Tate, "These elements of CRT represent a beginning point" (1997, p. 235). The written documentation and critique of education policies, practices, and institutional structures are visible outcomes of critical race theory. Our published works become a form of resistance that Angela Harris calls "writing back" (1994). Writing back entails unraveling majoritarian tales, re-framing historical events, and questioning the very concepts of race and libera-tion, which remain at the center of critical race theory scholarship. It is through the process of "writing back" that scholars have the power to shift discourses on students of color, policy outcomes, and school practices; and, with those shifts, scholars create possible moments for empowerment.

However, critical race theorists understand that those moments of empower-ment must be cultivated over time and within community. In order to reach the goal of racial justice, critical race scholars also take on the role of activists. Most often, the role of scholar activist goes unseen and holds little value in the academy. Scholar activism is the time spent growing trusting relationships with community members, school personnel, parents, and students. It requires scholars to honor reciprocal agreements with the people who are participating in their research. Scholar activists ask the question: "How can we help?" Depending on the project, the answer to this question may be lengthy. Because of the nature of the unseen work, the roles scholars continue to play in the communities they research may not be easily connected to their chapter. However, several authors offer our readers a glimpse of what it means to be a scholar activist.

The projects conducted by Delgado Bernal et al. demonstrate the roles scholar activists play in the field. The three authors recount research projects that force them to embrace "a state of in-betweenness, contradictions, and liminality." The authors experience a particular set of tensions because of their conflicting sets of accountabilities. In this instance, the authors question their ability to balance the needs of the participants with their positions as university professors, mothers, and Latina feminists. Moreover, the unseen work involved in their chapter is the time and resources it takes to develop the relationships they so value. As described in Stovall's chapter, these trusting relationships take years to develop. It was Stovall's previous work in Chicago communities that led community leaders to seek his help in building a school. Relatedly, Dixson (Dixson, James and Frieson) describes the ways that local communities depend on her expertise and resources in their fight for quality schools in the aftermath of Katrina and the influx of charter schools across the New Orleans. Brayboy and Chin describe a similar positioning of identity in their chapter as they tell the story of how an indigenous university professor struggles to serve the needs of local tribal communities while maintain-ing his professional responsibilities.

What goes unsaid in these chapters is that these authors describe projects that may not yield data for years, or the data collection has ended and the authors have remained in those contexts. For critical race theorists, the data collection becomes secondary to the larger empowerment project and using their academic privileges to create greater equity and access for students of color. Harris explains:

> At the same time, CRT inherits from traditional civil rights scholarship a commitment to a vision of liberation from racism through right reason.

Despite the difficulty of separating legal reasoning and institutions from their racist roots, CRT's ultimate vision is redemptive, not deconstructive.

(1994, 794)

For critical race scholar activists, part of the redemptive project is the use of their own bodies to facilitate change, regardless of the value the experience is given by their institutions.

The Future of Critical Race Methods

Throughout this volume, scholars explicated their methodological approaches to engaging in CRT research. In many cases, the researchers also problematized the use of traditional methodological approaches in critical race research (e.g. Dixson et al., Chapter 6; Stovall, Chapter 7). Despite these detailed discussions, we have only scratched the surface in that there is not enough space to discuss all of the significant critical race methodological issues in this volume. Additional conversations are needed to address a variety of areas.

One significant discussion that was explored in this text was the combining of CRT and quantitative methods as well as mixed methods. Although there has been initial discussion regarding QuantCrit (Crawford et al., in this volume) and critical race quantitative intersectionality (Covarrubias et al., in this volume), more details are needed on how to appropriately combine quantitative methods and CRT. How does a researcher combine CRT with sophisticated statistical approaches (e.g. Hierarchical Linear Modeling (HLM), Structural Equation Modeling (SEM)? What role does CRT play in scale development and validation? What constitutes a quality quantitative CRT study? Similarly, more work is needed regarding the combining of CRT and mixed methods or critical race mixed methods (DeCuir-Gunby & Schutz, in this volume). Most mixed methods approaches are quantitative dominant and take a positivist or post-positivist stance. Also, like most post-positivist research, world-views are not discussed (Creswell & Plano Clark, 2018). Only recently are mixed methods researchers becoming receptive to qualitative-dominant approaches to mixed methods research and discussing world-views within their research, including more critical or transformative frameworks (Hesse-Biber, 2010). As such, where is the place for CRT within traditional mixed methods discourse? Should critical race mixed methods approaches be qualitative-dominant or can they be quantitative-dominant approaches?

Although most CRT research utilizes qualitative research approaches and many of the chapters in this volume have addressed issues pertaining to qualitative methods, more work is clearly needed within this area. As illustrated by many of the chapters in this text, prolonged time in the field is essential to taking a critical race approach. Thus, the further exploration of methods such as ethnographies are essential. Critical race ethnographic work such as Duncan's (2002) study on

African American male students' experiences at City High School serves as a useful example on how to combine CRT and ethnographic methods. Scholars have also used portraiture to extend the use of ethnographic methods with CRT (Chapman, 2005, 2007; Dixson, 2005; Lynn & Jennings, 2009). In addition to critical race ethnographies, the field needs to embrace the use of visual methods. Not all data is collected in written format. For example, Pérez Huber and Solórzano's (2015) powerful work on visual racial microaggressions demonstrates how CRT and visual methods can be used to challenge the negative portrayals of Mexicans in children's literature. Similarly, various researchers are utilizing documentaries, another form of visual imagery, in order to illustrate what written words alone are not always able to capture. Documentaries such as *Stolen Education*, which examines the school experiences of Mexican-American children in Texas who testified in *Hernandez et al. v. Driscoll Consolidated Independent School District*, a school desegregation case, or *Precious Knowledge,* which focuses on the Mexican-American studies program at Tucson High School and the subsequent Ethnic Studies ban in Arizona, are prime examples of how CRT can be combined with documentary methods.

Final Thoughts

In 1989 Stacey Latisaw and Johnny Gil sang the love song "Where do we go from here," questioning the strength of their romantic relationship in troubled times.

> *Where do we go from here, my love*
> *Do we walk away*
> *Do we keep on trying?*
> *After the feeling's gone, my love*

And, as local, national, and world politics rapidly change, many of us, as critical race theorists, have asked the question, "where do we go from here?" in regards to how can we use CRT to fight for the rights and humanity of people of color. Indeed, just as the song talks of love and struggle, those of us who call ourselves critical race theorists, consider our scholarship an act of love, struggle, and hope as we continue to dedicate our work to gaining racial justice.

The editors of this book also recognize that there are scholars who began working with CRT and have moved on to inhabit other theoretical homes. For those scholars, "the love is gone." For some, critical race theory is not an easy framework and may be considered too rigid, overly concerned with issues of race and ethnicity, or past its usefulness. However, when critical race theory is masterfully done, the scholarship has the potential to change the way people understand issues of race and racism and help to empower racially marginalized communities.

To generate more scholars who can masterfully use critical race theory, the editors created a collective set of works that demonstrates how scholars are using critical race theory and different research methods to combat the many ways racism and ethnocentrism are manifested in educational spaces. While we hold firm to the power of stories and the naming of oppression and resistance through the voices of racially marginalized groups, we recognize the need to enlist as many tools as possible enact social change and community empowerment.

The authors in the book are breaking new methodological ground in order to increase access and equity for students of color. The chapters provide readers with new strategies to interrogate historical and present-day instantiations of racism in education. As critical race theorists we decided not to "walk away" from the challenge of pairing CRT with new methods; rather we will "keep on trying" to strengthen modalities of research using CRT by giving readers an expansive vision of critical race theory and its growth in the field of education. We build on Derrick Bell's contention about the satisfaction of doing meaningful education research that utilizes a CRT framework. He states:

> The work, they say, speaks for itself and is its own legitimation. It was written to record experience and insight that are often unique and prior to this new work, too little heard. There is sufficient satisfaction for those who write in the myriad methods of critical race theory that comes from the work itself.
>
> *(1995, p. 910)*

And although we recognize that we could not cover every facet of critical race theory that comprises the body of work in education research, it is our sincere hope that readers find this volume useful for building new projects focused on racial justice.

Note

1 The use of maps as a tool of oppression can be found in the over-sizing of Europe and the United States in most K-12 texts and materials. The authors remember when K-12 students were taught that Egypt was not part of Africa, but part of the Middle East. Moreover, the construction of "Middle-East" is politically and socially constructed through mapping.

References

Bell, D. A. (1995). Who's afraid of critical race theory. *University of Illinois Law Revview*, (4), 893–920.

Chapman, T. K. (2005). Expressions of "voice" in portraiture. *Qualitative Inquiry*, *11*(1), 27–51.

Chapman, T. K. (2007). Interrogating classroom relationships and events: Using portraiture and critical race theory in education research. *Educational Researcher*, *36*(3), 156–162.

Creswell, J., & Plano Clark, V. (2018). *Designing and conducting mixed methods research* (3rd ed.). Thousand Oaks, CA: Sage.

Dixson, A. D. (2005). Extending the metaphor: Notions of jazz in portraiture. *Qualitative Inquiry, 11*(1), 106–137.

Donnor, J. K., & Ladson-Billings, G. (2017). Critical race theory and the post-racial imaginary. In N. K. Denzin & Y. S. Lincoln (Eds.), *The Sage handbook of qualitative research* (5th ed.) (pp. 195–213). Thousand Oaks, CA: Sage.

Duncan, G. A. (2002). Beyond love: A critical race ethnography of the schooling of adolescent Black males. *Equity &Excellence in Education, 35*(2), 131–143.

Harris, A. P. (1994). Foreword: The jurisprudence of reconstruction, *California Law Review, 82*(4), 741–785.

Hesse-Biber, S. (2010). Qualitative approaches to mixed methods practice. *Qualitative Inquiry, 16*(6), 455–468.

Ladson-Billings, G. (2013). Critical race theory—What it is not! In Marvin Lynn & Adrienne D. Dixson, *Handbook of critical race theory in education* (pp. 34–47). Abingdon, UK: Routledge.

Ladson-Billings, G., & Donnor, J. (2005). The moral activist role of critical race theory scholarship. In N. K. Denzin & Y. S. Lincoln (Eds.), *The Sage handbook of qualitative research* (3rd ed.) (pp. 279–301). Thousand Oaks, CA: Sage.

Latisaw, S and Gil, J. (1989). Where do we go from here? Detroit, MI: Motown Records.

Lawrence, C. (2002). Foreword: Who are we? And why are we here? Doing Critical Race Theory in hard times. In F. Valdes, J. M. Culp & A. P. Harris (Eds.), *Crossroads, directions, and a new critical race theory* (pp. xi-xxi). Philadelphia, PA: Temple University Press.

Lynn, M., & Jennings, M. E. (2009). Power, politics, and critical race pedagogy: A critical race analysis of Black male teachers' pedagogy. *Race Ethnicity and Education, 12*(2), 173–196.

Pérez Huber, L., & Solórzano, D. G. (2015). Visualizing everyday racism: Critical race theory, visual microaggressions, and the historical image of Mexican banditry. *Qualitative Inquiry, 21*(3), 223–238.

Su, J. A., & Yamamoto, E. K. (2002). Critical coalitions: Theory and practice. In F. Valdes, J. M. Culp & A. P. Harris (Eds.), *Crossroads, directions, and a new critical race theory* (pp. 379–392). Philadelphia, PA: Temple University Press.

Tate, W. F. (1997). Critical race theory and education: History, theory, and implications. *Review of Research in Education, 22*, 191–243.

Valdes, F., Culp, J. M., & Harris, A. P. (2002). Introduction: Battles waged, won, and lost: Critical Race Theory at the turn of the millennium. In F. Valdes, J. M. Culp & A. P. Harris (Eds.), *Crossroads, directions, and a new critical race theory* (pp. 1–6). Philadelphia, PA: Temple University Press.

INDEX

Note: bold page numbers indicate tables; italic page numbers indicate figures; numbers preceded by n indicate chapter endnotes.

AAHAM (African American, heterosexual and male) perspective 34, 35, 36, 37, 38, 42
AAL (African American language) 36–37, 38, 40, 42, 45n2; omission of women in research on 35, 36–37; publications on 36
AAVL (African American Vernacular Language) 35, 37, 38
AAWL (African American Women's Language) 35, 36–37
academic language 77
access 4, 57, 130, 187
accountability 61, 104, 187; and jazz methodology 77, 79, 80, 82, 83; researcher 76, 104
achievement gap 99, 140–141
ACS (American Community Survey) 144, 147n1
action research 66, 68; participatory see PAR
activist scholars see scholar activism
Adelante Partnership 113–115, 119n3
admissions policies 5, 57, 129
ADS (American Dialect Society) 35
affirmative action policies 3
African American, heterosexual and male (AAHAM) perspective 34, 35, 36, 37, 38, 42

African American language see AAL
African American Vernacular Language (AAVL) 35, 37, 38
African American women see Black women
African American Women's Language (AAWL) 35, 36–37
African-American identity 30, 31, 44n1
African-American teacher burnout 69–71, 72; and Attribution theory 70; and counter-storytelling 70, 71; and racial incidents 70–71; and self-care 71
Akom, Antwi 66
Alameda Corridor (Los Angeles) 150, 157–158, 161n1, 161–162n8
Alcoff, L. 103, 104, 106
Alemán, Enrique 114, 138
Alridge, D. P. 26
ALVCS (American language variation/change and sociolinguistics) research 7, 34–44, 186; and AAHAM perspective 34, 35, 36, 37, 38, 42; and AAL/AAVL 35, 36–37, 38, 40, 42, 45n2; African American women ignored in 35, 36–38; and American Dialect Society 35–36; AmSp survey see American Speech survey; and CRT 40, 41, 44; and intersectionality 34, 37, 38, 40, 43, 44; and methods/methodologies 40; and

researcher identity 34, 44; and WHAM perspective 34, 35, 41, 44
American Community Survey (ACS) 144, 147n1
American Dialect Society (ADS) 35
American Speech (AmSp) survey 35, 39–43; Black authors in 41–42, **42, 43**; Black women in 41, 42, 44; CRT applied in 40, 41, 44; feature articles featuring POCs in 39–40, **39**; methods/ methodologies in 40; racist terminology in 40–41; WHAM as unmarked referent in 41; White representations of POCs in 40, 42, **43**, 44
Andrews, K. T. 14
Anzaldúa, Gloria 109, 112, 114, 118, 119n1, 139
Apple, M. W. 128
archives/archival documents 7, 24, 25, 26; and marginalized/undocumented people 29
Arizona 189
Armour, J. D. 16, 17
artefacts, material 24–25
AsianCrit 100–101, 102, 119n1
assimilation 59, 100, 101
Atlanta (Georgia) 31
Attribution theory 69
Austin, Regina 86
Ayers, W. C. 86

Bailey, Richard W. 35
Basso, Keith 56
Baugh, John 36, 41
Bell, Derrick 20, 52, 64, 88, 110, 143, 183, 190
Benavides Lopez, C. 110
Black criminality 15, 17
Black feminist scholarship 34, 37, 40, 44
Black teachers 29, 86, 186
Black women 34, 86; CRT researchers 99, 101, 167; ignored in research 7, 35, 37–38; and intersectionality 37, 89–90, 91; and language research 34, 35, 36–37; students 8, 102–103, 166, 169–175, 185–186
bodymindspirit 111, 113, 114
Bolivar County (Mississippi) 19, *see also Cowan v. Bolivar County Board of Education*
Bolton, Charles C. 15–16
Bottomore, T. 57
Bourdieu, P. 53
Brayboy, B. M. J. 54, 57

Britain (UK) 128, 129, 130–133, **131, 133**
brown body 111, 114
Brown v. Board of Education (1954) 7, 15, 16, 26, 68, 72; and counter-narrative 30–31
Brydon-Miller, M. 68

Calderón, D. 5
Calmore, J. O. 77
campus racial climates 5, 99, 102–107; and denial of racism 105
capacity building 59
cartographies, critical race 139, 150–161, 185; and color-lines *see* color-lines; and counter-cartographic narratives 155–160; and critical geography 151, 153, 156; and critical race spatial analysis *see* CRSA; and GIS technologies 8, 150–151, 154–155; and schools 154; transdisciplinary aspects of 153–154
case law 88; *see also specific cases*
CFTs (Chicana feminist theories) 7–8, 115, 116, 118, 119n1; and CRTs 109–110; five tools of 111–112, *see also* critical race feminista methodology
CFTs (critical feminist theories) 138
Charlottesville attack (2017) 28
charter schools 3
Chase, S. E. 87
Chicago 79, 187
Chicago Public Schools (CPS) 79, 82
Chicana feminist theories *see* CFTs
Chicano masculinities 113, 117–118
chóques 138, 143
CIRM (critical indigenous research methodologies) 7, 51–61; and counter-stories 53–61; and four Rs of research 53, 57, 60
Citizens Councils 14
citizenship 141, 144, 145
civil rights 6, 41, 67, 153, 187; diminishment of 52; in Mississippi 14
Clandinin, D. J. 87, 92
Cleveland High School (Mississippi) 19, 20
Coates, Jennifer 38
Collins, Patricia Hill 37, 183
colonialism 80, 84, 110, 111, 118, 153; and maps 154–155, 185, 190n1
colonization 51, 55, 56, 59, 60
colonized body 111
color-lines 151–153, 156, 161, 161n3; Alameda Corridor case study 157–158; Mexican American case study 158–160; resistance to 152–153

colorblindness 5, 19, 20, 38, 41, 184, 186; and statistics 129–130
community building 138, 146
community engagement 5, 8, 29, 113–115; and PAR 64–65, 66–67, 68; and post-Katrina New Orleans 66–67; and storytelling 55–56, 57, 58, 59
community nomination 29
community-based research 30–31, 144, 161, 187; and CRQI 138, 143, 144, 146; and jazz methodology 76, 77, 79–80
complexity, research 7
Connelly, F. M. 87, 92
conocimiento 111, 113, 116, 118
convivencia 112, 113–115
Cope, M. 154, 160
counter-narrative/-stories 7, 13, 20, 30–31, 41, 65; auto-ethnographic nature of 52; and CIRM 51, 52–53; and community engagement 55–56, 57, 58, 59; and CRMM 168, 169; of CRT researchers 101; and fiction 52; and intersectionality 90–91, 92–93, **93**; and jazz methodology 79; and *lengua* 112; and map-making 150; and material artefacts 25; as narrative research 87, 88; and Native scholarship *see* universities and counter-stories; and PAR 68, 70, 71; and power structures 61; purposes of 52, 61; and sociolinguistics 41, 42, 44
Covarrubias, Alejandro 140, 141
Cowan v. Bolivar County Board of Education (2012) 15, 17, 18–20; and curriculum 19–20; and school choice policies 18–19
CPS (Chicago Public Schools) 79, 82
Crampton, J. W. 155
Crawford v. Los Angeles Board of Education (1963) 157
Crenshaw, Kimberlé W. 4–5, 14, 37, 38, 56, 89–90
Crespino, Joseph 14, 21n2
Creswell, J. W. 167, 176n2
critical consciousness 66, 109
critical race praxis 8, 67–68, 71, 72
critical ethnography 77, 83
critical feminist theories (CFTs) 138
critical geography 151, 153, 156
critical indigenous research methodologies *see* CIRM
critical race feminista methodology 7–8, 109–119, 185; and Chicana feminist theories *see* CFTs; conceptualizing

112–113; and *conocimiento* 111, 113, 116, 118; and *convivencia* 112, 113–115; and CRT concepts/theories 110–111, 115, 116, 118, 119; in educational research 113; and healing 113, 115–117; and *nepantla* 112, 113–115, 118; and praxis 113, 118, 119; and *sitios y lenguas* 112, 117–118; and *testimonios* 113, 114, 115–116
Critical Race Intersectional Think Tank (CRITT) 138, 145, 146
critical race mixed methodology *see* CRMM
Critical Race Quantitative Intersectionality *see* CRQI
critical race spatial analysis *see* CRSA
critical race theory (CRT) 4–6; bridges between methodologies of 109–110, 111, 113, 118; and education *see* CRT research in education; four assumptions of 168; future of 188–190; as jazz methodology *see* jazz methodology; and mixed methods research *see* CRMM; praxis 8, 67–68, 71, 72; and race-based methodologies 98; Tribal *see* Tribal Critical Race Theory
CRITT (Critical Race Intersectional Think Tank) 138, 145, 146
CRMM (critical race mixed methodology) 8, 166–176; and counterstories 168; and CRT framework 166, 168–169, *170*, 174, 175, 176; and data analysis 166, 167, 168, 169, 174–175, 176; and data integration 174, 176; and explanatory sequential mixed methods design 166, 169, *170*, 174, 176; implications for implementing 175–176; and inquiry world-view 167–168, 169, 174–175; quantitative-/qualitative-dominant approaches 168–169, 175–176; and sequential mixed methods design 166, 169, *170*, 176; and validity/reliability/trustworthiness 175, 176
CRMM example study 169–175; context 172; data analysis 173–175; data integration in 174; instrumentation 171–172, 174; and Need for Relatedness scale *170*, 171, 172, 173–174; participants 172–173; quantitative/qualitative phases 171, 172, 173; and REMS 171–172, 173; research questions 169–170
CRQI (Critical Race Quantitative Intersectionality) 8, 138–147; as

anti-racist praxis 140; as community-based research 138, 143, 144, 146; and CRITT collective 138, 145, 146; defined 140; and educational pipelines 138, 139, 141, *142*, 143; and experiential knowledge/cultural intuition 139, 141, 143; and scyborg positionality 144; and statistical significance 140–141, 143; and structural transformation 143–144; tenets of 140–144; and *testimonios* 139, 145–146; as trans-sectional methodology 139, 146; and transformational ruptures/*chóques* 138, 143
CRSA (critical race spatial analysis) 8, 151, 155–161; Alameda Corridor case study 150, 157–158, 161n1, 161–162n8; and color-lines *see* color-lines; defined 155–156; and groundtruthing 160; housing segregation case study 158–160; and racial justice 160–161; requirements of 156; and schools as racialized spaces 154; segregated housing case study 158–160
CRT *see* critical race theory
CRT research in education 3–6, 13, 64–65; central principles in 5–6; eight operational constructs of 65; future of 8, 188–190; history/legal literature in *see* historical analysis; legal literature; mixed-method approach in *see* CRMM; mixed methods research; and participatory action research *see* PAR; qualitative methods in *see* qualitative CRT research methods; quantitative methods in *see* QuantCrit; and racial realism 110, 119n3; and racist nativism 110, 116, 117; and resistance theories 110–111; and social justice *see* social justice; team approach to *see* team-based CRT research
cultural intuition 115, 139, 141, 143
curriculum 5, 19–20, 99, 114
Czarniawska, B. 87

data collection/analysis 27, 40, 41, 71, 87, 187; and critical race feminista methodology 110, 114, 117; and CRMM 166, 167, 168, 169, 173–175; and CRQI 144, 145, 146; and interpretations 127; and intersectionality 139, 140, 141; and team-based CRT research 99, 101, 102, 104, *see also* statistics
data integration 174, 176

data triangulation 7, 27, 79
DataFerret 144, 147n2
decolonizing methodologies 58, 139
DeCuir, J. T. 88
DeCuir-Gunby, J. T. 169
deficit schooling practices 117
deficit theories 126–127, 134, 183
Delaney, D. 153
Delgado Bernal, D. 110, 114, 138, 187
Delgado, Richard 20, 52, 71, 86, 88, 89, 183
Deloria, Vine 53, 58
desegregation 15, 18–20, 68, 157, 189; and CRT research 26–27; and curriculum 19–20; and school choice policies 18–19, 20; White antipathy to 7
Dill, B. T. 143
Dillard, C. B. 106
Dis/ability Critical Race Theory (DisCrit) 126
Dixson, Adrienne D. 5, 13, 65, 72, 77, 78, 82, 88, 127
document analysis 7
Donnor, J. K. 13, 14, 17–18, 185
double-consciousness 91, 98
Douglass, Frederick 151
Du Bois, W. E. B. 151–152, 161n3
Duncan, G. A. 107, 188–189

East Side High School (Mississippi) 19–20
Ebonics Controversy (1996–1997) 36
education: colonization in 55, 56, 59, 60; and critical race theory research *see* CRT research in education; and equity/access *see* access; equity; higher *see* higher education
education policy 5, 68
education reform research 7
educational justice 83, 88–89
educational performance 128, 130–132, **131**, 133, **133**, 134, 140–141; and structural inequalities 139
educational pipelines 138, 139, 141, *142*, 143, 144–145
Elwood, S. 154
employment 16, 130
empowerment 106, 110, 116, 183, 185, 187
environmental justice 66
epistemologies 4, 7, 9; and cartography 151, 154, 160; Chicana feminist 111, 112; experiential 6, 65–66; indigenous 70; positivist 65, 154, 160; racist 98; and

researcher's identity 26, 27–28, 97, 102, 106–107
equity 4, 8, 68, 126, 127, 187
ethnic studies 3, 156, 189
ethnography 139, 188–189
Eurocentrism 27, 127, 190n1
experiential knowledge 6, 65–66, 69, 92, 94, 98, 110, 115, 127, 141, 143
explanatory sequential mixed methods design 166, 169, *170*, 174, 176

federal Indian law 54
feminism 7–8, 83, 89, 139; as racist/classist 37, 38
feminist geographers 151, 154
FHA (Federal Housing Administration) 158–159
Foster, Michele 29, 86
Freeman, Alan 88

Gaddis, J. L. 28
gender 29, 43, 45n2, 65, 76; and intersectionality 37, 38, 89, 90, 91, 94; and racial microaggressions 168
genesis amnesia 53, 56
geographic information systems *see* GIS
Georgetown University 57
Gibson, Kean 41
Gillborn, David 130, 132, 134
Ginwright, Shawn 76, 77, 79
GIS (geographic information systems) 8, 150–151, 156, 157; critiques of 154–155; and PPGIS 161; and subversive cartographies/racial justice 160–161
Gotanda, N. 4–5
Gramsci, A. 56
grants deeds 158
Greater Lawndale/Little Village School of Social Justice *see* SOJO
grounded visualization 160
groundtruthing 160
Guba, E. G. 24
Guinier, Lani 59
gun violence 79

Harris, Angela P. 88, 187
Harvey, D. 153
Hayes, J. R. 16
healing 113, 115–117
hegemony 41, 56
Hernandez et al. v. Driscoll Consolidated Independent School District 189
heteronormativity 118

hierarchies of oppression 90, **92**, 93, **93**
higher education 3, 5, 97, 112, 113; access to 130–132; outcomes **131**, 132, 141, *142, see also* universities and counter-stories
Highlander Folk School (Tennessee) 66
historical analysis 7, 15, 24–31; and archives 24, 26; importance in CRT of 20–21, 24; and material artifacts 24–25; missing from CRT educational research 13–14; and oral history *see* oral history; and PAR 68–69; and records/documents *see* historical records/documents; and representations of contemporary Black education 30–31; and researcher *see* researcher identity
historical records/documents 28–29; absence of 28, 29; and community nomination 29; distinction between 24; and narrative process 29–30; and oral history 24–25, 29, 31; and primary/secondary sources 29
Hmong identity 100, 104
Home Owners Loan Corporation (HOLC) 158, 159
Horton, Myles 66
housing 16, 145, 147n1, 154; and color-lines 158–160
Huff, Darrell 126
Hughes, S. 88
human rights 68, 145
Human Subjects Review panels 79

identity 30, 31, 44n1, 100, 104, 168, 187; and communities/collective histories 167; and intersectionality 91, 92, 94; researcher *see* researcher identity
immigration status 110, 141
indigenous communities 7, 66, 139, *see also* CIRM; Native scholarship
Indigo Williams, et al v. Phil Bryant, et al (2017) 14
inquiry world-view 167–168, 169, 174–175
Institutional Review Boards (IRBs) 60, 79
intersectionality 7, 34, 37, 38, 40, 43, 44, 109, 188; and identity 91, 92, 94; and jazz methodology 76; as method 91, 92; as multiplicative praxis 94; and narrative research 86, 88–93, **92**, **93**, 94; and power/oppression 89, 139; three forms of 37, 90, 93; and transformation 143–144, *see also* CRQI

jazz methodology 7, 76–84; and academic language 77; and accountability/responsibility 77, 79, 80, 82, 83; and communities 76, 77, 79–82; and counter-stories 79; and CRT 76, 77–79, 82, 83, 84; and field notes/student journaling 79, 80, 81, 82; and intersectionality 76; jazz concepts in 78, 81; and member-checking/data triangulation 79; and reflexivity 81–83; and reframing facilitator/learner roles 82, 83; and self-determination 82, 83–84; and students' presentation 81; and YPAR/critical race methodology 76, 77, 83
Jennings, M. E. 88

K-12 education 5, 64, 99, 100, 185, 190n1
K-16 education 113
Katrina, Hurricane see New Orleans
Keating, AnaLouise 109, 111, 113, 118
Knigge, L. 154, 160
knowledge 6, 70, 83, 106–107, 111, 167; experiential see experiential knowledge; Native 58, 186; and power 139; production 112, 138, 151; of self 84; situated 160, see also epistemologies
Kobayashi, A. 153
Kohlman, M. H. 143
Krygier, J. 155
Kwan, M. 154, 160

Ladson-Billings, Gloria 5, 13, 14, 65, 88, 98, 183–184, 185
Lakoff, Robin 38
Lanehart, S. L. 38
Lara, A. 141
Lara, Irene 111, 119n1
LatCrit 101–102, 119n1, 138
Latinas/os/Latinx people 3, 91, 101–102, 104, 110, 119n2; and CRQI 141, 144–147; use of terms 162n9, see also critical race feminista methodology; Mexican Americans
law 5, 67, 88, 89, see also case law; legal literature
Lawrence, C. R. III 68
Ledesma, M. C. 5
Lefebvre, H. 153
legal literature: importance in CRT of 15, 20, 21; missing from CRT educational research 13–14, see also case law
Leitner, H. 154
lengua 112, 117

liminality 57, 112, 138, 143, 187
Lincoln, Y. S. 24
linguistics see sociolinguistics
Los Angeles 150, 157–160; housing segregation in 158–160; resistance to segregation in 152–153, see also Alameda Corridor
Lowry, S. 129
Lynn, M. 65, 88, 127

McCloskey, D. N. 140
McCoy, D. L. 5
MacKinnon, C. A. 89, 91
Macpherson, G. 129
magnet schools 19–20, 26
Maguire, P. 68
Malagón, M. C. 110
maps: appraisal/residential security 158–159; and colonialism 154–155, 185, 190n1, see also cartographies, critical race
masculinity 117, 118
master narrative 29, 70, 88, 91, 92, 93
Matsuda, M. 64, 68, 91
member checking 7, 27, 79
merit, democratic 59
meritocracy 5, 105, 145, 184, 185, 186
Mexican Americans 119n2, 141, 144, 158–160, 189
microaggressions see racial microaggressions
Mills, C. 81
miscegenation 15
Mississippi 14–21; Cowan v. Bolivar County Board of Education (2012) 15, 17, 18–20; history of White reaction to Black education in 14–18; intergenerational impact of White racism in 14, 17–18, 20; legacy of White racism in 14, 15; race-neutral/freedom of choice policies in 18; Reconstruction era 14, 15, 17; segregationism in 14, 15–16
mixed methods research 4, 8, 166, 185–186, 188, see also CRMM
Montagu, Ashley 16–17
Morris, J. E. 26–27, 30–31
mortgages 158–159
multicultural education 3
multiple consciousness 93, 94, 98

narrative research 7, 86–94, 186; counterstory as see counter-narrative/-story; as inquiry/process 92, **93**; interdisciplinary/qualitative approach of

87; and intersectionality 86, 88–93, **92**, **93**, 94; and master narrative 29, 70, 88, 91, 92, 93; and multiple identities 91; overview of 87–88; as phenomenon/inquiry 87, 92, 93–94
National Association for the Advancement of Colored People (NAACP) 67
Native scholarship 40, 42, 139, 187; and TribalCrit 54, **55**, 57, 61, *see also* universities and counter-stories
Native Teacher Training Program (NTTP) 54
Naughton, J. 129
Negrophobia: and intelligence 16–17; and segregationism in education 16, 20–21; and self-defence cases 17
neoliberalism 38, 41, 44
nepantla 112, 113–115, 118, 138, 143
New Deal 158
New Orleans, post-Katrina 66–68, 72, 187
news media 125, 126, 130
NTTP (Native Teacher Training Program) 54

Obama, Barack 28
objectivity 5, 16, 26, 27–28, 44, 71–72, 77, 78, 97, 184, 186; and statistics 129–130, 140–141, 185
oppression 28, 97, 100, 107, 169, 186; in Chicano communities 110–111, 112–113, 115, 116, 117, 118, 119; and counter stories 52, 54, 61, 71; CRT's mission to end 6, 64, 88; multiple/intersecting 76, 89, 90, 91, **92**, 93, **93**, 109; and PAR 61, 65, 66; permanence of 30; and statistics/quantitative methods 126, 127, 140
oral history 24–25, 29, 31, 117, 145; and PAR 68–69, *see also testimonios*
Ovarian Psycos Bicycle Brigade (O.V.A.S.) 152–153
over-surveillance/neglect binary 117–118

P-20 education 66
paperson, la 144
parents 114
Parker, Arthur C. 58
Parker, L. 65
participatory action research (PAR) 7, 64–72, 186; and African-American teacher burnout *see* African-American teacher burnout; and community engagement 64–65, 66–67, 68; and critical consciousness 66; and CRT 65–66, 68–69, 71, 72; and educational

history 68–69; and post-Katrina New Orleans 66–68, 72; and social/racial justice 65, 67, 68, 69, 72; youth (YPAR) 7, 76, 77
participatory research 66, 77
Passeron, J. C. 53
Patterson, J.T. 16
Peake, L. 153
Peller, G. 4–5
Pérez, Emma 112, 119n1
Pérez Huber, L. 110, 116, 189
Pillow, W. 98
pláticas 114
police brutality 64
political intersectionality 37, 90
Polkinghorne, D. E. 87
positivism/post-positivism 4, 65, 154, 160, 188
post-racial America 28, 30
power structures/relations 4, 26, 31, 51, 56–57, 61; and cartography 151, 154–155; and CRMM 169, 176; and intersectionality 89, 91, 139, 144; and PAR 65; in research process 103–104, 106; and statistics 126–127, 128, 141; and symbolic force 57
PPGIS (public participation geographic information science) 161
praxis 55, 113, 118, 119, 156; anti-oppressive 127; critical race 8, 67–68, 71, 72; and CRQI 138, 140, 146; and four Rs of research 53; intersectional 91, 92; multiplicative 94
predominately White institutions (PWIs) 167, 171, 172, 173, 175
prisons 52, 152
property rights 5, 158
public participation geographic information science (PPGIS) 161

qualitative CRT research methods 3, 4, 7, 65, 79, 87, 188; and CRMM 167, 168–169
QuantCrit 4, 8, 185–186, 188; and centrality of racism 126, 127–128; and CRMM 167, 168–171; five principles of 126–127; and social justice 134, 135, *see also* CRQI; statistics
quantitative criticalism 144

race-neutral educational policies 18
race/racism: centrality of 126, 127–128; construction of *see* social constructions; experienced by CRT researchers

100–101; and intelligence 16–17;
interdisciplinary approach to 6; and
law 5; normality/ordinariness of 168,
171; and other forms of subordination
5; permanence of 41, 44, 69, 110; and
"scientific" claims 134; spatial aspects of
see cartographies, critical race
Racial and Ethnic Microaggressions Scale
(REMS) 171–172, 173
racial justice 3, 4, 6, 72, 106, 107, 110,
184, 189, 190; and GIS 160–161; and
scholar activism 67, 114–115, 134,
186–188; and statistics 128, *see also*
social justice
racial marking 19
racial microaggressions 5, 8, 52, 72, 145,
189; in CRMM study 166, 168, *170*,
171–174, 175; instrument for measuring
(REMS) 171–172, 173, 174
racial realism 110, 119n3
racially restrictive covenants 158, 162n10
racist nativism 110, 116, 117
Reconstruction era 14, 15, 17, 52
redlining 158, 162n10
reflexivity 26, 81–83, 113, 160
regression analyses 132–133, **133**
relatedness *170*, 171, 172, 173–174
REMS (Racial and Ethnic
Microaggressions Scale) 171–172,
173
representational intersectionality 37, 38,
90
research: four Rs of 53, 57, 60; and power
65
researcher accountability 76
researcher identity 7, 25–28, 34, 167–168;
and childhood educational experiences
26; and co-construction 27, 77; and
contextualization/storytelling 28;
and educational iconography 27; and
epistemologies 26, 27–28; and member
checking/data triangulation 27
researcher vulnerability 111
researcher-participant reciprocity 7
residential security maps 158–160
resiliency 111, 114, 115
resistance 38, 67, 69, 79, 110–111, 112,
115, 152, 187
Riessman, C. 92
Rodricks, D. J. 5
Rousseau Anderson, C. K. 5, 13, 65
ruptures, transformative 138

St Louis (Missouri) 31
Sampson, Henry 7, 53–61, 186
San Joaquin Valley (California) 8, 144–145
Scheurich, J. 98
scholar activism 67, 114–115, 134,
186–188
school buildings, as expressions of White
dominance 27
school choice policies 18–19, 20
school climate/culture 5, 114
school discipline 114, 117, 186
school finance 3, 5
Schubert, W. H. 86
Schutz, P. A. 169
scyborg positionality 144
segregation in education 14, 15–16, 20,
30; and color-line concept 152; and
contemporary CRT research 31; as
emblematic of Negrophobia 16
segregationism in education: *see also
Cowan v. Bolivar County Board of
Education*
self-determination 59, 60, 66, 69, 82,
83–84
Shelly v. Kramer (1948) 158
Shepp, Archie 77
Silver, J. W. 15
sitios y lenguas 112, 113, 117–118
Slattery, P. 102
slavery 52, 56, 57
Smith, L. T. 154–155
Smith, Linda Tuhiwai 58
social class 28, 29, 31, 37, 38
social constructions 38, 88, 104–105, 110,
111, 128, 134, 168; of difference 140;
of masculinity 117, 118; statistics as
126–127, 128–130
social justice 6, 65, 68, 69, 72, 83, 110,
113, 162n9, 184; and CRMM 169; and
statistics 126, 127, 129, 134, *see also* racial
justice
sociolinguistics 7, 38; and researcher
identity 34, *see also* ALVCS research
Soja, E. W. 153
SOJO (School of Social Justice, Greater
Lawndale High School, Chicago) 78,
79, 80
Solórzano, Daniel G. 25, 30, 65, 79, 80, 97,
110, 155, 160, 189
space, discursive/theorizing 34, 70, 76,
97, 119, 139; and jazz methodology 78,
81, 82–83; methodological *nepantla* as

112, 113–115, 118, 138; and narrative research 90–91, 92, **92**, 94; *sitios y lenguas* as 112, 113, 117–118
Span, Christopher M. 17
Spanish Conquest 111
spatial analysis *see* CRSA
spiritual activism 111
Stage, F. K. 141, 144
Stanley, C. A. 102
statistics 125–135; and assumptions of objectivity 129–130, 140–141, 185; lack of scrutiny of 128, 135, 135n2; principled ambivalent position to 133–134; and questions/asked/not asked 130–132; and regression analyses 132–133, **133**; and significance 140–141, 143; as social constructions 126–127, 128–129, 130; Trump's misuse of 125, 134–135; and White supremacy 126–127, 128, 141
Steele, M. J. 126
Stefancic, Jean 86, 88, 89
storytelling 6, 52, 56, 61, 86, 183–184; counter- *see* counter-narrative/-stories, *see also* narrative research
structural intersectionality 37, 90
student protests 64
subjectivities 44, 69, 78, 111, 151, 160, 167–168, *see also* researcher identity
Supreme Court 38, *see also Brown v. Board of Education*
symbolic force 57

Tannen, Deborah 38
Tashakkori, A. 167
Tate, William 5, 13, 65, 88, 184–185, 186
teacher burnout 71, *see also* African-American teacher burnout
team-based CRT research 7, 97–107; and counter-stories 101, 103, 106; date collection/analysis in 99, 101, 102, 104, 105, 106; and denial of racism on campus 105; details of research team 99–102; details of study 99; generational issues in 99, 104–105; and multi-racial aspects of research 102–103; and problem of single researchers 98; and racial justice 106, 107; and researcher epistemologies/ontologies 97, 102, 106–107; and speaking for others/allowing voices to be heard 103–105

Teranishi, R. T. 100
testimonios 113, 114, 115–116, 139, 145–146
Thomas, K. 4–5
Torre, Maria 66
trans-sectional methodologies 139, 146, *see also* CRQI
Tribal Critical Race Theory (TribalCrit) 54, 55, 57, 61
Trinidad Galván, R. 112, 119n1
Trump, Donald 28, 125, 134–135
Tucson (Arizona) 189
Tyson, C. 106

undocumented people 8, 113, 116
universities and counter-stories 53–61, 186; and colonization 55, 56, 59, 60; and community engagement 55–56; and genesis amnesia 53, 56; and Institutional Review Boards (IRBs) 60; and slavery 56, 57; and TribalCrit 54, 55, 57, 61
U.S. Commission on Civil Rights 18
U.S.-Mexican War 111

Vélez, V. 110, 140, 155–156, 160
voice 5, 6, 13, 20, 65; and intersectionality 90, 91, **92**, 93, **93**, 94
voucher system 3

Waco (Texas) 68–69, 72
Watts Rebellion (1965) 157
ways of knowing *see* epistemologies
WHAM (white, heterosexual and male) perspective 34, 35, 41, 44
White flight 157
White nationalism 3, 28
White racial victimization 130–132
White racism 13, 21n1; and colorblindness 5, 19, 20; intergenerational impact of 14, 17, 20; and school segregation 7, 14, 15–16, *see also* Negrophobia
White supremacy 4–5, 8, 41, 80, 88, 111; and statistics 126–127, 128, 141, 185
Whiteness 8, 13–21, 90, 110; and space *see* cartographies, critical race, *see also* WHAM
Wilder, Craig Steven 56
Williams, Patricia 52, 86
Williams, R. A. 51
Williams-Johnson, M. R. 169

Wilson, Shawn 58
Wing, A. K. 89, 94
women of color *see* Black women
Woodson, Carter G. 30

Yamamoto, E. K. 67, 71, 72
Yosso, T. J. 25, 30, 65, 79, 80, 97

Young, M. D. 98
youth participatory action research
    (YPAR) 7, 76, 77, 83
youth work 77

Zamudio, M. 30
Ziliak, S. 140